# THE MISSIONARY JOURNEY OF

_____

Serving as a Missionary for

## THE CHURCH OF JESUS CHRIST OF LATTER-DAY SAINTS

_in the_ _____

_Mission_

_This record is of my missionary experiences_

_from_ _____ , _until_ _____

         (date)                          (date)

"I am called of God. My authority is above that of the kings of the earth. By revelation I have been selected as a personal representative of the Lord Jesus Christ. He is my Master and he has chosen me to represent him. To stand in his place, to say and do what he himself would say and do if he personally were ministering to the very people to whom he has sent me. My voice is his voice, and my acts are his acts; my words are his words and my doctrine is his doctrine. My commission is to do what he wants done. To say what he wants said. To be a living modern witness in word and deed of the divinity of his great and marvelous latter-day work." - Elder Bruce R. McConkie

# MISSIONARY CALLING

I was interviewed by Bishop/Branch President
_____ on _____

Then I was interviewed by Stake President
_____ on _____

I received my mission call on _____

to the _____ mission

I was set apart as a missionary by _____

on _____

Here's some things I remember from that
experience and how I felt: _____
_____
_____
_____
_____
_____
_____
_____
_____
_____

I received my patriarchal blessing on _____
_____ through the hands of
_____

I received my Temple Endowment on_____
_____ at the _____

temple

*Where and on what date did you open
your mission call?* _____

*Describe that experience. How did you feel?*
_____
_____
_____
_____
_____
_____
_____
_____
_____
_____

*Names of family and friends who were there:*

_____  _____
_____  _____
_____  _____
_____  _____
_____  _____
_____  _____
_____  _____
_____  _____
_____  _____
_____  _____
_____  _____
_____  _____
_____  _____
_____  _____
_____  _____
_____  _____
_____  _____

# MISSIONARY GOALS

(WHAT KIND OF MISSIONARY DO YOU WANT TO BE? HOW WILL YOU GET THERE? WHAT ARE YOU COMMITTING TO DO? WHO WILL YOU BECOME?)

_____
_____
_____
_____
_____
_____
_____
_____
_____
_____
_____
_____
_____
_____
_____
_____
_____
_____

# YOUR TESTIMONY DAY 1

(YOU WILL HAVE AN OPPORTUNITY TO WRITE YOUR TESTIMONY AT THE END OF THIS JOURNAL AS YOU FINISH YOUR MISSION JOURNEY)

_____
_____
_____
_____
_____
_____
_____
_____
_____
_____
_____
_____
_____
_____
_____
_____

# ORDINANCES PERFORMED

| Name | Ordinance | Date | Place |
|------|-----------|------|-------|
|      |           |      |       |
|      |           |      |       |
|      |           |      |       |
|      |           |      |       |
|      |           |      |       |
|      |           |      |       |
|      |           |      |       |
|      |           |      |       |
|      |           |      |       |
|      |           |      |       |
|      |           |      |       |
|      |           |      |       |
|      |           |      |       |
|      |           |      |       |
|      |           |      |       |
|      |           |      |       |
|      |           |      |       |
|      |           |      |       |
|      |           |      |       |
|      |           |      |       |

# ORDINANCES PERFORMED

| Name | Ordinance | Date | Place |
|------|-----------|------|-------|
|      |           |      |       |

# CHRONOLOGICAL LIST OF MISSIONARY COMPANIONS

Name                        Area(s)                        Dates you
                                                           served together

_____

Contact info:

_____

_____

_____

Name                        Area(s)                        Dates you
                                                           served together

_____

Contact info:

_____

_____

_____

Name                        Area(s)                        Dates you
                                                           served together

_____

Contact info:

_____

_____

_____

Name                        Area(s)                        Dates you
                                                           served together

_____

Contact info:

_____

_____

_____

# CHRONOLOGICAL LIST OF
# MISSIONARY COMPANIONS

| Name | Area(s) | Dates you served together |
|---|---|---|

Contact info:

| Name | Area(s) | Dates you served together |
|---|---|---|

Contact info:

| Name | Area(s) | Dates you served together |
|---|---|---|

Contact info:

| Name | Area(s) | Dates you served together |
|---|---|---|

Contact info:

# CHRONOLOGICAL LIST OF MISSIONARY COMPANIONS

Name      Area(s)    Dates you served together

_____

Contact info:

_____

_____

_____

Name      Area(s)    Dates you served together

_____

Contact info:

_____

_____

_____

Name      Area(s)    Dates you served together

_____

Contact info:

_____

_____

_____

Name      Area(s)    Dates you served together

_____

Contact info:

_____

_____

_____

# CHRONOLOGICAL LIST OF MISSIONARY COMPANIONS

Name                    Area(s)              Dates you served together

_____

Contact info:

_____

_____

_____

Name                    Area(s)              Dates you served together

_____

Contact info:

_____

_____

_____

Name                    Area(s)              Dates you served together

_____

Contact info:

_____

_____

_____

Name                    Area(s)              Dates you served together

_____

Contact info:

_____

_____

_____

# NAMES, ADDRESSES, AND CONTACT INFO OF OTHERS

Name and info

_____
_____
_____
_____

Name and info

_____
_____
_____
_____

Name and info

_____
_____
_____
_____

Name and info

_____
_____
_____
_____

Name and info

_____
_____
_____
_____

Name and info

_____
_____
_____
_____

Name and info

_____
_____
_____
_____

Name and info

_____
_____
_____
_____

Name and info

_____
_____
_____
_____

Name and info

_____
_____
_____
_____

Name and info

_____
_____
_____
_____

Name and info

_____
_____
_____
_____

Name and info

_____
_____
_____
_____

Name and info

_____
_____
_____
_____

# NAMES, ADDRESSES, AND CONTACT INFO OF OTHERS

*Name and info*

_____
_____
_____
_____

*Name and info*

_____
_____
_____
_____

*Name and info*

_____
_____
_____
_____

*Name and info*

_____
_____
_____
_____

*Name and info*

_____
_____
_____
_____

*Name and info*

_____
_____
_____
_____

*Name and info*

_____
_____
_____
_____

*Name and info*

_____
_____
_____
_____

*Name and info*

_____
_____
_____
_____

*Name and info*

_____
_____
_____
_____

*Name and info*

_____
_____
_____
_____

*Name and info*

_____
_____
_____
_____

*Name and info*

_____
_____
_____
_____

*Name and info*

_____
_____
_____
_____

# NAMES, ADDRESSES, AND CONTACT
# INFO OF OTHERS

*Name and info*

_____
_____
_____
_____

*Name and info*

_____
_____
_____
_____

*Name and info*

_____
_____
_____
_____

*Name and info*

_____
_____
_____
_____

*Name and info*

_____
_____
_____
_____

*Name and info*

_____
_____
_____

*Name and info*

_____
_____
_____

*Name and info*

_____
_____
_____
_____

*Name and info*

_____
_____
_____
_____

*Name and info*

_____
_____
_____
_____

*Name and info*

_____
_____
_____
_____

*Name and info*

_____
_____
_____
_____

*Name and info*

_____
_____
_____

*Name and info*

_____
_____
_____

# NAMES, ADDRESSES, AND CONTACT INFO OF OTHERS

*Name and info*

_____

_____

_____

_____

*Name and info*

_____

_____

_____

_____

*Name and info*

_____

_____

_____

_____

*Name and info*

_____

_____

_____

_____

*Name and info*

_____

_____

_____

_____

*Name and info*

_____

_____

_____

_____

*Name and info*

_____

_____

_____

_____

*Name and info*

_____

_____

_____

_____

*Name and info*

_____

_____

_____

_____

*Name and info*

_____

_____

_____

_____

*Name and info*

_____

_____

_____

_____

*Name and info*

_____

_____

_____

_____

*Name and info*

_____

_____

_____

_____

*Name and info*

_____

_____

_____

_____

# NAMES, ADDRESSES, AND CONTACT INFO OF OTHERS

*Name and info*

_____
_____
_____
_____

*Name and info*

_____
_____
_____
_____

*Name and info*

_____
_____
_____
_____

*Name and info*

_____
_____
_____
_____

*Name and info*

_____
_____
_____
_____

*Name and info*

_____
_____
_____
_____

*Name and info*

_____
_____
_____
_____

*Name and info*

_____
_____
_____
_____

*Name and info*

_____
_____
_____
_____

*Name and info*

_____
_____
_____
_____

*Name and info*

_____
_____
_____
_____

*Name and info*

_____
_____
_____
_____

*Name and info*

_____
_____
_____
_____

*Name and info*

_____
_____
_____
_____

# FAVORITE QUOTES FROM YOUR MISSION

# FAVORITE QUOTES FROM YOUR MISSION

# FUNNY THINGS YOUR MISSION PRESIDENT AND OTHERS SAID

# TENDER MERCIES & MIGHTY MIRACLES

# TENDER MERCIES & MIGHTY MIRACLES

# BAPTISM PAGES

*(WRITE ABOUT PEOPLE AND DETAILS OF THEIR CONVERSION STORIES)*

# BAPTISM PAGES

*(WRITE ABOUT PEOPLE AND DETAILS OF THEIR CONVERSION STORIES)*

# BAPTISM PAGES

*(WRITE ABOUT PEOPLE AND DETAILS OF THEIR CONVERSION STORIES)*

# BAPTISM PAGES

*(WRITE ABOUT PEOPLE AND DETAILS OF THEIR CONVERSION STORIES)*

# Great Messages on the Atonement of Jesus Christ

1 Nephi 11

2 Nephi 1:15

2 Nephi 2

2 Nephi 4

2 Nephi 9

2 Nephi 26:24

2 Nephi 28

2 Nephi 31

Jacob 4

Enos 1

Omni 1:26

Mosiah 3–5

Mosiah 27

Alma 5

Alma 34

Alma 36

Alma 42

Helaman 3

Helaman 5:9–12

3 Nephi 27

Ether 3

Ether 12:27

Moroni 7

Moroni 10

Others:

# MEMBERSHIP BLESSINGS

Blessed by _____

Baptized by _____

Confirmed by _____

## PRIESTHOOD ORDINATIONS

Deacon _____

Teacher _____

Priest _____

Elder _____

## PRIESTHOOD LINE OF AUTHORITY

On _____ I was ordained

an Elder by _____

who was ordained by _____

_____

_____

_____

_____

_____

_____

_____

who was ordained by Joseph Smith Junior, who
was ordained by Peter, James, and John, who
were set apart by Jesus Christ.

BOOM! Welcome to missionary life! It is truly an honor to wear the name of Jesus Christ over your heart. You are set apart—literally set apart from the world to devote your time, talents and energies to the greatest work in the world! Yes, missionary work is challenging and can feel overwhelming at first as you start at the home MTC… but it is SO rewarding! Commit to obedience—it's the first law of heaven. Earn the trust of God. Look for the good in your companion and those in your district. Participate and commit to going "all-in." You will experience joy as you search inward, turn outward, look upward, and press forward. With the help of the Godhead, you've got this!

DATE: _____

MEMORIES MADE, TOUGH TIMES, & LESSONS LEARNED:

Stressed   Angry   Tired   Sad   Happy   Excited

_____
_____
_____
_____
_____
_____
_____
_____

What are you grateful for today? _____

*Before you can serve the Master, you must first master the servant.*

REMEMBER! WAIT TO WRITE BELOW UNTIL THIS SAME DATE NEXT YEAR!

DATE: _____

MEMORIES MADE, TOUGH TIMES, & LESSONS LEARNED:

Stressed   Angry   Tired   Sad   Happy   Excited

_____
_____
_____
_____
_____
_____
_____

Prompt of the day: (you can answer this one now rather than wait for 1 year)
What inspired you to serve a mission? Reflect on the spiritual experiences and personal growth that led you to this decision.

_____
_____
_____
_____
_____

What are you grateful for today? _____

What kind of missionary do you truly want to be? Forget yourself and let God know you are ready and willing to say and do whatever He wants said and done. Commit to doing things His way. Remember, this mission is not about you. It was never about you. Lose yourself in this great work and you will find Jesus. Jesus changes everything. He can and will change your heart if you give it to Him. Elder Neal A. Maxwell said it this way, "Please, submit your will to God. It is the only gift you've got to give. And the sooner it is placed on the altar, the better it will be for all." Offer your whole soul to the Lord. Your burdens will be lifted and your heart will be healed. Give Him your heart. Completely. Alma 5:7. What are the first 5 words? How does that happen?

DATE: _____

MEMORIES MADE, TOUGH TIMES, & LESSONS LEARNED:

Stressed   Angry   Tired   Sad   Happy   Excited

_____
_____
_____
_____
_____
_____
_____
_____

What are you grateful for today? _____

*Obedience is the price. Faith is the power. Love is the motive. The Spirit is the key. Now is the time. I am His messenger. My mission is the place.*
*Jesus is the Reason.*

REMEMBER! WAIT TO WRITE BELOW UNTIL THIS SAME DATE NEXT YEAR!

DATE: _____

MEMORIES MADE, TOUGH TIMES, & LESSONS LEARNED:

Stressed   Angry   Tired   Sad   Happy   Excited

_____
_____
_____
_____
_____
_____
_____
_____

Prompt of the day: (you can answer this one now rather than wait for 1 year)
Describe a lesson or principle from the Preach My Gospel manual that has stood out to you during your time in the MTC. How do you plan to apply this in your missionary service?

_____
_____
_____
_____
_____

What are you grateful for today? _____

If you want to make progress as a missionary and in life, keep track of that progress by journaling. Then you can reflect on what happened as you continue to write during the second half of your mission on the bottom half of each page. There is power in journaling your journey and noticing and remembering the hand of the Lord in your life. Write down what you are learning, how you feel, and testimony-building experiences. Reflect on how great and important this work is and whose work it is. It's the Lord's work. Nothing else even approaches it in significance. And you have been called to carry it forward today in a time of urgency and opportunity that we have never seen before. The time goes fast. Make each moment count. Then return with honor.

DATE: _____

MEMORIES MADE, TOUGH TIMES, & LESSONS LEARNED:  Stressed  Angry  Tired  Sad  Happy  Excited

_____
_____
_____
_____
_____
_____
_____
_____
_____

What are you grateful for today? _____

*"Save for those few who defect to perdition after having known a fulness, there is no habit, no addiction, no rebellion, no transgression, no offense exempted from the promise of complete forgiveness." - Boyd K. Packer*

DATE: _____

MEMORIES MADE, TOUGH TIMES, & LESSONS LEARNED:  Stressed  Angry  Tired  Sad  Happy  Excited

_____
_____
_____
_____
_____
_____
_____
_____

Prompt of the day: (you can answer this one now rather than wait for 1 year)
What are your first impressions about home MTC. What aspects are easier or more difficult than you anticipated? What was surprising?

_____
_____
_____
_____

What are you grateful for today? _____

As a missionary, writing a letter to yourself can be a powerful way to reflect on your journey and set intentions for your future. In this letter, express your hopes and aspirations for who you want to become by the end of your mission. Share your fears and worries, acknowledging the challenges you may face and the uncertainties of the future. Reflect on what is important to you at this moment, whether it's your relationship with God, your mission goals, or your personal growth. Seal the letter and open it on your last day as a missionary to see how far you've come and to remind yourself of the person you aspire to be.

DATE: _____

MEMORIES MADE, TOUGH TIMES, & LESSONS LEARNED:

Stressed   Angry   Tired   Sad   Happy   Excited

_____
_____
_____
_____
_____
_____
_____
_____

What are you grateful for today? _____

"*When we love God with all our hearts, He turns our hearts to the well-being of others in a beautiful, virtuous cycle.*" - Russell M. Nelson

DATE: _____

MEMORIES MADE, TOUGH TIMES, & LESSONS LEARNED:

Stressed   Angry   Tired   Sad   Happy   Excited

_____
_____
_____
_____
_____
_____
_____
_____

Prompt of the day: (you can answer this one now rather than wait for 1 year)
How do you feel about the mission call you received? What excites you most about serving in your assigned area?

_____
_____
_____
_____

What are you grateful for today? _____

"Anyone who does any kind of missionary work will have occasion to ask, Why is this so hard? Why doesn't it go better? Why can't our success be more rapid? Why aren't there more people joining the Church? It is the truth. We believe in angels. We trust in miracles. Why don't people just flock to the font? You will have occasion to ask those questions. I have thought about this a great deal. I offer this as my personal feeling. I am convinced that missionary work is not easy because salvation is not a cheap experience. Salvation never was easy. We are The Church of Jesus Christ, this is the truth, and He is our Great Eternal Head. How could we believe it would be easy for us when it was never, ever easy for Him? It seems to me that missionaries and mission leaders have to spend at least a few moments in Gethsemane. Missionaries and mission leaders have to take at least a step or two toward the summit of Calvary." – Jeffrey R. Holland

DATE: _____

MEMORIES MADE, TOUGH TIMES, & LESSONS LEARNED:

Stressed  Angry  Tired  Sad  Happy  Excited

_____
_____
_____
_____
_____
_____
_____
_____

What are you grateful for today? _____

"As you demonstrate the charity that true followers of Jesus Christ manifest, the Lord will magnify your efforts beyond your loftiest imagination...Peacemakers thwart the adversary." - Russell M. Nelson

DATE: _____

MEMORIES MADE, TOUGH TIMES, & LESSONS LEARNED:

Stressed  Angry  Tired  Sad  Happy  Excited

_____
_____
_____
_____
_____
_____
_____

Prompt of the day: (you can answer this one now rather than wait for 1 year)
Describe a goal you have set for yourself during your time in the MTC. How do you plan to achieve this goal?

_____
_____
_____
_____
_____

What are you grateful for today? _____

Staying consistent with daily habits and study routines is key to your success on the mission! Even when distractions tempt you, prioritize your spiritual and educational growth. Set aside distractions each day as you dive into the scriptures during personal study. By staying disciplined and focused, you'll make the most of every opportunity to learn and serve. Keep up the great work!

DATE: _____

MEMORIES MADE, TOUGH TIMES, & LESSONS LEARNED:

Stressed   Angry   Tired   Sad   Happy   Excited

_____
_____
_____
_____
_____
_____
_____
_____

What are you grateful for today? _____

"But perhaps even more important than speaking is listening. These people are not lifeless objects disguised as a baptismal statistic. They are children of God, our brothers and sisters, and they need what we have. Be genuine. Reach out sincerely. Ask these friends what matters most to them. What do they cherish, and what do they hold dear? And then listen." - Jeffrey R. Holland

DATE: _____

MEMORIES MADE, TOUGH TIMES, & LESSONS LEARNED:

Stressed   Angry   Tired   Sad   Happy   Excited

_____
_____
_____
_____
_____
_____
_____
_____

Prompt of the day: (you can answer this one now rather than wait for 1 year)
Write down things you are nervous for or worry about.

_____
_____
_____
_____
_____

What are you grateful for today? _____

Use various techniques to help you memorize scriptures, lessons, and other important information. Break down the material into smaller chunks and review it regularly. Use mnemonic devices, repetition, and visualization to aid in memorization. Find a method that works best for you and stick with it. Remember that memorizing takes time and effort, so be patient and persistent in your efforts. Use these skills if you are studying a language as well!

DATE: _____

MEMORIES MADE, TOUGH TIMES, & LESSONS LEARNED: 

Stressed  Angry  Tired  Sad  Happy  Excited

_____
_____
_____
_____
_____
_____
_____
_____

What are you grateful for today? _____

*"Our message to the world is simple and sincere: we invite all of God's children on both sides of the veil to come unto their Savior, receive the blessings of the holy temple, have enduring joy, and qualify for eternal life." - Russell M. Nelson*

DATE: _____

MEMORIES MADE, TOUGH TIMES, & LESSONS LEARNED: 

Stressed  Angry  Tired  Sad  Happy  Excited

_____
_____
_____
_____
_____
_____
_____
_____

Prompt of the day: (you can answer this one now rather than wait for 1 year)
Be sure to write down the names of those in your MTC district. What lessons are you learning from them?

_____
_____
_____
_____
_____

What are you grateful for today? _____

Commit yourself fully to the Lord and His work. By giving your all and forgetting yourself, you will find true happiness, clarity of purpose, and a newfound appreciation for the people and culture you serve. This commitment will change your life forever. Elder Jeffery R. Holland once said, paraphrasing the Savior, "Do you love me? Well then, feed my sheep, and do it forever." Press on every day, giving it your best. The Savior loves you.

DATE: _____

MEMORIES MADE, TOUGH TIMES, & LESSONS LEARNED:

Stressed  Angry  Tired  Sad  Happy  Excited

_____
_____
_____
_____
_____
_____
_____
_____
_____

What are you grateful for today? _____

*"When our priorities are out of order we lose power." - Gene R. Cook*

*(read that one again)*

DATE: _____

MEMORIES MADE, TOUGH TIMES, & LESSONS LEARNED:

Stressed  Angry  Tired  Sad  Happy  Excited

_____
_____
_____
_____
_____
_____
_____
_____
_____

Prompt of the day: (you can answer this one now rather than wait for 1 year) How do you feel about prayer so far? Describe how often you pray and what you are praying for.

_____
_____
_____
_____
_____

What are you grateful for today? _____

Embrace the challenges and find joy in serving the Lord, regardless of the circumstances you face. Missionary work can be difficult at times, but remember that through dedicated service, you will feel the love and warmth of the Spirit in your life. This divine guidance and support will bring you happiness and fulfillment as you strive to share the gospel message with others. Stay focused on your purpose, rely on the Lord's strength, and cherish the personal growth and spiritual experiences that come from selflessly serving God and his children. Your faithful efforts will be a source of great blessings and joy throughout your mission and beyond.

DATE: _____

MEMORIES MADE, TOUGH TIMES, & LESSONS LEARNED:

Stressed    Angry    Tired    Sad    Happy    Excited

_____
_____
_____
_____
_____
_____
_____
_____

What are you grateful for today? _____

"If you serve a mission faithfully and well, you will be a better husband [or wife], you will be a better father, you will be a better student, a better worker in your chosen vocation. Love is of the essence of this missionary work. Selflessness is of its very nature. Self-discipline is its requirement. Prayer opens its reservoir of power." - Gordon B. Hinckley

DATE: _____

MEMORIES MADE, TOUGH TIMES, & LESSONS LEARNED:

Stressed    Angry    Tired    Sad    Happy    Excited

_____
_____
_____
_____
_____
_____
_____
_____

Prompt of the day: (you can answer this one now rather than wait for 1 year) What are a few things you have learned from your MTC instructors? Jot their names down and be sure to thank them often.

_____
_____
_____
_____
_____

What are you grateful for today? _____

Remember that the Lord loves and values each missionary. You are precious to Him, and He will bless you with His protection, direction, and connection as you strive to live worthily and serve faithfully. Every missionary brings different personalities, talents, gifts, skills, and work ethic to the table. Lay down all that you have and let the Lord work with it. Don't be discouraged if you can't get the language down right away, or if your teaching skills aren't where you want them. Give yourself grace. Pray for patience. You are doing great!

DATE: _____

MEMORIES MADE, TOUGH TIMES, & LESSONS LEARNED:

Stressed   Angry   Tired   Sad   Happy   Excited

_____
_____
_____
_____
_____
_____
_____
_____

What are you grateful for today? _____

*"You will learn the necessity of obedience. One day you are going to find out that the key to leadership is followship, and it comes from obedience. If you will learn to follow, the rules and regulations [of the mission] are just like an armor. Wear it well, and it will protect you."*
*- Boyd K. Packer*

DATE: _____

MEMORIES MADE, TOUGH TIMES, & LESSONS LEARNED:

Stressed   Angry   Tired   Sad   Happy   Excited

_____
_____
_____
_____
_____
_____
_____
_____

Prompt of the day: (you can answer this one now rather than wait for 1 year)
Write down some of the most important lessons you have learned so far and who taught you those lessons.

_____
_____
_____
_____
_____

What are you grateful for today? _____

As you write, think about what President Henry B. Eyring did as he posed this question each day, "Have I seen the hand of God reaching out to touch [my life] today?" "As I kept at it," President Eyring recalled, "something began to happen. As I would cast my mind over the day, I would see evidence of what God had done for one of us that I had not recognized in the busy moments of the day. As that happened, and it happened often, I realized that trying to remember had allowed God to show me what He had done. More than gratitude began to grow in my heart. Testimony grew. I became ever more certain that our Heavenly Father hears and answers prayers. I felt more gratitude for the softening and refining that come because of the Atonement of the Savior Jesus Christ."

DATE: _____

MEMORIES MADE, TOUGH TIMES, & LESSONS LEARNED:

Stressed    Angry    Tired    Sad    Happy    Excited

_____
_____
_____
_____
_____
_____
_____
_____

What are you grateful for today? _____

"The blessings of having the Holy Ghost in your life are enormous. It will lead, guide, enlighten, show, bless, teach, comfort, testify, witness to, and literally purify you. In your life as a missionary, you cannot succeed in any phase of work without the Holy Ghost. You cannot teach (see D&C 42:14; 50:17-22) or be directed in the work." - Ed Pinegar

DATE: _____

MEMORIES MADE, TOUGH TIMES, & LESSONS LEARNED:

Stressed    Angry    Tired    Sad    Happy    Excited

_____
_____
_____
_____
_____
_____
_____

Prompt of the day: (you can answer this one now rather than wait for 1 year)
Describe a moment when you felt the Spirit strongly since your MTC experience. How did this experience strengthen your testimony?

_____
_____
_____
_____
_____

What are you grateful for today? _____

Early in your mission you may have some hesitancy at what to say or do in finding or teaching situations. When you feel nervous or unsure what to say or do, just testify of Jesus Christ. Share a simple heartfelt testimony of your Savior and of His love for those you come in contact with. You may also share brief relatable experiences from your own life that people might be able to relate to. Share what you know to be true. Keep it simple. Always have a silent prayer in your heart to know what to say or do. But never walk away from an opportunity to bear testimony of Jesus.

DATE: _____

MEMORIES MADE, TOUGH TIMES, & LESSONS LEARNED:

Stressed   Angry   Tired   Sad   Happy   Excited

_____
_____
_____
_____
_____
_____
_____
_____

What are you grateful for today? _____

"In this work there must be commitment. There must be devotion. We are engaged in a great eternal struggle that concerns the very souls of the sons and daughters of God. We are not losing. We are winning. We will continue to win if we will be faithful and true. We can do it. We must do it. We will do it. There is nothing the Lord has asked of us that in faith we cannot accomplish." - Gordon B. Hinckley

DATE: _____

MEMORIES MADE, TOUGH TIMES, & LESSONS LEARNED:

Stressed   Angry   Tired   Sad   Happy   Excited

_____
_____
_____
_____
_____
_____
_____
_____

Prompt of the day: (you can answer this one now rather than wait for 1 year)
How has your testimony grown just in the short amount of time you have been a missionary?

_____
_____
_____
_____

What are you grateful for today? _____

Gratitude. This one is HUGE. So huge that there are going to be different types of happy hacks that focus on gratitude. Let's start with this one. Write down and reflect on 3 good things that happened today and why they happened. Try it every day for a week or two. The key is to be specific and jot down something different each time. Don't rush through it. Positivity is boosted in the process not in just going through the motions.

DATE: _____

MEMORIES MADE, TOUGH TIMES, & LESSONS LEARNED:

Stressed   Angry   Tired   Sad   Happy   Excited

_____
_____
_____
_____
_____
_____
_____

What are you grateful for today? _____

*"In order to ask with real intent or to act with full purpose of heart, we must always make an accompanying commitment." - Dallin H. Oaks*

DATE: _____

MEMORIES MADE, TOUGH TIMES, & LESSONS LEARNED:

Stressed   Angry   Tired   Sad   Happy   Excited

_____
_____
_____
_____
_____
_____
_____

Prompt of the day: (you can answer this one now rather than wait for 1 year)
Write about a time when you had to rely on your faith to overcome a difficult situation or challenge while in the MTC.

_____
_____
_____
_____

What are you grateful for today? _____

Recognize that feeling stress or discomfort when adjusting to missionary life is normal. Be patient with yourself as you learn to adapt to new responsibilities and environments, trusting that the Spirit will guide and support you through this transition. Remember that many missionaries experience four stages of adjustment: anticipation, discovering the unexpected, "I can do this," and emotional self-reliance. Understand that each stage is a natural part of the process and that with time, faith, and effort, you will develop the resilience and confidence needed to thrive as a missionary.

DATE: _____

MEMORIES MADE, TOUGH TIMES, & LESSONS LEARNED:

Stressed  Angry  Tired  Sad  Happy  Excited

_____
_____
_____
_____
_____
_____
_____
_____

What are you grateful for today? _____

"Now, the Atonement of Christ is the most basic and fundamental doctrine of the gospel, and it is the least understood of all our revealed truths. Many of us have a superficial knowledge and rely upon the Lord and His goodness to see us through the trials and perils of life. But if we are to have faith like that of Enoch and Elijah, we must believe what they believed, know what they knew, and live as they lived." - Bruce R. McConkie

DATE: _____

MEMORIES MADE, TOUGH TIMES, & LESSONS LEARNED:

Stressed  Angry  Tired  Sad  Happy  Excited

_____
_____
_____
_____
_____
_____
_____
_____

Prompt of the day: (you can answer this one now rather than wait for 1 year)
Have you felt homesick at all? Either way, write down your feelings and what it's like being away from home.

_____
_____
_____
_____
_____

What are you grateful for today? _____

Your service as a missionary will not only brings countless blessings to the lives of those you serve, but the windows of heaven will be opened and you will grow and change in wonderful ways. Your family will be blessed for your service. Your future family and children will be blessed. You are laying the spiritual foundation for your posterity for generations to come! The worth of souls is great! God is with you in every decision, and effort that you make as a missionary. Make wise choices, and be sure to rely on the Spirit. Never forget to include the Lord in HIS own work!

DATE: _____

MEMORIES MADE, TOUGH TIMES, & LESSONS LEARNED:

Stressed   Angry   Tired   Sad   Happy   Excited

_____
_____
_____
_____
_____
_____
_____
_____

What are you grateful for today? _____

"The gospel of Jesus Christ is a gospel of repentance. Because of the Savior's Atonement, His gospel provides an invitation to keep changing, growing, and becoming more pure. It is a gospel of hope, of healing, and of progress. Thus, the gospel is a message of joy! Our spirits rejoice with every small step forward we take." - Russell M. Nelson

DATE: _____

MEMORIES MADE, TOUGH TIMES, & LESSONS LEARNED:

Stressed   Angry   Tired   Sad   Happy   Excited

_____
_____
_____
_____
_____
_____
_____
_____

Prompt of the day: (you can answer this one now rather than wait for 1 year)
How have your perceptions of the missionary lifestyle changed since you started the MTC?

_____
_____
_____
_____
_____

What are you grateful for today? _____

Adjusting to missionary life can be challenging for some. Be open with your feelings and share them with your companion, your family, and even mission president. Explore scriptural examples of prophets and others who were called to do things beyond their perceived capabilities, and learn from their faith and reliance on God. Consider the experiences of Moses, Jeremiah, Alma, and others who felt inadequate but trusted in the Lord's strength. Seeking advice and insight from those who have faced similar challenges can provide valuable perspective and encouragement as you navigate the ups and downs of missionary service.

DATE: _____

MEMORIES MADE, TOUGH TIMES, & LESSONS LEARNED:  Stressed   Angry   Tired   Sad   Happy   Excited

_____
_____
_____
_____
_____
_____
_____
_____

What are you grateful for today? _____

*"The setting apart may be taken literally; it is a setting apart from sin, apart from the carnal; apart from everything which is crude, low, vicious, cheap, or vulgar; set apart from the world to a higher plane of thought and activity. The blessing is conditional upon faithful performance." - Spencer W. Kimball*

DATE: _____

MEMORIES MADE, TOUGH TIMES, & LESSONS LEARNED:  Stressed   Angry   Tired   Sad   Happy   Excited

_____
_____
_____
_____
_____
_____
_____
_____

Prompt of the day: (you can answer this one now rather than wait for 1 year)
Lessons in Humility: Reflect on a lesson in humility you've learned during your mission so far.

_____
_____
_____
_____

What are you grateful for today? _____

Be patient with yourself as you adapt to a new schedule. Give yourself time to acclimate to the routine and don't be too hard on yourself if things don't go perfectly at first. Stay organized and prioritize your tasks to make the most of your time. Remember that adjusting to a new schedule is a process, and it's okay to seek help and guidance from your companions, family, and leaders.

DATE: _____

MEMORIES MADE, TOUGH TIMES, & LESSONS LEARNED:

Stressed  Angry  Tired  Sad  Happy  Excited

_____
_____
_____
_____
_____
_____
_____
_____

What are you grateful for today? _____

*"When the Lord delivers this person to your view, just chat—about anything. You can't miss. You don't have to have a prescribed missionary message. Your faith, your happiness, the very look on your face is enough to quicken the honest in heart. Haven't you ever heard a grandmother talk about her grandchildren? That's what I mean—minus the photographs! The gospel will just tumble out. You won't be able to contain yourself!" - Jeffrey R. Holland*

DATE: _____

MEMORIES MADE, TOUGH TIMES, & LESSONS LEARNED:

Stressed  Angry  Tired  Sad  Happy  Excited

_____
_____
_____
_____
_____
_____
_____
_____

Prompt of the day: (you can answer this one now rather than wait for 1 year)
Today's Teaching Reflections: Describe an impactful teaching moment from today. What did you learn about yourself, your companion, or those you taught?

_____
_____
_____
_____
_____

What are you grateful for today? _____

Keep up the writing in this or other journals. It's a great way to process challenging experiences and feelings. Recording your thoughts, insights, and spiritual impressions can provide perspective and help you recognize personal growth and blessings throughout your mission. Use this journal as a safe space to express your struggles, fears, and triumphs. As you reflect on your experiences and see the hand of the Lord in your life, you will gain a deeper appreciation for your mission and the ways in which you are learning and growing.

DATE: _____

MEMORIES MADE, TOUGH TIMES, & LESSONS LEARNED:

Stressed   Angry   Tired   Sad   Happy   Excited

_____
_____
_____
_____
_____
_____
_____
_____

What are you grateful for today? _____

"*I believe that in his justice and mercy he will give us the maximum reward for our acts, give us all that he can give, and in the reverse, I believe that he will impose upon us the minimum penalty which it is possible for him to impose.*" - *J. Reuben Clark*

DATE: _____

MEMORIES MADE, TOUGH TIMES, & LESSONS LEARNED:

Stressed   Angry   Tired   Sad   Happy   Excited

_____
_____
_____
_____
_____
_____
_____
_____

Prompt of the day: (you can answer this one now rather than wait for 1 year)
The Role of the Holy Ghost: Write about a time when you felt guided by the Holy Ghost in an unmistakable way.

_____
_____
_____
_____

What are you grateful for today? _____

Time to discover Your. Core. Four. We're talking about your values! Not things you value. It's more character traits of the person you want to be. Think about what you want people at your funeral to think and say about you. Those are your values! Want to be happier? Align your thoughts, words, and behaviors with your values. Here are a few examples of values, but feel free to look up other values or think about the person you truly want to be. Write down Your. Core. Four. Values below. Then strive to live true to these at all times and in all places! Examples: compassion, humility, positivity, appreciation, loyalty, forgiving, generosity, kindness, honesty, hard worker, loving, selfless, integrity, trustworthy, friendly...

1.                                          3.
2.                                          4.

DATE: _____

MEMORIES MADE, TOUGH TIMES, & LESSONS LEARNED:

Stressed   Angry   Tired   Sad   Happy   Excited

_____
_____
_____
_____
_____
_____
_____
_____

What are you grateful for today? _____

"It is a great experience to learn that it is not your mission — it is the Lord's mission. . . . You will find through challenge, through work, through study, and through the difficulties and disappointments that you face that it is the Lord's mission. You will come to know that." - Boyd K. Packer

DATE: _____

MEMORIES MADE, TOUGH TIMES, & LESSONS LEARNED:

Stressed   Angry   Tired   Sad   Happy   Excited

_____
_____
_____
_____
_____
_____
_____
_____

Prompt of the day:
Spiritual Insights: Share a spiritual insight or testimony you gained this week. How did this insight come to you, and how has it affected your perspective?

_____
_____
_____
_____
_____

What are you grateful for today? _____

The sooner you learn to love the people in your mission, the happier you will be. Fast and pray earnestly for charity—the greatest gift of all. Ask for the ability to see others as God sees them and to love them unconditionally. Lose yourself in the service of the people you meet. By focusing on their needs and serving them selflessly, you will develop a deep love and compassion for them. At the end of your mission or at transfers, you will miss them. Remember that true love is not just a feeling but an action, and as you serve with all your heart, you will find that your love for the people grows immensely. Be sure to thank God regularly for allowing you to feel a small portion of what He feels for the same people you both love.

DATE: _____

MEMORIES MADE, TOUGH TIMES, & LESSONS LEARNED:

Stressed   Angry   Tired   Sad   Happy   Excited

_____
_____
_____
_____
_____
_____
_____
_____

What are you grateful for today? _____

*"The Creator of the seas, sands, and endless stars is reaching out to you this very day! He is offering the grand recipe for happiness, peace, and eternal life!" - Dieter F. Uchtdorf*

DATE: _____

MEMORIES MADE, TOUGH TIMES, & LESSONS LEARNED:

Stressed   Angry   Tired   Sad   Happy   Excited

_____
_____
_____
_____
_____
_____
_____
_____

Prompt of the day: (OK! WAIT to answer the rest of the prompts on the bottom half of this journal until 1 year from now!)

Gratitude for Unseen Support: Reflect on the unseen support you've received during your mission and express gratitude for those who have supported you from afar.

_____
_____
_____
_____

What are you grateful for today? _____

Focus on helping others and sharing the gospel with those who will listen. Despite facing rejection or difficult conditions, find satisfaction in knowing that you are doing what you can to teach the gospel of Jesus Christ and bless the lives of others. Rejection is hard. But every time it happens think of Christ. Elder Holland stated, "I believe that missionaries and investigators, to come to the truth, to come to salvation, to know something of this price that has been paid, will have to pay a token of that same price. For that reason, I don't believe missionary work has ever been easy, nor that conversion is, nor that retention is, nor that continued faithfulness is. I believe it is supposed to require some effort, something from the depths of our soul."

DATE: _____

MEMORIES MADE, TOUGH TIMES, & LESSONS LEARNED:   Stressed   Angry   Tired   Sad   Happy   Excited

_____
_____
_____
_____
_____
_____
_____

What are you grateful for today? _____

*"I bear witness that there is nothing more important than honoring the covenants you make, or may make, in the temple. No matter where you are on the covenant path, I urge you to qualify and become eligible to attend the temple. Visit as frequently as circumstances will allow." - Henry B. Eyring*

DATE: _____

MEMORIES MADE, TOUGH TIMES, & LESSONS LEARNED:   Stressed   Angry   Tired   Sad   Happy   Excited

_____
_____
_____
_____
_____
_____
_____

Prompt of the day:
Companion Dynamics: Reflect on your relationship with your current companion. What strengths do they bring to your mission, and how do you complement each other?

_____
_____
_____
_____

What are you grateful for today? _____

Find joy in your unique missionary journey: Embrace the unique experiences and challenges of your mission. Remember that your path is tailored to your personal growth and development. Instead of comparing yourself to other missionaries or expectations, focus on learning and growing from your own journey. Trust that God has a plan for you and that every experience, whether positive or difficult, can teach you valuable lessons. As you find joy in your individual mission, you'll discover a sense of purpose and fulfillment.

DATE: _____

MEMORIES MADE, TOUGH TIMES, & LESSONS LEARNED:

Stressed    Angry    Tired    Sad    Happy    Excited

_____
_____
_____
_____
_____
_____
_____
_____
_____

What are you grateful for today? _____

*"One of the paramount purposes of Jesus's ministry was to reveal to mortals "what God our Eternal Father is like, ... to reveal and make personal to us the true nature of His Father, our Father in Heaven." - Dallin H. Oaks*

DATE: _____

MEMORIES MADE, TOUGH TIMES, & LESSONS LEARNED:

Stressed    Angry    Tired    Sad    Happy    Excited

_____
_____
_____
_____
_____
_____
_____
_____

Prompt of the day:

Adapting Gospel Messages: Reflect on how you've adapted gospel messages to be more relatable to those you teach.

_____
_____
_____
_____

What are you grateful for today? _____

Use the correct, full name of the Church - The Church of Jesus Christ of Latter-day Saints. This is more than just a name change; it is an invitation to center yourself and your faith more fully in Christ. By using the complete name of the Church, you bear witness of Jesus Christ's central role in the Restoration. You also help others understand that this is His Church, guided by Him. Embrace this inspired counsel from our prophet and let it deepen your own discipleship.

DATE: _____

MEMORIES MADE, TOUGH TIMES, & LESSONS LEARNED:

Stressed   Angry   Tired   Sad   Happy   Excited

_____
_____
_____
_____
_____
_____
_____
_____

What are you grateful for today? _____

*"None of us will honor our Heavenly Father and our Savior more than by serving as a devoted, compassionate missionary, 'For them that honour me I will honour.' 1 Samuel 2:30 . - Thomas S. Monson.*

DATE: _____

MEMORIES MADE, TOUGH TIMES, & LESSONS LEARNED:

Stressed   Angry   Tired   Sad   Happy   Excited

_____
_____
_____
_____
_____
_____
_____
_____

Prompt of the day:

Overcoming Challenges: Write about a challenge you faced this week and how you overcame it. What did this experience teach you about reliance on the Lord?

_____
_____
_____
_____

What are you grateful for today? _____

There may be times on your mission when you think to yourself, or even look up to the heavens in frustration and cry: "This isn't what I signed up for!" When we followed the Savior in the premortal existence, perhaps we had a glimpse of what mortality might be like. Perhaps this is not what we expected, but maybe THIS IS what we signed up for. Regardless of your current circumstances on your mission, one of the greatest truths I have learned over the last few decades is this: Jesus Changes Everything. You may not be able to see clearly how it all fits together or how it all ends. Please remember that you signed up for this on the right team. Things may be bitter, but they will eventually be better. Because JESUS changes everything.

DATE: _____

MEMORIES MADE, TOUGH TIMES, & LESSONS LEARNED:

Stressed  Angry  Tired  Sad  Happy  Excited

_____
_____
_____
_____
_____
_____
_____
_____

What are you grateful for today?

*"How profoundly grateful I am for the experience of that mission. I touched the lives of a few who have, over the years, expressed appreciation. That has been important. But I have never been greatly concerned over the number of baptisms that I had or that other missionaries had. My satisfaction has come from the assurance that I did what the Lord wanted me to do and that I was an instrument in His hands for the accomplishment of His purposes." - Gordon B. Hinckley*

DATE: _____

MEMORIES MADE, TOUGH TIMES, & LESSONS LEARNED:

Stressed  Angry  Tired  Sad  Happy  Excited

_____
_____
_____
_____
_____
_____
_____
_____

Prompt of the day:

Personal Revelation in Mission Work: Share an experience of receiving personal revelation that guided your mission work.

_____
_____
_____
_____
_____

What are you grateful for today? _____

Embrace the unique challenges of missionary life as opportunities for personal growth and spiritual development. Rely on the Lord's guidance and strength to navigate through the difficulties you may face, such as adjusting to a new culture, learning a language, or living with a companion 24/7. Remember that these challenges are designed to help you become a more effective servant of the Lord and to deepen your faith in Him. Trust that He will support you every step of the way and that these experiences will shape you into the missionary He wants you to be. Give the Lord your loyalty. He will stretch you and trim you to the missionary He wants you to become.

DATE: _____

MEMORIES MADE, TOUGH TIMES, & LESSONS LEARNED:

Stressed   Angry   Tired   Sad   Happy   Excited

_____
_____
_____
_____
_____
_____
_____
_____

What are you grateful for today? _____

"It has never been more imperative to know how the Spirit speaks to you than right now. In the Godhead, the Holy Ghost is the messenger. He will bring thoughts to your mind which the Father and Son want you to receive. He is the Comforter. He will bring a feeling of peace to your heart. He testifies of truth and will confirm what is true as you hear and read the word of the Lord." - Russell M. Nelson

DATE: _____

MEMORIES MADE, TOUGH TIMES, & LESSONS LEARNED:

Stressed   Angry   Tired   Sad   Happy   Excited

_____
_____
_____
_____
_____
_____
_____
_____

Prompt of the day:
Cultural Experiences: The Role of Mentorship in Missionary Work: Share your experiences with mentorship, either as a mentor or being mentored, during your mission.

_____
_____
_____
_____
_____

What are you grateful for today? _____

When you find yourself struggling with the challenges of missionary life, don't hesitate to reach out to your companion, mission leaders, or other trusted mentors for support and guidance. Remember that they have likely faced similar difficulties and may have valuable insights and advice to share. Be humble and open in expressing your concerns and feelings and be willing to listen to their counsel and perspective. Draw strength from their testimonies and experiences and allow their love and encouragement to bolster your own faith and resolve. As you do so, you will find that you are not alone in your struggles, and that there is always someone ready and willing to help you along the way.

DATE: _____

MEMORIES MADE, TOUGH TIMES, & LESSONS LEARNED:

Stressed   Angry   Tired   Sad   Happy   Excited

_____
_____
_____
_____
_____
_____
_____
_____
_____

What are you grateful for today? _____

*"We are here to assist our Father in His work and His glory, 'to bring to pass the immortality and eternal life of man' (Moses 1:39). Your obligation is as serious in your sphere of responsibility as is my obligation in my sphere." - Gordon B. Hinckley*

DATE: _____

MEMORIES MADE, TOUGH TIMES, & LESSONS LEARNED:

Stressed   Angry   Tired   Sad   Happy   Excited

_____
_____
_____
_____
_____
_____
_____
_____

Prompt of the day:
Missionary Work's Physical Challenges: Write about the physical challenges of missionary work and how you've adapted.

_____
_____
_____
_____
_____

What are you grateful for today? _____

Look upward, press forward and reach outward to your companion, mission leaders, or trusted friends and family for support. It's essential to recognize that feelings of discouragement and inadequacy are common, and you're not alone in your struggles. Share your concerns and lean on the support of those who care about you. Engage in uplifting activities with your companion, such as studying the scriptures, sharing testimony, or setting small, achievable goals together. Remember that your mission is a time of growth and learning, and it's okay to ask for help when you need it.

DATE: _____

MEMORIES MADE, TOUGH TIMES, & LESSONS LEARNED:

Stressed   Angry   Tired   Sad   Happy   Excited

_____
_____
_____
_____
_____
_____
_____
_____
_____

What are you grateful for today? _____

*"The gospel net to gather scattered Israel is expansive. There is room for each person who will fully embrace the gospel of Jesus Christ. Each convert becomes one of God's covenant children, whether by birth or by adoption. Each becomes a full heir to all that God has promised the faithful children of Israel!" - Russell M. Nelson*

DATE: _____

MEMORIES MADE, TOUGH TIMES, & LESSONS LEARNED:

Stressed   Angry   Tired   Sad   Happy   Excited

_____
_____
_____
_____
_____
_____
_____
_____

Prompt of the day:

Service Stories: Share a story of a service project or act of kindness you participated in. How did it impact those you served and your own heart?

_____
_____
_____
_____

What are you grateful for today? _____

Pray always. When someone is speaking in a sacrament meeting, offer a sincere prayer for them that they will have the Spirit to be with them. Repeat the words of the sacrament prayer in your mind when they are spoken each sacrament meeting but replace the words we/them with "me." Pray for your investigators by name every night, and while you're teaching a lesson and your companion is teaching, pray for them in your heart, and pray for the people you are teaching, in your mind. Pray for those in your district, pray for your president. Pray for the other missionaries in your ward at home. Make a prayer roll of your own. Write down names. Pray for them. Open your heart at night and pray like you've never prayed, not for you, but for others. Plead for God to feel His love for others, to see them differently, and then you'll treat them differently. And then you will slowly experience that mighty change of heart, without even realizing it.

DATE: _____

MEMORIES MADE, TOUGH TIMES, & LESSONS LEARNED:

Stressed   Angry   Tired   Sad   Happy   Excited

_____
_____
_____
_____
_____
_____
_____
_____

What are you grateful for today? _____

*"Nothing is more liberating, more ennobling, or more crucial to our individual progression than is a regular, daily focus on repentance. Repentance is not an event; it is a process. It is the key to happiness and peace of mind. When coupled with faith, repentance opens our access to the power of the Atonement of Jesus Christ." - Russell M. Nelson*

DATE: _____

MEMORIES MADE, TOUGH TIMES, & LESSONS LEARNED:

Stressed   Angry   Tired   Sad   Happy   Excited

_____
_____
_____
_____
_____
_____
_____
_____

Prompt of the day:
Reflecting on Leadership Styles: Reflect on the different leadership styles you've encountered on your mission and what you've learned from them.

_____
_____
_____
_____

What are you grateful for today? _____

Refuse to be average. Those are the words I remember writing on a piece of paper and posting on the wall of every missionary apartment where I served. Whether it's reading, praying, studying or contacting, being an average cleaner, or being the average missionary who just does the bare minimum, give your best at whatever you're doing. Speaking at a zone conference? Give it your best effort. President Gordon B. Hinckley once said, "Do the best you can. But I want to emphasize that it be the very best. We are too prone to be satisfied with mediocre performance. We are capable of doing so much better."

DATE: _____

MEMORIES MADE, TOUGH TIMES, & LESSONS LEARNED:  Stressed  Angry  Tired  Sad  Happy  Excited

_____
_____
_____
_____
_____
_____
_____
_____

What are you grateful for today? _____

*"I plead with you to come unto Him so that He can heal you! He will heal you from sin as you repent. He will heal you from sadness and fear. He will heal you from the wounds of this world." - Russell M. Nelson*

DATE: _____

MEMORIES MADE, TOUGH TIMES, & LESSONS LEARNED:  Stressed  Angry  Tired  Sad  Happy  Excited

_____
_____
_____
_____
_____
_____
_____

Prompt of the day:
Language Learning: If you're learning a new language, reflect on your progress and any funny or enlightening moments you've had while communicating.

_____
_____
_____
_____
_____

What are you grateful for today? _____

Look forward to the blessings of missionary service: Anticipate the growth, learning, and miracles that will come from your missionary efforts. Set goals and make plans for your personal development and the progress of those you teach. As you look forward to these experiences with faith and enthusiasm, you'll find a renewed sense of motivation and purpose. Embrace the challenges and opportunities that lie ahead, knowing that they will stretch you and shape you into the disciple of Christ you are meant to become.

DATE: _____

MEMORIES MADE, TOUGH TIMES, & LESSONS LEARNED:

Stressed  Angry  Tired  Sad  Happy  Excited

_____
_____
_____
_____
_____
_____
_____
_____

What are you grateful for today? _____

"As members of the Lord's Church, we must take missionary work more seriously. The Lord's commission to 'preach the gospel to every creature' (Mark 16:15) will never change in our dispensation. We have been greatly blessed with the material means, the technology, and an inspired message to bring the gospel to all men. More is expected of us than any previous generation. Where 'much is given much is required.' (D&C 82:3.)" - Ezra Taft Benson

DATE: _____

MEMORIES MADE, TOUGH TIMES, & LESSONS LEARNED:

Stressed  Angry  Tired  Sad  Happy  Excited

_____
_____
_____
_____
_____
_____
_____

Prompt of the day:

Fostering a Positive Mindset: How do you foster a positive mindset, especially on tough days?

_____
_____
_____
_____
_____

What are you grateful for today? _____

Practicing emotional self-reliance involves recognizing when you can manage emotional pressures independently and when it's wise to seek help. This skill allows you to develop resilience and maintain a healthy emotional state. Remember, it's okay to ask for support when needed; this is a sign of strength, not weakness. Striking this balance helps you navigate life's challenges more effectively, knowing when to rely on your own coping mechanisms and the Lord, and when to lean on the support of others for guidance and comfort.

DATE: _____

MEMORIES MADE, TOUGH TIMES, & LESSONS LEARNED:

Stressed    Angry    Tired    Sad    Happy    Excited

_____
_____
_____
_____
_____
_____
_____

What are you grateful for today? _____

*"We can literally change the world—one person and one interaction at a time. How? By modeling how to manage honest differences of opinion with mutual respect and dignified dialogue." - Russell M. Nelson*

DATE: _____

MEMORIES MADE, TOUGH TIMES, & LESSONS LEARNED:

Stressed    Angry    Tired    Sad    Happy    Excited

_____
_____
_____
_____
_____
_____

Prompt of the day:

Teaching Techniques: Reflect on a teaching technique or approach you tried this week. How effective was it, and what would you do differently next time?

_____
_____
_____
_____

What are you grateful for today? _____

As a missionary, you are going to make mistakes. Own up to your mistakes. In challenging situations, take responsibility without making excuses. Avoid blaming others—companions, members, or others. Acknowledge your role in the problem and focus on improving. Shifting blame is common but blaming is a completely useless activity. Instead of faulting a companion for being late or saying something embarrassing at a dinner appointment, search inward and notice where you can improve. Recognize your power to make better choices, including a better investment of your time to learning and studying. If something truly seems unfair, seek solutions instead of just complaining about it.

DATE:_____

MEMORIES MADE, TOUGH TIMES, & LESSONS LEARNED:

Stressed   Angry   Tired   Sad   Happy   Excited

_____
_____
_____
_____
_____
_____
_____
_____
_____

What are you grateful for today? _____

"...where there is a prayerful heart, a hungering after righteousness, a forsaking of sins, and obedience to the commandments of God, the Lord pours out more and more light until there is finally power to pierce the heavenly veil. ... A person of such righteousness has the priceless promise that one day he shall see the Lord's face and know that he is." - Spencer W. Kimball

DATE:_____

MEMORIES MADE, TOUGH TIMES, & LESSONS LEARNED:

Stressed   Angry   Tired   Sad   Happy   Excited

_____
_____
_____
_____
_____
_____
_____
_____

Prompt of the day:

Experiencing Forgiveness: Share an experience where forgiveness played a key role in your mission, either giving or receiving it.

_____
_____
_____
_____
_____

What are you grateful for today? _____

Be vigilant and don't hesitate to voice concerns about missionaries displaying worrisome signs. If you notice a companion or other missionary becoming withdrawn, making comments about suicide, sending troubling messages, or exhibiting sudden shifts in mood or behavior, promptly inform your mission president or other leader. Your proactive response could alter a dangerous course or even save a life. Mental health matters tremendously, so remain aware of the wellbeing of your fellow missionaries, as well as members and others you minister to. If something seems amiss, speak up immediately. Expressing care and getting help could make an immense difference for someone struggling. Trust your instincts and have the courage to act.

DATE: _____

MEMORIES MADE, TOUGH TIMES, & LESSONS LEARNED:

Stressed   Angry   Tired   Sad   Happy   Excited

_____
_____
_____
_____
_____
_____
_____
_____

What are you grateful for today? _____

"To the faithful, comfort comes from the knowledge that no blessings will be withheld from any who love the Lord and strive earnestly to keep His commandments. We will be judged by our deeds and the desires of our hearts — in the Lord's merciful way and time." - Russell M. Nelson

DATE: _____

MEMORIES MADE, TOUGH TIMES, & LESSONS LEARNED:

Stressed   Angry   Tired   Sad   Happy   Excited

_____
_____
_____
_____
_____
_____
_____

Prompt of the day:

Personal Growth: Share a story that highlights the importance of patience in your missionary efforts.

_____
_____
_____
_____

What are you grateful for today? _____

Acknowledge that while you may not be able to alter someone's difficult journey, you can make sure they don't walk it alone. Be willing to walk together and share the load, just as the Savior lifts and supports us. Some challenges may not be resolved quickly or easily, but your consistent presence and support can make a significant difference in the lives of those who are struggling. Listen to their concerns, offer words of encouragement, and pray with and for them. By being a faithful friend and a steadfast witness of Christ, you can help lighten their burdens and bring hope to their souls.

DATE: _____

MEMORIES MADE, TOUGH TIMES, & LESSONS LEARNED:

Stressed    Angry    Tired    Sad    Happy    Excited

_____
_____
_____
_____
_____
_____
_____
_____

What are you grateful for today? _____

*"Immersing ourselves regularly in the truths of the Book of Mormon can be a life-changing experience...When I think of the Book of Mormon, I think of the word power. The truths of the Book of Mormon have the power to heal, comfort, restore, succor, strengthen, console, and cheer our souls." - Russell M. Nelson*

DATE: _____

MEMORIES MADE, TOUGH TIMES, & LESSONS LEARNED:

Stressed    Angry    Tired    Sad    Happy    Excited

_____
_____
_____
_____
_____
_____
_____

Prompt of the day:

Gratitude for Companions: Express gratitude for a current or former companion and what they've taught you.

_____
_____
_____
_____

What are you grateful for today? _____

Embrace "I don't know." If you're not sure about a question, admit it instead of speculating. Saying, "I'm not sure" or "Let me get back to you" is okay. Rushed opinions or wrong answers can cause problems. You're not required to answer immediately, especially if you haven't looked into the issue or don't know the facts, principles, or doctrines. Humility and maturity lies in recognizing your knowledge limits. It's totally fine to admit you're not sure about something and then do some studying to boost your understanding before sharing your opinion on a topic. It's better to take time to learn it than fake it!

DATE: _____

MEMORIES MADE, TOUGH TIMES, & LESSONS LEARNED: 

Stressed   Angry   Tired   Sad   Happy   Excited

_____
_____
_____
_____
_____
_____
_____
_____

What are you grateful for today? _____

"Men and women who turn their lives over to God will discover that He can make a lot more out of their lives than they can. He will deepen their joys, expand their vision, quicken their minds, strengthen their muscles, lift their spirits, multiply their blessings, increase their opportunities, comfort their souls, raise up friends, and pour out peace. Whoever will lose his life in the service of God will find eternal life." - Ezra Taft Benson

DATE: _____

MEMORIES MADE, TOUGH TIMES, & LESSONS LEARNED:

Stressed   Angry   Tired   Sad   Happy   Excited

_____
_____
_____
_____
_____
_____
_____

Prompt of the day:

Prayer Insights: Share how your understanding or appreciation of prayer has evolved. Describe a recent prayer experience that was particularly meaningful.

_____
_____
_____
_____
_____

What are you grateful for today? _____

Remember what Elder Jeffrey R. Holland has taught—that missionary work is not easy because salvation is not a cheap experience. Just as Christ suffered in Gethsemane and on Calvary, missionaries and investigators must put forth effort and sacrifice to come to the truth and experience salvation. You should expect challenges and difficulties, knowing that you are standing with the Savior, who endured all things. Conversion requires something from the depths of the soul, and you must be willing to pay a token of the price Christ paid to help others come unto Him. Your own conversion is the most important conversion on your mission.

DATE: _____

MEMORIES MADE, TOUGH TIMES, & LESSONS LEARNED:

Stressed   Angry   Tired   Sad   Happy   Excited

_____
_____
_____
_____
_____
_____
_____
_____

What are you grateful for today? _____

*"One of God's greatest gifts to us is the joy of trying again, for no failure ever need be final. Even if we've been a conscious, deliberate sinner or have repeatedly faced failure and disappointment, the moment we decide to try again, the Atonement of Christ can help us." - Dale G. Renlund*

DATE: _____

MEMORIES MADE, TOUGH TIMES, & LESSONS LEARNED:

Stressed   Angry   Tired   Sad   Happy   Excited

_____
_____
_____
_____
_____
_____
_____

Prompt of the day:
The Impact of Music in Worship: Reflect on the impact of music in worship and missionary work.

_____
_____
_____
_____

What are you grateful for today? _____

Find joy in your gospel study as a missionary: Make your personal gospel study a source of joy and inspiration during your mission. Approach your study with enthusiasm, curiosity, and a desire to learn. Seek to deepen your understanding of gospel principles, scriptural truths, and the words of modern prophets. As you find joy in your gospel study, you'll be better prepared to teach others with clarity, conviction, and love. Your study will also strengthen your own testimony and help you find answers to life's questions.

DATE: _____

MEMORIES MADE, TOUGH TIMES, & LESSONS LEARNED:

Stressed   Angry   Tired   Sad   Happy   Excited

_____
_____
_____
_____
_____
_____
_____
_____

What are you grateful for today? _____

*"Faith never demands an answer to every question but seeks the assurance and courage to move forward, sometimes acknowledging, 'I don't know everything, but I do know enough to continue on the path of discipleship.'" - Neil L. Anderson*

DATE: _____

MEMORIES MADE, TOUGH TIMES, & LESSONS LEARNED:

Stressed   Angry   Tired   Sad   Happy   Excited

_____
_____
_____
_____
_____
_____
_____

Prompt of the day:
Miracle Moments: Write about a "miracle" moment you witnessed or experienced. How did it strengthen your faith or testimony?

_____
_____
_____
_____

What are you grateful for today? _____

Be patient and understanding with others' imperfections, just as you hope they would be with yours. Recognize that everyone is on their own journey of growth and change, and it is not your place to judge their mistakes or shortcomings. Instead, focus on extending love, empathy, and compassion to those you serve, remembering that Christ's Atonement is for everyone. As a missionary, you will encounter people from all walks of life, each with their own struggles and challenges. By treating them with kindness and understanding, you will create an environment where they feel safe to learn, grow, and draw closer to the Savior.

DATE: _____

MEMORIES MADE, TOUGH TIMES, & LESSONS LEARNED:

Stressed    Angry    Tired    Sad    Happy    Excited

_____
_____
_____
_____
_____
_____
_____
_____

What are you grateful for today? _____

"*The pure doctrine of Christ is powerful. It changes the life of everyone who understands it and seeks to implement it in his or her life. The doctrine of Christ helps us find and stay on the covenant path. Staying on that narrow but well-defined path will ultimately qualify us to receive all that God has. Nothing could be worth more than all our Father has!*" - Russell M. Nelson

DATE: _____

MEMORIES MADE, TOUGH TIMES, & LESSONS LEARNED:

Stressed    Angry    Tired    Sad    Happy    Excited

_____
_____
_____
_____
_____
_____
_____
_____

Prompt of the day:

Appreciating Simple Blessings: Write about a simple blessing you've come to appreciate more deeply on your mission.

_____
_____
_____
_____

What are you grateful for today? _____

Trust in the Lord's plan for you. He knows you, loves you, and will guide you through this experience. Keep your faith strong and rely on Him for strength and guidance. Remember that your mission is not just about teaching others but also about your own personal growth and development. Trust that the challenges and experiences you encounter are part of His plan to shape you into the person He wants you to become. Embrace each day with faith and confidence, knowing that the Lord is with you every step of the way. EVERY step.

DATE: _____

MEMORIES MADE, TOUGH TIMES, & LESSONS LEARNED:

Stressed   Angry   Tired   Sad   Happy   Excited

_____
_____
_____
_____
_____
_____
_____
_____

What are you grateful for today? _____

*"...these are the latter days. If you and I are to withstand the forthcoming perils and pressures, it is imperative that we each have a firm spiritual foundation built upon the rock of our Redeemer, Jesus Christ. So I ask each of you, how firm is your foundation? And what reinforcements to your testimony and understanding of the gospel are needed?" - Russell M. Nelson*

DATE: _____

MEMORIES MADE, TOUGH TIMES, & LESSONS LEARNED:

Stressed   Angry   Tired   Sad   Happy   Excited

_____
_____
_____
_____
_____
_____
_____
_____

Prompt of the day:

Study Insights: Reflect on a recent study session that was particularly impactful. What did you learn, and how do you plan to apply this knowledge?

_____
_____
_____
_____

What are you grateful for today? _____

Actively seek and expect miracles in your missionary work. Have faith that the Lord will do His part as you do yours. Recognize that miracles come by faith, and teaching by the Spirit is one of the most effective ways to invite the Lord's influence into the lives of those you teach. Pray for opportunities to witness the Lord's hand in your work, and be open to the promptings of the Spirit as you teach and testify. Trust that as you exercise faith and invite others to do the same, you will see the power of God manifest in miraculous ways.

DATE: _____

MEMORIES MADE, TOUGH TIMES, & LESSONS LEARNED:

Stressed   Angry   Tired   Sad   Happy   Excited

_____
_____
_____
_____
_____
_____
_____
_____

What are you grateful for today? _____

*"I am asking us to interact with others in a higher, holier way. Please listen carefully. 'If there is anything virtuous, lovely, or of good report or praiseworthy' that we can say about another person—whether to his face or behind her back—that should be our standard of communication." - Russell M. Nelson*

DATE: _____

MEMORIES MADE, TOUGH TIMES, & LESSONS LEARNED:

Stressed   Angry   Tired   Sad   Happy   Excited

_____
_____
_____
_____
_____
_____
_____
_____

Prompt of the day:

Handling Conflict: Share how you've handled conflict in a constructive way during your mission.

_____
_____
_____
_____

What are you grateful for today? _____

Avoid the harmful practice of rating others' appearances or participating in "rating games." This objectifying behavior is hurtful and inappropriate, especially as representatives of Christ. Never ask others to rate your looks, as your worth extends far beyond superficial judgments. Commenting on the attractiveness of fellow missionaries may seem harmless but can severely damage self-esteem and lead to negative thoughts. Instead, view each person as a child of God with inherent value beyond their physical traits. Refuse to engage in these games and actively discourage them to promote a healthier perspective rooted in spiritual qualities.

DATE: _____

MEMORIES MADE, TOUGH TIMES, & LESSONS LEARNED:   Stressed   Angry   Tired   Sad   Happy   Excited

_____
_____
_____
_____
_____
_____
_____
_____

What are you grateful for today? _____

*"If you are not...seeking the Lord through daily prayer and gospel study, you leave yourself vulnerable to philosophies that may be intriguing but are not true. Even Saints who are otherwise faithful can be derailed by the steady beat of Babylon's band." - Russell M. Nelson*

DATE: _____

MEMORIES MADE, TOUGH TIMES, & LESSONS LEARNED:   Stressed   Angry   Tired   Sad   Happy   Excited

_____
_____
_____
_____
_____
_____
_____

Prompt of the day:
Community Interactions: Describe a meaningful interaction you had with someone in the community. What did this interaction teach you about love, acceptance, or empathy?

_____
_____
_____
_____
_____

What are you grateful for today? _____

Myth: All missionaries need to be extroverted and naturally outgoing. Reality: All missionaries come with diverse personalities. Introverted individuals can also be effective missionaries, often excelling in deep, one-on-one conversations. While being comfortable talking to people is helpful, the most important qualities for a missionary are a sincere love for others, a strong testimony, and a willingness to serve. Both introverts and extroverts can develop the skills needed to connect with people and share the gospel effectively in their own unique ways.

DATE: _____

MEMORIES MADE, TOUGH TIMES, & LESSONS LEARNED:

Stressed  Angry  Tired  Sad  Happy  Excited

_____
_____
_____
_____
_____
_____
_____
_____

What are you grateful for today? _____

"Speaking from the perspective of eternity, eternal life is the greatest of all the gifts of God. But narrowing the perspective to this life only, the gift of the Holy Ghost is the greatest gift a mortal can enjoy" - Bruce R. McConkie

DATE: _____

MEMORIES MADE, TOUGH TIMES, & LESSONS LEARNED:

Stressed  Angry  Tired  Sad  Happy  Excited

_____
_____
_____
_____
_____
_____
_____
_____

Prompt of the day:

Gospel Discussions with Youth: Reflect on a gospel discussion with youth and what it taught you about engaging with younger audiences.

_____
_____
_____
_____
_____

What are you grateful for today? _____

What is the key to becoming a Christlike missionary? It is your willingness to see, feel, and act as Jesus sees, feels, and acts. It's called Charity. That is the key to missionary work. How do you get it? There are no shortcuts. There is only one source for this precious gift: Moroni 7:47: "Pray unto the Father with all the energy of heart, that ye may be filled with this love, which he has bestowed upon all who are true followers of Jesus Christ; that ye may become the sons of God." We cannot create charity ourselves. We can make ourselves humble. We can withhold judgement. We can feel compassion for others. Then we must call on God "with all the energy of heart" for the heavenly gift of charity, which only He can give. Charity is the gift that changes everything, especially in missionary work.

DATE: _____

MEMORIES MADE, TOUGH TIMES, & LESSONS LEARNED:

Stressed　Angry　Tired　Sad　Happy　Excited

_____
_____
_____
_____
_____
_____
_____
_____

What are you grateful for today? _____

*"What a marvelous and wonderful thing it is, this powerful conviction that says the Church is true. It is God's holy work. He overrules in the things of His kingdom and in the lives of His sons and daughters. This is the reason for the growth of the Church. The strength of this cause and kingdom is not found in its temporal assets, impressive as they may be. It is found in the hearts of its people. That is why it is successful. That is why it is strong and growing." - Gordon B. Hinckley*

DATE: _____

MEMORIES MADE, TOUGH TIMES, & LESSONS LEARNED:

Stressed　Angry　Tired　Sad　Happy　Excited

_____
_____
_____
_____
_____
_____
_____

Prompt of the day:
Leadership Lessons: Write about the importance of self-care in maintaining your mental, physical, and spiritual health during your mission.

_____
_____
_____
_____

What are you grateful for today? _____

Do maintain a positive and optimistic attitude as often as possible, even when faced with challenges. Positivity can be contagious and uplifting, to your companion or to other missionaries. Just know, it is okay to have hard days and hard moments throughout your mission! That is completely normal! Don't bottle up your emotions or feel like you have to put on a brave face all the time. It's okay to have difficult days and to reach out for support when needed.

DATE: _____

MEMORIES MADE, TOUGH TIMES, & LESSONS LEARNED:

Stressed  Angry  Tired  Sad  Happy  Excited

_____
_____
_____
_____
_____
_____
_____
_____
_____

What are you grateful for today? _____

*"Pray in the name of Jesus Christ about your concerns, your fears, your weaknesses—yes, the very longings of your heart. And then listen! Write the thoughts that come to your mind. Record your feelings and follow through with actions that you are prompted to take. As you repeat this process day after day, month after month, year after year, you will "grow into the principle of revelation." - Russell M. Nelson*

DATE: _____

MEMORIES MADE, TOUGH TIMES, & LESSONS LEARNED:

Stressed  Angry  Tired  Sad  Happy  Excited

_____
_____
_____
_____
_____
_____
_____
_____

Prompt of the day:
Embracing Diversity: Share your experiences and lessons learned from embracing diversity during your mission.

_____
_____
_____
_____

What are you grateful for today? _____

Find joy in the power of prayer as a missionary: Make prayer a constant source of strength and joy during your mission. Develop a habit of praying fervently and sincerely, seeking guidance, comfort, and inspiration. Pray for your investigators, your companion, and your own spiritual growth. As you communicate with your Heavenly Father, you'll feel His love and support. You'll find joy in the answers to your prayers and in the peace that comes from aligning your will with His.

DATE: _____

MEMORIES MADE, TOUGH TIMES, & LESSONS LEARNED:

Stressed   Angry   Tired   Sad   Happy   Excited

_____
_____
_____
_____
_____
_____
_____
_____

What are you grateful for today? _____

"Everything we believe and every promise God has made to His covenant people come together in the temple. In every age, the temple has underscored the precious truth that those who make covenants with God and keep them are children of the covenant." - Russell M. Nelson

DATE: _____

MEMORIES MADE, TOUGH TIMES, & LESSONS LEARNED:

Stressed   Angry   Tired   Sad   Happy   Excited

_____
_____
_____
_____
_____
_____
_____
_____

Prompt of the day:
Homesickness and Coping: Write about moments of homesickness or longing for familiar comforts. How do you cope with these feelings, and what does this teach you about reliance on the Lord and His plan? _____

_____
_____
_____

What are you grateful for today? _____

Label your emotions. As a missionary, you may experience various emotions, including stress, anxiety, and frustration. Research suggests that labeling these emotions can help reduce their intensity. When you feel stressed, take a moment to pause and describe your feelings without judgment. This practice can prevent an emotional downward spiral and help you manage stress more effectively. Remember not to criticize yourself for the emotions you experience. The more you practice labeling your emotions, the more automatic it will become, rewiring your brain for better emotional regulation. Give it a try and see how it can benefit your mission.

DATE: _____

MEMORIES MADE, TOUGH TIMES, & LESSONS LEARNED:

Stressed     Angry     Tired     Sad     Happy     Excited

_____
_____
_____
_____
_____
_____
_____
_____

What are you grateful for today? _____

"Whenever I hear anyone, including myself, say, "I know the Book of Mormon is true," I want to exclaim, "That's nice, but it is not enough!" We need to feel, deep in "the inmost part" of our hearts, that the Book of Mormon is unequivocally the word of God. We must feel it so deeply that we would never want to live even one day without it." - Russell M. Nelson

DATE: _____

MEMORIES MADE, TOUGH TIMES, & LESSONS LEARNED:

Stressed     Angry     Tired     Sad     Happy     Excited

_____
_____
_____
_____
_____
_____
_____
_____

Prompt of the day:

Personal Prayer Journey: Reflect on how your personal prayer journey has evolved during your mission.

_____
_____
_____
_____
_____

What are you grateful for today? _____

Express gratitude to the Lord and others to counteract feelings of jealousy or discouragement. When you find yourself comparing your success to other missionaries, shift your focus to what you have and what is going right in your own work. Remember that the Lord is in charge of His work, and avoid measuring your worth or success based on the outward results of your efforts compared to others. Genuinely express gratitude for the opportunities and blessings you have been given, and let that gratitude empower you to continue serving with enthusiasm and love.

DATE: _____

MEMORIES MADE, TOUGH TIMES, & LESSONS LEARNED:

Stressed    Angry    Tired    Sad    Happy    Excited

_____
_____
_____
_____
_____
_____
_____
_____

What are you grateful for today? _____

*"It's very important that the messenger be worthy of the message. We ask you to look a certain way and act a certain way because of the message." - Jeffrey R. Holland*

DATE: _____

MEMORIES MADE, TOUGH TIMES, & LESSONS LEARNED:

Stressed    Angry    Tired    Sad    Happy    Excited

_____
_____
_____
_____
_____
_____
_____

Prompt of the day:
Scripture that Touched You: Share a scripture that has touched you deeply during your mission. Why does it resonate with you, and how have you shared this with others?

_____
_____
_____
_____
_____

What are you grateful for today? _____

Embrace the power of testimony as a missionary: Recognize the joy and strength that come from bearing your testimony of the gospel. Take every opportunity to share your witness of Jesus Christ, the Book of Mormon, and the restored Church. As you testify of these truths, you'll feel the confirming power of the Holy Ghost and a deepening of your own conviction. Find joy in the knowledge that your testimony can touch hearts and change lives, including your own.

DATE: _____

MEMORIES MADE, TOUGH TIMES, & LESSONS LEARNED:

Stressed  Angry  Tired  Sad  Happy  Excited

_____
_____
_____
_____
_____
_____
_____
_____

What are you grateful for today? _____

*"While we take the gospel of Christ to all people, we do not oppose other churches. If you meet someone who challenges our right to the title Christian, do not confront them. Teach them peaceably. We have but to remain humble and peaceable followers of Christ, for He has promised, 'I will fight your battles.'" - Boyd K. Packer*

DATE: _____

MEMORIES MADE, TOUGH TIMES, & LESSONS LEARNED:

Stressed  Angry  Tired  Sad  Happy  Excited

_____
_____
_____
_____
_____
_____
_____
_____

Prompt of the day:

Witnessing Acts of Charity: Write about witnessing an act of charity that deeply moved you.

_____
_____
_____
_____

What are you grateful for today? _____

Do focus on your efforts to help people come unto Christ (I think that is part of your mission purpose...). Recognize that success is measured by your dedication, love, and service, not just numbers. Trust that the Lord sees your hard work and will bless you and those you serve. Don't fall into the trap of defining success solely by baptisms or church attendance. Your success is NOT determined by these metrics alone. The Lord is watching your efforts to help people come unto Him. Be careful not to compare your success with others. Everyone is going to have a different mission experience. Let yours be YOURS!

DATE: _____

MEMORIES MADE, TOUGH TIMES, & LESSONS LEARNED: Stressed  Angry  Tired  Sad  Happy  Excited

_____
_____
_____
_____
_____
_____
_____
_____

What are you grateful for today? _____

"*The ability to qualify for, receive, and act on personal revelation is the single most important skill that can be acquired in this life...It requires a conscious effort to diminish distractions, but having the Spirit of revelation makes it possible to prevail over opposition and persist in faith through difficult days and essential routine tasks. ... With [personal revelation] we cannot fail; without it we cannot succeed.*" - Julie B. Beck

DATE: _____

MEMORIES MADE, TOUGH TIMES, & LESSONS LEARNED: Stressed  Angry  Tired  Sad  Happy  Excited

_____
_____
_____
_____
_____
_____
_____
_____

Prompt of the day:
Planning and Goal Setting: Discuss how you approach planning and goal setting in your mission. How do these practices contribute to your effectiveness and spiritual growth?

_____
_____
_____
_____
_____

What are you grateful for today? _____

Prioritize sleep for peak performance. Missionaries can reduce stress by prioritizing sleep. Research shows that missing just 90 minutes of sleep can reduce alertness by 33%. High achievers often average 8 hours and 36 minutes of sleep each night, recognizing its importance for peak performance and reaching full potential. As a missionary, view adequate sleep not as laziness but as a critical component of success. By following the mission rules and making sleep a priority, you can better manage stress and serve others more effectively.

DATE: _____

MEMORIES MADE, TOUGH TIMES, & LESSONS LEARNED:

Stressed   Angry   Tired   Sad   Happy   Excited

_____
_____
_____
_____
_____
_____
_____
_____
_____

What are you grateful for today? _____

*"The Lord knows you and loves you. He is your Savior and your Redeemer. He leads and guides His Church. He will lead and guide you in your personal life if you will make time for Him in your life— each and every day." - Russell M. Nelson*

DATE: _____

MEMORIES MADE, TOUGH TIMES, & LESSONS LEARNED:

Stressed   Angry   Tired   Sad   Happy   Excited

_____
_____
_____
_____
_____
_____
_____
_____

Prompt of the day:
The Role of the Atonement: Reflect on a personal experience that deepened your understanding of the Atonement of Jesus Christ.

_____
_____
_____
_____
_____

What are you grateful for today? _____

Remember "AIM." It stands for an "All-In Missionary." Decide early on to go "all-in." Let go of lesser things. Don't secretly text others on days you shouldn't. Be obedient and you will be blessed. Refuse to be average. Don't just go through the motions and count down your days left. Rise up and be the best you can be. The Lord prepared people for you to teach, and they are waiting. They have been waiting since the premortal existence. Pray to find them. Commit to AIM.

DATE: _____

MEMORIES MADE, TOUGH TIMES, & LESSONS LEARNED:

Stressed  Angry  Tired  Sad  Happy  Excited

_____
_____
_____
_____
_____
_____
_____
_____

What are you grateful for today? _____

*"Be patient with yourself. Perfection comes not in this life, but in the next life. Don't demand things that are unreasonable, but demand of yourself improvement. As you let the Lord help you through that, He will make the difference." - Russell M. Nelson*

DATE: _____

MEMORIES MADE, TOUGH TIMES, & LESSONS LEARNED:

Stressed  Angry  Tired  Sad  Happy  Excited

_____
_____
_____
_____
_____
_____
_____
_____

Prompt of the day:
Weekly Reflections: At the end of each week, summarize your feelings, experiences, and lessons learned. What are you grateful for, and what are your goals for the coming week?

_____
_____
_____
_____

What are you grateful for today? _____

Immersing yourself in missionary work can be a source of strength and happiness. By staying focused on your purpose and working diligently, you'll find that worries and challenges seem less daunting. Remember, the work you're doing is meaningful and part of the greatest work and gathering occurring today! Your efforts are making a difference. As you continue to serve with dedication and commitment, you'll find that the Spirit accompanies you, bringing joy and peace even in difficult times. Stay focused on your mission and the work at hand, trust that the Lord is taking care of things at home, and you'll find that you are able to overcome challenges and find success in your efforts.

DATE: _____

MEMORIES MADE, TOUGH TIMES, & LESSONS LEARNED:

Stressed    Angry    Tired    Sad    Happy    Excited

_____
_____
_____
_____
_____
_____
_____
_____
_____

What are you grateful for today? _____

*"We can pray to be of one heart and one mind with the Lord's anointed and with our loved ones. We can pray for mutual understanding and respect between ourselves and our neighbors. If we really care for others, we should pray for them." - Russell M. Nelson*

DATE: _____

MEMORIES MADE, TOUGH TIMES, & LESSONS LEARNED:

Stressed    Angry    Tired    Sad    Happy    Excited

_____
_____
_____
_____
_____
_____
_____
_____
_____

Prompt of the day:

Learning Through Service: Share a moment when you learned something significant through an act of service.

_____
_____
_____
_____

What are you grateful for today? _____

Seek personal revelation. President Russell M. Nelson has said multiple times, "I plead with you to increase your spiritual capacity to receive revelation." Take time each day to seek personal revelation through prayer and scripture study. The guidance you receive will help you make decisions and navigate challenges. Personal revelation is a powerful tool in missionary work, guiding you to those who are ready to receive the message of the gospel. Cultivate a habit of seeking guidance from the Spirit in all aspects of your mission, and you'll find that you're better able to discern God's will and follow His direction.

DATE: _____

MEMORIES MADE, TOUGH TIMES, & LESSONS LEARNED:    Stressed   Angry   Tired   Sad   Happy   Excited

_____
_____
_____
_____
_____
_____
_____
_____

What are you grateful for today? _____

*"You covenant to always remember the Savior. In situations that are highly charged and filled with contention, I invite you to remember Jesus Christ. Pray to have the courage and wisdom to say or do what He would. As we follow the Prince of Peace, we will become His peacemakers." - Russell M. Nelson*

DATE: _____

MEMORIES MADE, TOUGH TIMES, & LESSONS LEARNED:    Stressed   Angry   Tired   Sad   Happy   Excited

_____
_____
_____
_____
_____
_____
_____

Prompt of the day:

Testimony Evolution: Share a situation that required significant patience and understanding, and how you navigated it.

_____
_____
_____
_____

What are you grateful for today? _____

Show compassion to those you serve, recognizing that many people struggle with mental illness, addiction, family challenges, and other difficulties. Strive to be a source of comfort and support, just as the Savior would. Remember that approximately one in five adults experiences mental illness every year, and many others face challenges such as pornography addiction, divorce, and single parenthood. As a missionary, you have the opportunity to be a light in the lives of those who are suffering, offering them the hope and healing that come through the gospel of Jesus Christ.

DATE: _____

MEMORIES MADE, TOUGH TIMES, & LESSONS LEARNED:

Stressed    Angry    Tired    Sad    Happy    Excited

_____
_____
_____
_____
_____
_____
_____
_____

What are you grateful for today? _____

"I would like to suggest five specific actions we can take to help us maintain positive spiritual momentum...Get on the covenant path and stay there... Discover the joy of daily repentance...Learn about God and how He works... Seek and expect miracles...End conflict in your personal life." - Russell M. Nelson

DATE: _____

MEMORIES MADE, TOUGH TIMES, & LESSONS LEARNED:

Stressed    Angry    Tired    Sad    Happy    Excited

_____
_____
_____
_____
_____
_____
_____
_____

Prompt of the day:
Overcoming Language Misunderstandings: Write about a humorous or insightful language misunderstanding and what you learned from it.

_____
_____
_____
_____

What are you grateful for today? _____

Remember that it is completely normal to experience all kinds of ups and downs as a missionary. There will be days when you feel on top of the world, and others when you feel discouraged or overwhelmed. Embrace these experiences as opportunities for growth and learning. Lean on your faith and the support of your companions and leaders during challenging times. Celebrate the successes (with ice cream?) and learn from the setbacks, knowing that each experience is helping you become a better missionary.

DATE: _____

MEMORIES MADE, TOUGH TIMES, & LESSONS LEARNED:

Stressed    Angry    Tired    Sad    Happy    Excited

_____
_____
_____
_____
_____
_____
_____
_____

What are you grateful for today? _____

*"I say, choose faith. Choose faith over doubt, choose faith over fear, choose faith over the unknown and the unseen, and choose faith over pessimism." - Dallin H. Oaks*

DATE: _____

MEMORIES MADE, TOUGH TIMES, & LESSONS LEARNED:

Stressed    Angry    Tired    Sad    Happy    Excited

_____
_____
_____
_____
_____
_____
_____
_____

Prompt of the day:
Daily Acts of Kindness: Write about a small act of kindness you performed or witnessed today. How did it make you feel?

_____
_____
_____
_____
_____

What are you grateful for today? _____

Be open to learning, stretching, and growth. The mission is a place for learning and growth, both spiritually and personally. Be open to new experiences, ideas, and perspectives. Embrace the teachings and guidance you receive and be willing to change and improve. This attitude of openness and humility will not only enhance your missionary experience but also benefit you throughout your life. Approach each day with a sense of curiosity and a willingness to learn from those around you. Seek out opportunities for growth and development, both spiritually and personally, and be open to the lessons they bring.

DATE: _____

MEMORIES MADE, TOUGH TIMES, & LESSONS LEARNED:

Stressed  Angry  Tired  Sad  Happy  Excited

_____
_____
_____
_____
_____
_____
_____
_____

What are you grateful for today? _____

"The assaults of the adversary are increasing exponentially, in intensity and in variety. Our need to be in the temple on a regular basis has never been greater. I plead with you to take a prayerful look at how you spend your time...I promise you that the Lord will bring the miracles He knows you need as you make sacrifices to serve and worship in His temples." - Russell M. Nelson

DATE: _____

MEMORIES MADE, TOUGH TIMES, & LESSONS LEARNED:

Stressed  Angry  Tired  Sad  Happy  Excited

_____
_____
_____
_____
_____
_____
_____
_____

Prompt of the day:

Adapting Gospel Teaching to Various Ages: Reflect on your experiences adapting gospel teaching to different age groups.

_____
_____
_____
_____

What are you grateful for today? _____

Take care of your physical and mental health. Read that again. Seriously, this is one of the most important investments you'll make. When you're running low on mental fuel, your entire life will be affected in negative ways. Take care of your body and brain - and there's all kinds of tips out there, including tons of them here in this journal!!

DATE: _____

MEMORIES MADE, TOUGH TIMES, & LESSONS LEARNED:

Stressed   Angry   Tired   Sad   Happy   Excited

_____
_____
_____
_____
_____
_____
_____

What are you grateful for today? _____

*"Mortality is a master class in learning to choose the things of greatest eternal import. Far too many people live as though this life is all there is. However, your choices today will determine three things: where you will live throughout all eternity, the kind of body with which you will be resurrected, and those with whom you will live forever. So, think celestial."*
*- Russell M. Nelson*

DATE: _____

MEMORIES MADE, TOUGH TIMES, & LESSONS LEARNED:

Stressed   Angry   Tired   Sad   Happy   Excited

_____
_____
_____
_____
_____
_____
_____

Prompt of the day:
Learning from Rejection: Reflect on a recent rejection or setback in your missionary work. What did you learn from this experience?

_____
_____
_____
_____

What are you grateful for today? _____

Dr. Sue Johnson, one of the most respected marriage scholars, once stated, "The greatest gift we can give another person is our emotionally attuned attention and our timely responsiveness." Your attention and responsiveness. For decades, countless people said the greatest gift in marriage and family was one's time. However, in our day of technology distractions, we believe the greater gift is your attention. As a missionary, you can spend time with others without paying attention to them. Learn to listen with love, aim for understanding, reflect what you hear with compassion, and respond in Christlike ways. Be timely in your responses to others' requests. Return phone calls and texts promptly. Don't just give the Lord your time. Offer your heart and your attention as one of the greatest gifts you can truly give.

DATE: _____

MEMORIES MADE, TOUGH TIMES, & LESSONS LEARNED:

Stressed   Angry   Tired   Sad   Happy   Excited

_____
_____
_____
_____
_____
_____
_____
_____

What are you grateful for today? _____

"The Lord's message is for everyone. This is a global work. ... The message is to invite all God's children on both sides of the veil to come unto their Savior and enjoy the blessings of the temple, have enduring joy, and qualify for eternal life. And that will bring hope, help, and lift to all people." - Russell M. Nelson

DATE: _____

MEMORIES MADE, TOUGH TIMES, & LESSONS LEARNED:

Stressed   Angry   Tired   Sad   Happy   Excited

_____
_____
_____
_____
_____
_____
_____
_____

Prompt of the day:
Cultural Celebrations: Describe a cultural celebration you participated in and how it enriched your mission experience.

_____
_____
_____
_____
_____
_____

What are you grateful for today? _____

Make stress your friend. In her TED talk "How to Make Stress Your Friend," Kelly McGonigal suggests embracing stress rather than fearing it. By changing your attitude towards stress and recognizing it as a helpful response, missionaries can become stronger, more social, and healthier. Stress encourages the release of oxytocin, the "cuddle hormone," enhancing empathy, social support, and protecting the cardiovascular system. Embracing stress can lead to better health and resilience during your mission.

DATE: _____

MEMORIES MADE, TOUGH TIMES, & LESSONS LEARNED:

Stressed   Angry   Tired   Sad   Happy   Excited

_____
_____
_____
_____
_____
_____
_____
_____

What are you grateful for today? _____


*"The intensity of our desire to share the gospel is a great indicator of the extent of our personal conversation." - Dallin H. Oaks*


DATE: _____

MEMORIES MADE, TOUGH TIMES, & LESSONS LEARNED:

Stressed   Angry   Tired   Sad   Happy   Excited

_____
_____
_____
_____
_____
_____
_____

Prompt of the day:
Inspiring Individuals: Describe someone you've met on your mission who inspires you. What qualities do they possess that you admire?

_____
_____
_____
_____

What are you grateful for today? _____

Find joy in your personal growth as a missionary: Recognize that your mission is a time of incredible personal growth and development. Embrace the opportunities to learn new skills, overcome challenges, and stretch yourself beyond your comfort zone. Celebrate your progress and the Christlike attributes you are developing. As you find joy in your personal growth, you'll approach your missionary service with greater enthusiasm and purpose. Remember that you are becoming the person God wants you to be, and that your mission is a vital part of that process.

DATE: _____

MEMORIES MADE, TOUGH TIMES, & LESSONS LEARNED:

Stressed　Angry　Tired　Sad　Happy　Excited

_____
_____
_____
_____
_____
_____
_____
_____
_____

What are you grateful for today? _____

"The power of these priesthood keys is infinite and breathtaking. Consider how your life would be different if priesthood keys had not been restored to the earth. Without priesthood keys, you could not be endowed with the power of God...none of us would have access to essential ordinances and covenants that bind us to our loved ones eternally and allow us eventually to live with God...Priesthood keys distinguish The Church of Jesus Christ of Latter-day Saints from any other organization on earth." - Russell M. Nelson

DATE: _____

MEMORIES MADE, TOUGH TIMES, & LESSONS LEARNED:

Stressed　Angry　Tired　Sad　Happy　Excited

_____
_____
_____
_____
_____
_____
_____
_____

Prompt of the day:

Personal Sacrifices of Missionary Work: Reflect on the personal sacrifices you've made for missionary work and how they've shaped your character.

_____
_____
_____
_____
_____

What are you grateful for today? _____

Recognize that as long as you are striving to do your best, repenting when needed, and working diligently, you can consider yourself a successful missionary, regardless of whether people accept your message. Focus on developing Christlike attributes, obeying with exactness, and serving others at every opportunity. Trust that when you have done your very best, you can feel certain that the Lord is pleased with your efforts, even if you experience disappointments. Find confidence and peace in knowing that you are accepted by the Lord as you strive to serve Him faithfully.

DATE: _____

MEMORIES MADE, TOUGH TIMES, & LESSONS LEARNED:

Stressed   Angry   Tired   Sad   Happy   Excited

_____
_____
_____
_____
_____
_____
_____
_____

What are you grateful for today? _____

"To be sure, there may be times when you feel as though the heavens are closed. But I promise that as you continue to be obedient, expressing gratitude for every blessing the Lord gives you, and as you patiently honor the Lord's timetable, you will be given the knowledge and understanding you seek. Every blessing the Lord has for you—even miracles—will follow. That is what personal revelation will do for you." - Russell M. Nelson

DATE: _____

MEMORIES MADE, TOUGH TIMES, & LESSONS LEARNED:

Stressed   Angry   Tired   Sad   Happy   Excited

_____
_____
_____
_____
_____
_____
_____
_____

Prompt of the day:
Adapting to Change: How have you adapted to a significant change during your mission (e.g., a new area, companion, or rule)? What helped you through this transition?

_____
_____
_____
_____
_____

What are you grateful for today? _____

Try a cold shower. Just hear us out. Missionaries can increase their stress resilience by challenging themselves with a cold shower. After your usual warm shower, switch the water to a cold temperature and endure it for 15 to 30 seconds, focusing on your breathing. Recognize that physical stress doesn't have to trigger psychological stress. Choose to keep a relaxed mind amid the shock, reminding yourself that your body is built to adapt and benefit from this experience. By embracing discomfort and practicing mindfulness in a controlled setting, you'll be better prepared to handle unexpected stressors during your mission. Give it a try!

DATE: _____

MEMORIES MADE, TOUGH TIMES, & LESSONS LEARNED:

Stressed    Angry    Tired    Sad    Happy    Excited

_____
_____
_____
_____
_____
_____
_____
_____

What are you grateful for today? _____

"I plead with you who have distanced yourselves from the Church and with you who have not yet really sought to know that the Savior's Church has been restored. Do the spiritual work to find out for yourselves, and please do it now. Time is running out." - Russell M. Nelson

DATE: _____

MEMORIES MADE, TOUGH TIMES, & LESSONS LEARNED:

Stressed    Angry    Tired    Sad    Happy    Excited

_____
_____
_____
_____
_____
_____
_____

Prompt of the day:

Spiritual Gifts: Write about a spiritual gift you've discovered or developed during your mission.

_____
_____
_____
_____
_____

What are you grateful for today? _____

Respect other's apartments and living areas. As you get to know other missionaries, members and others you teach, stay respectful of their places. Always knock. Don't assume you can help yourself to their snacks or food whenever you want. Respect their shoe policy and don't put your feet up on furniture. If you make a mess, clean it up. If you break something, replace it. When missionaries get too comfortable, they tend to get too casual. Strive to be a guest that people look forward to having over—start with respect and asking about the living space rules.

DATE: _____

MEMORIES MADE, TOUGH TIMES, & LESSONS LEARNED:

Stressed  Angry  Tired  Sad  Happy  Excited

_____
_____
_____
_____
_____
_____
_____
_____

What are you grateful for today? _____

*"The time is long overdue for a massive flooding of the earth with the Book of Mormon for the many reasons which the Lord has given. In this age of electronic media and mass distribution of the printed word, God will hold us accountable if we do not now move the Book of Mormon in a monumental way." - Ezra Taft Benson*

DATE: _____

MEMORIES MADE, TOUGH TIMES, & LESSONS LEARNED:

Stressed  Angry  Tired  Sad  Happy  Excited

_____
_____
_____
_____
_____
_____
_____
_____

Prompt of the day:
Unexpected Joys: Share a moment of unexpected joy or humor you experienced. How did it brighten your day or lighten your burdens?

_____
_____
_____
_____

What are you grateful for today? _____

Myth: Missionaries have all the answers to theological questions. Reality: Recognize that you are well-trained but will continue to learn and grow. You might not have all the answers and you'll often learn alongside those you teach/teach with. When faced with difficult questions, rely on the Holy Spirit, study resources, and church leaders' wisdom. You aren't expected to be perfect, but to share the truth you know and grow together with your companion.

DATE: _____

MEMORIES MADE, TOUGH TIMES, & LESSONS LEARNED:

Stressed  Angry  Tired  Sad  Happy  Excited

_____
_____
_____
_____
_____
_____
_____
_____
_____

What are you grateful for today? _____

*"If we as a people and as individuals are to have access to the power of the Atonement of Jesus Christ—to cleanse and heal us, to strengthen and magnify us, and ultimately to exalt us—we must clearly acknowledge Him as the source of that power. We can begin by calling His Church by the name He decreed." - Russell M. Nelson*

DATE: _____

MEMORIES MADE, TOUGH TIMES, & LESSONS LEARNED:

Stressed  Angry  Tired  Sad  Happy  Excited

_____
_____
_____
_____
_____
_____
_____
_____

Prompt of the day:
The Role of Compassion in Missionary Work: Reflect on moments when compassion was pivotal in your interactions and teaching.

_____
_____
_____
_____

What are you grateful for today? _____

Respect your mission president and other leaders. They invest a great deal of time preparing trainings, assignments, and activities to support your growth as a missionary. If you interrupt or cause distractions, it can hinder the learning experience for everyone. Same with missionaries called as leaders. Contribute to a positive training environment by listening attentively, participating actively, and avoiding distractions—including your phone. Encourage your fellow missionaries to do the same. Remember, your leaders are people with feelings. They notice when you aren't listening or being disrespectful. Be sure to express your gratitude to them—they may rarely hear it.

DATE: _____

MEMORIES MADE, TOUGH TIMES, & LESSONS LEARNED:

Stressed  Angry  Tired  Sad  Happy  Excited

_____
_____
_____
_____
_____
_____
_____
_____

What are you grateful for today? _____

"As I agonized over my inadequacies this week, I received a distinct impression which both chastened and comforted me: to focus not on what I can't do but rather on what I can do. I can testify of the plain and precious truths of the gospel." - Gary E. Stevenson

DATE: _____

MEMORIES MADE, TOUGH TIMES, & LESSONS LEARNED:

Stressed  Angry  Tired  Sad  Happy  Excited

_____
_____
_____
_____
_____
_____
_____

Prompt of the day:
Spiritual Practices: Beyond prayer and scripture study, what spiritual practices have you found meaningful on your mission?

_____
_____
_____
_____
_____

What are you grateful for today? _____

The promises found in Doctrine and Covenants 6:32-37 can be a source of strength and comfort during challenging times. These verses assure you of the Lord's presence, rewards for righteousness, and inheritance of the celestial kingdom as you faithfully keep His commandments. Find peace in the knowledge that God is always near, ready to bless you for your obedience, forgive you upon repentance, and grant you eternal life as you follow the teachings of Jesus Christ. Trust in these promises, and you will find the strength and courage to face any challenge that comes your way.

DATE: _____

MEMORIES MADE, TOUGH TIMES, & LESSONS LEARNED:

Stressed  Angry  Tired  Sad  Happy  Excited

_____
_____
_____
_____
_____
_____
_____
_____

What are you grateful for today? _____

"As you think celestial, you will view trials and opposition in a new light. When someone you love attacks truth, think celestial, and don't question your testimony...There is no end to the adversary's deceptions. Please be prepared. Never take counsel from those who do not believe. Seek guidance from voices you can trust—from prophets, seers, and revelators and from the whisperings of the Holy Ghost." - Russell M. Nelson

DATE: _____

MEMORIES MADE, TOUGH TIMES, & LESSONS LEARNED:

Stressed  Angry  Tired  Sad  Happy  Excited

_____
_____
_____
_____
_____
_____
_____

Prompt of the day:

Navigating Cultural Sensitivities: Reflect on a time when you had to navigate cultural sensitivities with wisdom and respect.

_____
_____
_____
_____

What are you grateful for today? _____

Find joy in the present moment as a missionary: Embrace the present moment during your mission. Instead of dwelling on the past or worrying about the future, focus on the opportunities and experiences right in front of you. Find joy in your daily interactions with companions, investigators, and members. Savor the small moments of beauty, laughter, and connection. As you learn to appreciate the present, you'll find a deeper sense of contentment and happiness in your missionary service.

DATE: _____

MEMORIES MADE, TOUGH TIMES, & LESSONS LEARNED:

Stressed  Angry  Tired  Sad  Happy  Excited

_____
_____
_____
_____
_____
_____
_____
_____

What are you grateful for today? _____

*"In every high-jumping competition there is a minimum height at which the competition starts. The high jumper cannot ask to start at a lower height. In the same way, you should not expect the standards to be lowered to allow you to serve a mission. If you want to be a missionary, you must be able to clear the minimum standards." - L. Tom Perry*

DATE: _____

MEMORIES MADE, TOUGH TIMES, & LESSONS LEARNED:

Stressed  Angry  Tired  Sad  Happy  Excited

_____
_____
_____
_____
_____
_____
_____

Prompt of the day:
Personal Revelation: Describe a time when you felt you received personal revelation. How did it come, and how did you respond?

_____
_____
_____
_____
_____

What are you grateful for today? _____

Do consider the concerns and feedback of local members. Actively listen to their perspectives and seek to understand the unique needs and challenges facing the community. Use this knowledge to adapt your approach and tailor your efforts to better serve those you are called to minister to. Don't ignore local concerns and feedback. By valuing their input, you can foster collaboration, strengthen community bonds, and enrich your missionary experience.

DATE: _____

MEMORIES MADE, TOUGH TIMES, & LESSONS LEARNED:

Stressed  Angry  Tired  Sad  Happy  Excited

_____
_____
_____
_____
_____
_____
_____
_____

What are you grateful for today? _____

*"Joy is powerful, and focusing on joy brings God's power into our lives. As in all things, Jesus Christ is our ultimate exemplar, 'who for the joy that was set before him endured the cross.' Think of that! In order for Him to endure the most excruciating experience ever endured on earth, our Savior focused on joy!" - Russell M. Nelson*

DATE: _____

MEMORIES MADE, TOUGH TIMES, & LESSONS LEARNED:

Stressed  Angry  Tired  Sad  Happy  Excited

_____
_____
_____
_____
_____
_____
_____
_____

Prompt of the day:

Gospel Parables in Modern Life: Write about a modern-day situation that reminded you of a gospel parable and its teachings.

_____
_____
_____
_____

What are you grateful for today? _____

Avoid being judgmental towards others, including your companion, investigators, or those who may reject your message. The Savior taught us not to condemn others but to forgive and show compassion. As a missionary, focus on loving and serving those around you, regardless of their actions or attitudes. By extending kindness and understanding, even in difficult situations, you can touch hearts and inspire change in ways you may never fully comprehend. Remember that your Christlike example of love and compassion can have a far-reaching impact on the lives of those you serve. Strive to see others as the Savior sees them, and treat them with the same kindness and respect you would hope to receive. Your unwavering commitment to kindness will not only bless the lives of others but will also help you grow in your own discipleship and spiritual development.

DATE: _____

MEMORIES MADE, TOUGH TIMES, & LESSONS LEARNED:

Stressed   Angry   Tired   Sad   Happy   Excited

_____
_____
_____
_____
_____
_____
_____
_____

What are you grateful for today? _____

*"We should remember that the Lord does not punish us for our sins; he simply withholds his blessings. We punish ourselves." - Theodore M. Burton*

DATE: _____

MEMORIES MADE, TOUGH TIMES, & LESSONS LEARNED:

Stressed   Angry   Tired   Sad   Happy   Excited

_____
_____
_____
_____
_____
_____
_____

Prompt of the day:

Influence of Music: Write about how music has influenced your mission. Is there a particular hymn or song that uplifts you?

_____
_____
_____
_____

What are you grateful for today? _____

Recognize that you can't do this alone. Sure, you can endure the rest of the time out there. Or you can enjoy this time. He wants you to be happy. Live like Jesus. Love like Jesus. Read about Him. And then, day by day, you'll become like Him and you'll discern His will for you and for those you are teaching.

DATE: _____

MEMORIES MADE, TOUGH TIMES, & LESSONS LEARNED:

Stressed   Angry   Tired   Sad   Happy   Excited

_____
_____
_____
_____
_____
_____
_____
_____

What are you grateful for today? _____

"Our message is so imperative, when you stop to think that the salvation, the eternal salvation of the world, rests upon the shoulders of this church. When all is said and done, if the world is going to be saved, we have to do it. There is no escaping from that. No other people in the history of the world have received the kind of mandate that we have received. We are responsible for all who have lived on this earth." - Gordon B. Hinckley

DATE: _____

MEMORIES MADE, TOUGH TIMES, & LESSONS LEARNED:

Stressed   Angry   Tired   Sad   Happy   Excited

_____
_____
_____
_____
_____
_____
_____
_____

Prompt of the day:

Missionary Work's Emotional Challenges: Share how you cope with the emotional challenges of missionary work.

_____
_____
_____
_____
_____

What are you grateful for today? _____

Do regularly express your appreciation for the members' support, kindness, and any assistance they provide. Gratitude can strengthen bonds and encourage continued collaboration. Write thank-you notes, deliver (yummy) cookies, and express gratitude through kind words and service. Don't take the members' support for granted or fail to acknowledge their efforts. Regularly show your appreciation and let them know how much their help means to you.

DATE: _____

MEMORIES MADE, TOUGH TIMES, & LESSONS LEARNED:

Stressed   Angry   Tired   Sad   Happy   Excited

_____
_____
_____
_____
_____
_____
_____
_____
_____

What are you grateful for today? _____

"*When we habitually understate the meaning of the Atonement, we take more serious risks than simply leaving one another without comforting reassurances—for some may simply drop out of the race, worn out and beaten down with the harsh and untrue belief that they are just not celestial material.*" - Bruce C. Hafen

DATE: _____

MEMORIES MADE, TOUGH TIMES, & LESSONS LEARNED:

Stressed   Angry   Tired   Sad   Happy   Excited

_____
_____
_____
_____
_____
_____
_____
_____

Prompt of the day:
Local Traditions: Share a local tradition you've experienced on your mission and how it has enriched your understanding of the people and culture.

_____
_____
_____
_____
_____

What are you grateful for today? _____

Take breaks and engage in stress-relief activities. This is another mental health checkup. Don't use breaks to procrastinate, but plan breaks and reward yourself when you have put in the time. Plus, breaks give your brain a chance to soak it all in. Physical activities are especially helpful for your brain AND your body. The key is to be "all-in" with whatever you are doing, whether it's studying or taking a break.

DATE: _____

MEMORIES MADE, TOUGH TIMES, & LESSONS LEARNED:

Stressed   Angry   Tired   Sad   Happy   Excited

_____
_____
_____
_____
_____
_____
_____
_____

What are you grateful for today? _____

*"The more you learn about the Savior, the easier it will be to trust in His mercy, His infinite love, and His strengthening, healing, and redeeming power. The Savior is never closer to you than when you are facing or climbing a mountain with faith." - Russell M. Nelson*

DATE: _____

MEMORIES MADE, TOUGH TIMES, & LESSONS LEARNED:

Stressed   Angry   Tired   Sad   Happy   Excited

_____
_____
_____
_____
_____
_____
_____

Prompt of the day:
Building Interfaith Relationships: Reflect on your experiences building relationships with people of other faiths.

_____
_____
_____
_____

What are you grateful for today? _____

Learn to genuinely apologize. A sincere apology doesn't include blame or excuses. For instance, with a humble heart you might say, "I'm truly sorry for what I did. I feel so bad. I hope for your forgiveness, understanding it may take time. How can I make it up to you?" Real apologies involve sincerity, a change of heart, and a genuine desire to restore what was damaged. A genuine apology, when done right, can restore relationships. Remember, people are more important than problems.

DATE: _____

MEMORIES MADE, TOUGH TIMES, & LESSONS LEARNED:

Stressed   Angry   Tired   Sad   Happy   Excited

_____
_____
_____
_____
_____
_____
_____
_____

What are you grateful for today? _____

*"Taking the Savior's name upon us includes declaring and witnessing to others—through our actions and our words—that Jesus is the Christ. Have we been so afraid to offend someone who called us "Mormons" that we have failed to defend the Savior Himself, to stand up for Him even in the name by which His Church is called?" - Russell M. Nelson*

DATE: _____

MEMORIES MADE, TOUGH TIMES, & LESSONS LEARNED:

Stressed   Angry   Tired   Sad   Happy   Excited

_____
_____
_____
_____
_____
_____
_____

Prompt of the day:

Companion's Best Qualities: Reflect on the best qualities of your current or a past companion. How have they influenced you for the better?

_____
_____
_____
_____

What are you grateful for today? _____

Take time to refortify yourself and build yourself back up when serving others leaves you feeling fatigued or drained. Remember that even Jesus experienced fatigue and recognized the need to care for Himself. Ministering to the needs of others can be emotionally and spiritually taxing, and it's important to practice self-care to avoid burnout. Make time for daily prayer, scripture study, and other activities that help you feel close to God. Seek the companionship of the Holy Ghost and rely on His comforting and sustaining power. Don't hesitate to reach out for support from your companion, mission leaders, family, or other trusted friends when you need it.

DATE: _____

MEMORIES MADE, TOUGH TIMES, & LESSONS LEARNED:

Stressed   Angry   Tired   Sad   Happy   Excited

_____
_____
_____
_____
_____
_____
_____
_____

What are you grateful for today? _____

*"Being righteous doesn't mean being perfect or never making mistakes. It means developing an inner connection with God, repenting of our sins and mistakes, and freely helping others." - Sharon Eubank*

DATE: _____

MEMORIES MADE, TOUGH TIMES, & LESSONS LEARNED:

Stressed   Angry   Tired   Sad   Happy   Excited

_____
_____
_____
_____
_____
_____
_____

Prompt of the day:
Teaching Through Music: Describe an experience where music was a powerful tool in teaching or testimony.

_____
_____
_____
_____

What are you grateful for today? _____

Do maintain clear and open communication with local members. Be transparent about your goals, needs, and how they can be involved in missionary efforts. Oftentimes, the members are willing to help, they just don't know where to start. Give them ideas on how they can share the gospel in small and simple means. Don't keep members in the dark about your plans or assume they don't want to be involved. Communicate openly and provide specific ways they can contribute to the work.

DATE: _____

MEMORIES MADE, TOUGH TIMES, & LESSONS LEARNED:

Stressed  Angry  Tired  Sad  Happy  Excited

_____
_____
_____
_____
_____
_____
_____
_____

What are you grateful for today? _____

"We can also pray daily for our own personal missionary experiences. Pray that under the divine management of such things, the missionary opportunity you want is already being prepared in the heart of someone who longs for and looks for what you have." - Jeffrey R. Holland

DATE: _____

MEMORIES MADE, TOUGH TIMES, & LESSONS LEARNED:

Stressed  Angry  Tired  Sad  Happy  Excited

_____
_____
_____
_____
_____
_____
_____
_____

Prompt of the day:
Faith in Action: Describe a situation where you or someone else put their faith into action in a way that inspired you.

_____
_____
_____
_____

What are you grateful for today? _____

Spend time in nature. Breathing fresh air and spending time outdoors, particularly in green spaces, can be a natural and effective way for missionaries to uplift their mood and alleviate stress. The serenity and beauty of nature can have a calming effect, helping to clear the mind and rejuvenate the spirit. Regularly schedule time to step outside, be it for a leisurely walk or a visit to a nearby park on P-day, to harness these benefits and enhance overall well-being during your mission.

DATE: _____

MEMORIES MADE, TOUGH TIMES, & LESSONS LEARNED:

Stressed   Angry   Tired   Sad   Happy   Excited

_____
_____
_____
_____
_____
_____
_____
_____

What are you grateful for today? _____

*"If you are criticizing others, you are weakening the Church. If you are building others, you are building the kingdom of God. As Heavenly Father is kind, we also should be kind to others." - Joseph B. Wirthlin*

DATE: _____

MEMORIES MADE, TOUGH TIMES, & LESSONS LEARNED:

Stressed   Angry   Tired   Sad   Happy   Excited

_____
_____
_____
_____
_____
_____
_____
_____

Prompt of the day:
Missionary Work and Personal Identity: Reflect on how missionary work has influenced your personal identity.

_____
_____
_____
_____

What are you grateful for today? _____

Maintain a relationship of love. Instead of viewing scripture study and prayer as checklist activities, approach them as opportunities to maintain a loving relationship with God. Keep the conversation with your Heavenly Father ongoing and sincere. Find joy in staying connected with Him, knowing that He is always there to guide and comfort you. Focus on Christ. Like Nephi, make it a priority to talk of, rejoice in, and seek Christ in all things. Let your scripture study and prayer be centered on getting to know Him better, understanding His teachings, and following His example. As you focus on Christ, you will find joy, peace, and direction in your missionary work and in your life.

DATE: _____

MEMORIES MADE, TOUGH TIMES, & LESSONS LEARNED:

Stressed   Angry   Tired   Sad   Happy   Excited

_____
_____
_____
_____
_____
_____
_____
_____

What are you grateful for today? _____

"Serving a full-time mission may seem difficult to us. Perhaps it requires that we give up important things for a moment. The Lord certainly knows this, and He will always be by our side." - Marcos A. Aidukaitis

DATE: _____

MEMORIES MADE, TOUGH TIMES, & LESSONS LEARNED:

Stressed   Angry   Tired   Sad   Happy   Excited

_____
_____
_____
_____
_____
_____
_____

Prompt of the day:
Lesson Learned from a Child: Share a lesson you learned from interacting with a child during your mission.

_____
_____
_____
_____

What are you grateful for today? _____

When you imitate other missionaries or others, or adopt behaviors that aren't genuinely yours, you lose the chance to truly connect with people. The most precious thing you can offer is your authentic self. Regardless of the situation or what you're doing, what you're actually sharing is a piece of who you are. Embracing and presenting your true self is key, as genuine interactions and connections stem from authenticity, not from playing a role or following a script. Don't' try to be something you're not. Be you. But be the very best you.

DATE: _____

MEMORIES MADE, TOUGH TIMES, & LESSONS LEARNED:

Stressed    Angry    Tired    Sad    Happy    Excited

_____
_____
_____
_____
_____
_____
_____
_____

## What are you grateful for today?

"To more effectively flood the earth with the Book of Mormon, we must begin by better preparing our missionaries. We need missionaries who come into the mission field with burning testimonies of it. Even more importantly, we need more missionaries-including member missionaries-who are truly converted and have had spiritual experiences with the Book of Mormon. A missionary will not be effective if he or she does not have a strong testimony of this sacred volume of scripture. Indeed, I believe a missionary's effectiveness and success is directly related to his or her own conversion to, testimony of, and love of the Book of Mormon." - Joseph B. Wirthlin

DATE: _____

MEMORIES MADE, TOUGH TIMES, & LESSONS LEARNED:

Stressed    Angry    Tired    Sad    Happy    Excited

_____
_____
_____
_____
_____
_____
_____
_____

## Prompt of the day:

Resilience in the Face of Adversity: Share a story of resilience in the face of adversity during your mission.

_____
_____
_____
_____
_____

## What are you grateful for today? _____

Cultivate a spirit of unity with your missionary companion: Work to build a strong, unified relationship with your missionary companion. Recognize that you are both children of God, called to serve together for a divine purpose. Seek to understand and appreciate your companion's strengths, talents, and perspectives. Communicate openly and honestly, resolving conflicts with patience and forgiveness. As you cultivate a spirit of unity, you'll experience the joy of working together in the Lord's vineyard and witnessing miracles in your missionary service.

DATE: _____

MEMORIES MADE, TOUGH TIMES, & LESSONS LEARNED:

Stressed    Angry    Tired    Sad    Happy    Excited

_____
_____
_____
_____
_____
_____
_____
_____

What are you grateful for today? _____

"It [Missionary work] is by definition the most important thing you can do in the world, in time or eternity. For this reason you are engaged in the saving of the human soul. And that is the highest and holiest work in the universe. That is the thing that God Himself said was His work and glory. It is the purpose for which the Savior came to the earth and gave His life and was resurrected to open those possibilities and promises of Eternal Life...You join those ranks! You join that brotherhood and sisterhood and it is as I said by definition, by theology, it is the most important thing you can do." - Jeffrey R. Holland

DATE: _____

MEMORIES MADE, TOUGH TIMES, & LESSONS LEARNED:

Stressed    Angry    Tired    Sad    Happy    Excited

_____
_____
_____
_____
_____
_____
_____
_____

Prompt of the day:

A Day in the Life: Document a typical day on your mission, highlighting moments of joy, challenge, and reflection.

_____
_____
_____
_____
_____

What are you grateful for today? _____

I know of a man who records his favorite team's baseball games. He records them and then he actually looks to see who won. If his team lost, he doesn't bother watching the game. But if they win, then he pops some popcorn, grabs his favorite drink and watches the game. He says that if things aren't looking very promising and his team is behind, he doesn't stress and worry, because he knows who wins in the end! Similarly, we know how all of this ends. We just don't know when the final buzzer will sound. Stay on the covenant path. Hold fast to the iron rod. The gospel is true. It's all true. Jesus Christ wins in the end. And you are on His team. Go invite others to join His team.

DATE: _____

MEMORIES MADE, TOUGH TIMES, & LESSONS LEARNED:

Stressed   Angry   Tired   Sad   Happy   Excited

_____
_____
_____
_____
_____
_____
_____
_____
_____

What are you grateful for today? _____

"We have come not to take away from you the truth and virtue you possess. We have come not to find fault with you nor to criticize you. We have not come here to berate you. . . . Keep all the good that you have, and let us bring to you more good." - George Albert Smith

DATE: _____

MEMORIES MADE, TOUGH TIMES, & LESSONS LEARNED:

Stressed   Angry   Tired   Sad   Happy   Excited

_____
_____
_____
_____
_____
_____
_____
_____

Prompt of the day:

The Power of Scripture Study: Write about a moment when scripture study was particularly powerful or enlightening.

_____
_____
_____
_____
_____

What are you grateful for today? _____

Stay connected to your purpose: Remember why you chose to serve a mission and keep that purpose at the forefront of your mind. When challenges arise, refocus on your purpose and let it motivate you to keep going. Reread your mission call letter from God's prophet. Your mission is more than just a long commitment; it's a sacred opportunity to serve the Lord and bring others to Him. Keep your purpose in mind in all that you do, and you'll find that it gives meaning and direction to your mission experience.

DATE: _____

MEMORIES MADE, TOUGH TIMES, & LESSONS LEARNED:

Stressed  Angry  Tired  Sad  Happy  Excited

_____
_____
_____
_____
_____
_____
_____
_____

What are you grateful for today? _____

*"What will happen as you more intentionally hear, hearken, and heed what the Savior has said and what He is saying now through His prophets? I promise that you will be blessed with additional power to deal with temptation, struggles, and weakness...And I promise that your capacity to feel joy will increase even if turbulence increases in your life."* - Russell M. Nelson

DATE: _____

MEMORIES MADE, TOUGH TIMES, & LESSONS LEARNED:

Stressed  Angry  Tired  Sad  Happy  Excited

_____
_____
_____
_____
_____
_____
_____
_____

Prompt of the day:

Missionary Work Innovations: Write about an innovative approach you took in your missionary work. How was it received?

_____
_____
_____
_____

What are you grateful for today? _____

Serve your companion with Christlike love and compassion, following the example of Ammon, who selflessly served King Lamoni despite their cultural differences. Look for opportunities to help your companion, whether it be through acts of kindness, words of encouragement, or sincere prayers on their behalf. As you put your companion's needs before your own and strive to be a true friend and support, you will find that your hearts will be knit together in unity and love. This bond of service will not only strengthen your relationship but also enhance your ability to work together effectively in the Lord's vineyard. Some of your companions may become lifelong friends.

DATE: _____

MEMORIES MADE, TOUGH TIMES, & LESSONS LEARNED:

Stressed   Angry   Tired   Sad   Happy   Excited

_____
_____
_____
_____
_____
_____
_____
_____

What are you grateful for today? _____

"Unfortunately, too often we concentrate so much on our own problems that we lose focus on the solution, our Savior Jesus Christ." - Milton R. Camargo

DATE: _____

MEMORIES MADE, TOUGH TIMES, & LESSONS LEARNED:

Stressed   Angry   Tired   Sad   Happy   Excited

_____
_____
_____
_____
_____
_____
_____
_____

Prompt of the day:

Handling the Pressure of Expectations: Reflect on handling the pressure of expectations, both personal and from others, during your mission.

_____
_____
_____
_____

What are you grateful for today? _____

Prioritize what matters most as a missionary: Focus on the essential aspects of your missionary work. Prioritize your spiritual growth, your relationships with companions and investigators, and your efforts to share the gospel. Don't get distracted by less important tasks or worries. Remember, your primary purpose is to invite others to come unto Christ. When you keep this at the forefront of your mind, you'll find greater clarity, purpose, and happiness in your mission.

DATE: _____

MEMORIES MADE, TOUGH TIMES, & LESSONS LEARNED:

Stressed    Angry    Tired    Sad    Happy    Excited

_____
_____
_____
_____
_____
_____
_____
_____

What are you grateful for today? _____

"I testify that Joseph Smith was and is the prophet of this last dispensation. It was he who, through the gift and power of God, translated this holy book. This is the book that will help to prepare the world for the Second Coming of the Lord...I testify with my whole soul that in a most miraculous and singular way, the Book of Mormon teaches us of Jesus Christ and His gospel." - Russell M. Nelson

DATE: _____

MEMORIES MADE, TOUGH TIMES, & LESSONS LEARNED:

Stressed    Angry    Tired    Sad    Happy    Excited

_____
_____
_____
_____
_____
_____
_____
_____

Prompt of the day:

Building Relationships: Reflect on how you've built relationships with those you teach and serve. What approaches have been most effective?

_____
_____
_____

What are you grateful for today? _____

Follow Church standards and mission rules regarding moral conduct, dress, and grooming. Just obey these. These standards result from prayerful consideration by Church leaders. By adhering to them, you demonstrate your devotion to serving God and others. Your appearance can influence your thoughts, feelings, and actions, so dress and groom in a way that reflects your commitment to the gospel.

DATE: _____

MEMORIES MADE, TOUGH TIMES, & LESSONS LEARNED:

Stressed  Angry  Tired  Sad  Happy  Excited

_____
_____
_____
_____
_____
_____
_____
_____

What are you grateful for today? _____

*"Please do not fear or delay repenting. Satan delights in your misery. Cut it short. Cast his influence out of your life! Start today to experience the joy of putting off the natural man. The Savior loves us always but especially when we repent." - Russell M. Nelson*

DATE: _____

MEMORIES MADE, TOUGH TIMES, & LESSONS LEARNED:

Stressed  Angry  Tired  Sad  Happy  Excited

_____
_____
_____
_____
_____
_____
_____

Prompt of the day:
Memorable Farewells: Share the story of a memorable farewell with someone you met during your mission.

_____
_____
_____
_____

What are you grateful for today? _____

Develop Christlike attributes as a missionary: Make your mission a time to actively develop and strengthen Christlike attributes. Focus on qualities such as faith, hope, charity, humility, patience, and diligence. Study the Savior's life and teachings, seeking to emulate His example in your daily interactions and service. As you strive to develop Christlike attributes, you'll find greater joy and fulfillment in your missionary work. Your growing Christlike character will be a light to others and a testament to the transformative power of the gospel.

DATE: _____

MEMORIES MADE, TOUGH TIMES, & LESSONS LEARNED:

Stressed    Angry    Tired    Sad    Happy    Excited

_____
_____
_____
_____
_____
_____
_____
_____

What are you grateful for today? _____

*"Adversities are temporary. What is permanent is what we become by the way we react to them." - Dallin H. Oaks*

DATE: _____

MEMORIES MADE, TOUGH TIMES, & LESSONS LEARNED:

Stressed    Angry    Tired    Sad    Happy    Excited

_____
_____
_____
_____
_____
_____
_____
_____

Prompt of the day:

Overcoming Language Barriers: If applicable, share a story about overcoming a language barrier in a memorable or humorous way.

_____
_____
_____
_____

What are you grateful for today? _____

Do be mindful of the commitments you make and strive to follow through on your promises. Be honest about what you can and cannot do, setting realistic expectations and boundaries. Keep your word to build trust and credibility, which are essential for fostering meaningful connections. Don't make promises you can't keep. Overcommitting or failing to deliver can erode trust and hinder your ability to serve effectively. Prioritize authenticity and integrity in your interactions with others. Stick to your word!

DATE: _____

MEMORIES MADE, TOUGH TIMES, & LESSONS LEARNED:

Stressed    Angry    Tired    Sad    Happy    Excited

_____
_____
_____
_____
_____
_____
_____
_____

What are you grateful for today? _____

*"The Lord is gathering those who are willing to let God prevail in their lives. The Lord is gathering those who will choose to let God be the most important influence in their lives...As an essential prelude to the Second Coming of the Lord, it is the most important work in the world!" - Russell M. Nelson*

DATE: _____

MEMORIES MADE, TOUGH TIMES, & LESSONS LEARNED:

Stressed    Angry    Tired    Sad    Happy    Excited

_____
_____
_____
_____
_____
_____
_____
_____

Prompt of the day:
Staying Energized: Write about strategies you use to stay energized and motivated in your daily missionary activities.

_____
_____
_____
_____

What are you grateful for today? _____

Incorporate the "Fun 15" concept into your missionary schedule by setting aside 15 minutes each day for enjoyable physical activity. This could include playing a sport with your companion, going for a brisk walk, or engaging in a friendly exercise challenge with other missionaries. Regular physical activity, even in short bursts, can boost your mood, reduce stress, and improve overall well-being. By making time for "Fun 15," you'll not only care for your physical health but also enhance your mental and emotional resilience as a missionary. Remember, a happy and healthy missionary is better equipped to serve the Lord and others.

DATE: _____

MEMORIES MADE, TOUGH TIMES, & LESSONS LEARNED:

Stressed   Angry   Tired   Sad   Happy   Excited

_____
_____
_____
_____
_____
_____
_____
_____

What are you grateful for today? _____

"When sore trials come upon us, it's time to deepen our faith in God, to work hard and to serve others. Then He will heal our broken hearts. He will bestow upon us personal peace and comfort. Those great gifts will not be destroyed, even by death." - Russell M. Nelson

DATE: _____

MEMORIES MADE, TOUGH TIMES, & LESSONS LEARNED:

Stressed   Angry   Tired   Sad   Happy   Excited

_____
_____
_____
_____
_____
_____
_____

Prompt of the day:

A Moment of Peace: Describe a moment of peace or stillness you experienced, and what it taught you about finding tranquility amidst busyness.

_____
_____
_____
_____

What are you grateful for today? _____

As a missionary, find inspiration by observing others serve selflessly. Take a moment to reflect on the Christlike examples of service you've witnessed from your leaders, fellow missionaries, and members. Recall how their acts of kindness touched your heart and motivated you to be more compassionate. When you come across inspiring stories of service, share them with your companion, investigators, or loved ones. Discussing these examples can uplift others and multiply the joy you feel. By focusing on the positive impact of service, you'll be motivated to find more opportunities to serve and share the love of Christ with others.

DATE: _____

MEMORIES MADE, TOUGH TIMES, & LESSONS LEARNED:

Stressed  Angry  Tired  Sad  Happy  Excited

_____
_____
_____
_____
_____
_____
_____
_____
_____

What are you grateful for today? _____

*"How, then, can we claim that joy? We can start by 'looking unto Jesus the author and finisher of our faith' 'in every thought.' We can give thanks for Him in our prayers and by keeping covenants we've made with Him and our Heavenly Father. As our Savior becomes more and more real to us and as we plead for His joy to be given to us, our joy will increase." - Russell M. Nelson*

DATE: _____

MEMORIES MADE, TOUGH TIMES, & LESSONS LEARNED:

Stressed  Angry  Tired  Sad  Happy  Excited

_____
_____
_____
_____
_____
_____
_____
_____

Prompt of the day:

The Role of Fasting: Reflect on a time when fasting played a significant role in your mission, either personally or as part of a collective effort.

_____
_____
_____
_____

What are you grateful for today? _____

Don't "ghost" or unexpectedly fail to show up for appointments or commitments. If you can't make it to a teaching appointment, meeting, activity, or meal, or if you're running late, promptly let people know. If you're driving, pull over safely and send a text, or have your companion make a quick phone call. When others are expecting you and you're behind schedule for any reason, it's a matter of courtesy to give them a heads up. Failing to communicate leaves people wondering what happened and can come across as rude or inconsiderate. A simple message goes a long way in showing respect for their time.

DATE: _____

MEMORIES MADE, TOUGH TIMES, & LESSONS LEARNED: 

Stressed  Angry  Tired  Sad  Happy  Excited

_____
_____
_____
_____
_____
_____
_____
_____

What are you grateful for today? _____

*"The Atonement is much more than a divine remedy to correct our sins after they are committed. The Atonement is, in fact, the most powerful motivational force in the world to be good from day to day and, when necessary, to repent when we have fallen short." - Tad R. Callister*

DATE: _____

MEMORIES MADE, TOUGH TIMES, & LESSONS LEARNED: 

Stressed  Angry  Tired  Sad  Happy  Excited

_____
_____
_____
_____
_____
_____
_____
_____

Prompt of the day:
Gratitude for Support: Write a letter of gratitude to someone who has supported you in your mission, whether from home or in the field.

_____
_____
_____
_____
_____

What are you grateful for today? _____

As missionaries, if part of your efforts involves social media or other online interactions, be extremely cautious about what you post. Remember that anything posted online leaves a permanent digital footprint that can be accessed long after you share it. Writing or posting content on social media may feel private in the moment, but it's a public forum. Exercise extra care online because screenshots can capture anything, even messages or posts you assumed were temporary. Also, keep in mind that your future employers, Church leaders, companions, and family may come across what you share online. If you wouldn't feel comfortable with them viewing it, it's best not to post it. Maintain the highest standards of conduct in your online presence as a representative of the Lord.

DATE: _____

MEMORIES MADE, TOUGH TIMES, & LESSONS LEARNED:

Stressed    Angry    Tired    Sad    Happy    Excited

_____
_____
_____
_____
_____
_____
_____
_____

What are you grateful for today? _____

"*We are taught that for those who do not repent, it is as though no redemption had been made. Consider the converse. For those who do repent—truly repent—it is as though no sin had been committed. 'I, the Lord, remember them no more.'*" - Kyle S. McKay

DATE: _____

MEMORIES MADE, TOUGH TIMES, & LESSONS LEARNED:

Stressed    Angry    Tired    Sad    Happy    Excited

_____
_____
_____
_____
_____
_____
_____
_____

Prompt of the day:
Dealing with Isolation: Share your experiences and coping strategies for dealing with feelings of isolation or loneliness.

_____
_____
_____
_____

What are you grateful for today? _____

Do respect the privacy and boundaries of local members. Be mindful of when it's appropriate to visit or contact them, especially in their homes. This same principle also goes for your friends that you teach, make sure not to step over any boundaries that they may have. Communication is KEY! Don't assume that everyone is comfortable with the same level of contact or sharing. Always ask permission and respect others' wishes regarding their privacy and boundaries.

DATE: _____

MEMORIES MADE, TOUGH TIMES, & LESSONS LEARNED:

Stressed  Angry  Tired  Sad  Happy  Excited

_____
_____
_____
_____
_____
_____
_____
_____

What are you grateful for today? _____

"But remember, the Lord has never required expert, flawless missionary efforts. Instead, "the Lord requireth the heart and a willing mind"...The important thing is that you don't give up; keep trying to get it right. You will eventually become better, happier, and more authentic. Talking with others about your faith will become normal and natural. In fact, the gospel will be such an essential, precious part of your lives that it would feel unnatural not to talk about it with others. That may not happen immediately—it is a lifelong effort. But it will happen." -Dieter F. Uchtdorf

DATE: _____

MEMORIES MADE, TOUGH TIMES, & LESSONS LEARNED:

Stressed  Angry  Tired  Sad  Happy  Excited

_____
_____
_____
_____
_____
_____
_____
_____

Prompt of the day:
Handling Disappointment: Reflect on a time you felt disappointed in yourself or your progress. How did you move forward?

_____
_____
_____
_____
_____

What are you grateful for today? _____

Be teachable: Approach each day with a teachable attitude, willing to learn from your experiences, your companions, and the people you meet. The truth is, you can learn something from every single person you meet. Be open to the positive influence of others. This attitude will help you grow and become a more effective missionary. Be open to feedback and correction and use every experience as an opportunity to learn and improve. Remember that your mission is a time of learning and growth, both spiritually and personally, so embrace every opportunity to learn and grow.

DATE: _____

MEMORIES MADE, TOUGH TIMES, & LESSONS LEARNED:

Stressed   Angry   Tired   Sad   Happy   Excited

_____
_____
_____
_____
_____
_____
_____
_____
_____

What are you grateful for today? _____

"...whenever any kind of upheaval occurs in your life, the safest place to be spiritually is living inside your temple covenants! Please believe me when I say that when your spiritual foundation is built solidly upon Jesus Christ, you have no need to fear. As you are true to your covenants made in the temple, you will be strengthened by His power." - Russell M. Nelson

DATE: _____

MEMORIES MADE, TOUGH TIMES, & LESSONS LEARNED:

Stressed   Angry   Tired   Sad   Happy   Excited

_____
_____
_____
_____
_____
_____
_____
_____

Prompt of the day:
Spiritual Preparation: Write about your spiritual preparation process for a particularly challenging or important day.

_____
_____
_____
_____

What are you grateful for today? _____

Practice mindfulness and gratitude as a missionary: Incorporate mindfulness and gratitude into your daily routine. Take time to notice the beauty of God's creations, the kindness of others, and the small blessings in your life. Keep writing in this journal, where you can record the things you're thankful for each day. As you practice being mindful and grateful, you'll develop a more positive outlook and a deeper appreciation for your missionary experience. You'll find joy in the simple things and recognize God's hand in your life.

DATE: _____

MEMORIES MADE, TOUGH TIMES, & LESSONS LEARNED:

Stressed  Angry  Tired  Sad  Happy  Excited

_____
_____
_____
_____
_____
_____
_____
_____

What are you grateful for today? _____

"Prayers ought to be vocal. If privacy is not practical, prayers should be silent utterances in one's heart. If there be any time we feel not to pray, we can be sure that hesitancy does not come from God, who yearns to communicate with His children at any and all times. When unsure how or what to pray about, begin and continue until the Spirit guides one into the prayer that should be offered. - Jeffrey R. Holland

DATE: _____

MEMORIES MADE, TOUGH TIMES, & LESSONS LEARNED:

Stressed  Angry  Tired  Sad  Happy  Excited

_____
_____
_____
_____
_____
_____
_____
_____

Prompt of the day:
Cultural Appreciation: Write about a cultural aspect or tradition you've come to appreciate and how it has expanded your worldview.

_____
_____
_____
_____

What are you grateful for today? _____

As a missionary, remember to give up your seat when needed. Whether on a crowded bus or in a packed venue, look for those who would appreciate it more—the elderly, the tired, or the weary. This small act of kindness can brighten someone's day and exemplify Christlike love. By sharing your seat, you spread the comforting spirit of the gospel and serve others as the Savior would. Let your actions reflect your faith and uplift those around you.

DATE: _____

MEMORIES MADE, TOUGH TIMES, & LESSONS LEARNED:

Stressed   Angry   Tired   Sad   Happy   Excited

_____
_____
_____
_____
_____
_____
_____
_____

What are you grateful for today? _____

"...the pure love of Christ is the answer to the contention that ails us today. Charity propels us 'to bear one another's burdens' rather than heap burdens upon each other. The pure love of Christ allows us 'to stand as witnesses of God at all times and in all things'—especially in tense situations. Charity allows us to demonstrate how men and women of Christ speak and act—especially when under fire." - Russell M. Nelson

DATE: _____

MEMORIES MADE, TOUGH TIMES, & LESSONS LEARNED:

Stressed   Angry   Tired   Sad   Happy   Excited

_____
_____
_____
_____
_____
_____
_____
_____

Prompt of the day:

Teaching and Learning Patience: Reflect on how teaching others has also taught you patience.

_____
_____
_____
_____

What are you grateful for today? _____

When you are transferred to a new area and attend church with unfamiliar people, look them in the eye and introduce yourself. Smile and greet new people with a firm handshake, even if it feels uncomfortable. Practice makes it easier. Not sure how? Try, "Hello, I'm Elder/Sister Taylor. I'm new in this area. What's your name?" This skill helps you not only in the mission field, but in life. Being new or not, getting to know new people can be tough. Saying hi confidently is a big plus. And first impressions are super important. Strive to go out of your way and greet people. Plus, it makes social situations better for everyone.

DATE: _____

MEMORIES MADE, TOUGH TIMES, & LESSONS LEARNED:  Stressed  Angry  Tired  Sad  Happy  Excited

_____
_____
_____
_____
_____
_____
_____
_____

What are you grateful for today? _____

*"For Latter-day Saints, Jesus Christ is joy! That is why our missionaries leave their homes to preach His gospel. Their goal is not to increase the number of Church members. Rather, our missionaries teach and baptize to bring joy to the people of the world!" - Russell M. Nelson*

DATE: _____

MEMORIES MADE, TOUGH TIMES, & LESSONS LEARNED:  Stressed  Angry  Tired  Sad  Happy  Excited

_____
_____
_____
_____
_____
_____
_____

Prompt of the day:
Divine Guidance: Share an experience where you felt divinely guided in your decisions or actions.

_____
_____
_____
_____

What are you grateful for today? _____

Try a seven-minute HIIT workout. Try relieving stress through a simple seven-minute high-intensity interval training (HIIT) session. This can be done in the mornings before studies or when you get home at night. Select exercises like jumping jacks, planks, push-ups, squats, or lunges, and alternate between 30 seconds of exercise and 10 seconds of rest for seven minutes. Embrace the challenge and discomfort, focusing on each interval to metabolically burn through stress. This customizable workout positively stresses your body, regardless of fitness level. Remember, your body thrives on this effort, making it an effective stress reliever.

DATE: _____

MEMORIES MADE, TOUGH TIMES, & LESSONS LEARNED:  Stressed  Angry  Tired  Sad  Happy  Excited

_____
_____
_____
_____
_____
_____
_____
_____

What are you grateful for today? _____

"The adversary never stops attacking. So, we can never stop preparing! The more self-reliant we are—temporally, emotionally, and spiritually—the more prepared we are to thwart Satan's relentless assaults." - Russell M. Nelson

DATE: _____

MEMORIES MADE, TOUGH TIMES, & LESSONS LEARNED:  Stressed  Angry  Tired  Sad  Happy  Excited

_____
_____
_____
_____
_____
_____
_____
_____

Prompt of the day:
The Importance of Laughter: Share a time when laughter eased a difficult situation or brought people together.

_____
_____
_____
_____

What are you grateful for today? _____

Recognize your unique gifts, strengths, and talents. Missionaries often compare themselves to others who excel in various areas. However, it's crucial to remember that no one is perfect at everything. Everyone has unique talents and skills. Take time to identify your strengths and enjoy them. Have fun exploring your abilities and consider how you can use them to serve others. That's what truly matters. Focusing on your own talents, rather than comparing yourself to others, can help reduce stress and increase your sense of purpose. Embrace your individuality and let your talents shine as you serve God and those around you.

DATE: _____

MEMORIES MADE, TOUGH TIMES, & LESSONS LEARNED:

Stressed   Angry   Tired   Sad   Happy   Excited

_____

_____

_____

_____

_____

_____

_____

What are you grateful for today? _____

*"The Lord's way is the only way for us to experience enduring happiness. His way brings sustained comfort to our souls and perennial peace to our homes."* - Russell M. Nelson

DATE: _____

MEMORIES MADE, TOUGH TIMES, & LESSONS LEARNED:

Stressed   Angry   Tired   Sad   Happy   Excited

_____

_____

_____

_____

_____

_____

_____

Prompt of the day:

Sabbath Observance: Reflect on the importance of Sabbath observance during your mission. How has it provided rest and renewal?

_____

_____

_____

_____

What are you grateful for today? _____

You will never have as many people praying for you as you do now as a missionary. There's an army of angels on the other side praying for you and there's a ward or branch army fasting and praying for you back home. Pray for help and pray for others and remember that hundreds of thousands of people are praying for you in temples across the world. Pray for eyes to see and recognize the tender mercies and the many micro answers to prayers. Prayer is real. He hears your thoughts and your silent prayers and those prayers when you are face down on the floor in tears. He hears every single one. Please never forget how many people are praying for you. You have access to God's power, strength, mercy, and protection. Stay on the Lord's side of the line and the windows of heaven will remain open to you.

DATE: _____

MEMORIES MADE, TOUGH TIMES, & LESSONS LEARNED:

Stressed    Angry    Tired    Sad    Happy    Excited

_____
_____
_____
_____
_____
_____
_____
_____

What are you grateful for today? _____

"Trials will only give us the knowledge necessary to understand the minds of the ancients. For my part, I think I never could have felt as I now do, if I had not suffered the wrongs that I have suffered. All things shall work together for good to them that love God." - Joseph Smith

DATE: _____

MEMORIES MADE, TOUGH TIMES, & LESSONS LEARNED:

Stressed    Angry    Tired    Sad    Happy    Excited

_____
_____
_____
_____
_____
_____
_____
_____

Prompt of the day:

Maintaining a Missionary Mindset: Reflect on how you maintain a missionary mindset even on difficult days.

_____
_____
_____
_____
_____
_____

What are you grateful for today? _____

Stay connected with home. While it's important to focus on your missionary work, staying connected with family and friends can provide emotional support and encouragement. Schedule time on P-day to communicate with loved ones and be sure to share your experiences with them. Their support can help you stay motivated and connected to your roots. Keeping in touch with home can also provide a sense of stability and continuity amidst the changes and challenges of missionary life. Use technology to your advantage, whether it's through video calls, emails, or letters, to stay connected with your loved ones. Knowing this, be obedient! Don't respond to messages from back home unless you have permission. God wants you ALL in.

DATE: _____

MEMORIES MADE, TOUGH TIMES, & LESSONS LEARNED:

Stressed  Angry  Tired  Sad  Happy  Excited

_____
_____
_____
_____
_____
_____
_____
_____

What are you grateful for today? _____

"I am optimistic about the future. It will be filled with opportunities for each of us to progress, contribute, and take the gospel to every corner of the earth. But I am also not naive about the days ahead. We live in a world that is complex and increasingly contentious...If we are to have any hope of sifting through the myriad of voices and the philosophies of men that attack truth, we must learn to receive revelation." - Russell M. Nelson

DATE: _____

MEMORIES MADE, TOUGH TIMES, & LESSONS LEARNED:

Stressed  Angry  Tired  Sad  Happy  Excited

_____
_____
_____
_____
_____
_____
_____

Prompt of the day:
Physical and Spiritual Sustenance: How do you balance physical and spiritual sustenance to maintain your energy and focus?

_____
_____
_____
_____

What are you grateful for today? _____

As you wake up each morning, kneel on the floor and pray to your Heavenly Father. Thank Him. And then ask humbly and sincerely, "Father, what would Thou have me do? Where should we go today? Who should we serve? Who needs us today?" Then be still. Notice the nudges and follow the feelings. Follow every prompting.

DATE: _____

MEMORIES MADE, TOUGH TIMES, & LESSONS LEARNED:

Stressed   Angry   Tired   Sad   Happy   Excited

_____
_____
_____
_____
_____
_____
_____
_____

What are you grateful for today? _____

*"If you do not magnify your calling, God will hold you responsible for those you might have saved, had you done your duty." - John Taylor*

DATE: _____

MEMORIES MADE, TOUGH TIMES, & LESSONS LEARNED:

Stressed   Angry   Tired   Sad   Happy   Excited

_____
_____
_____
_____
_____
_____
_____
_____

Prompt of the day:

The Impact of Journaling: Write about how keeping a journal during your mission has impacted your experience and growth.

_____
_____
_____
_____

What are you grateful for today? _____

As a missionary, it's easy to feel overwhelmed by the many tasks and responsibilities you face daily. Procrastination can lead to feelings of guilt, inadequacy, and stress, hindering your ability to serve effectively. To overcome this, try breaking down your larger goals into smaller, manageable steps. Focus on completing one task at a time, whether it's studying a chapter of scripture, preparing for a lesson, or reaching out to a struggling investigator. Celebrate each small victory along the way, as this will help you maintain motivation and a sense of progress. By consistently taking small steps forward, you'll build momentum and confidence in your ability to fulfill your missionary duties. Remember, success as a missionary comes through steady, daily efforts in serving the Lord and bringing others unto Christ. Embrace the power of small and simple things, trusting that your diligent efforts will yield great results in the Lord's work.

DATE: _____

MEMORIES MADE, TOUGH TIMES, & LESSONS LEARNED:

Stressed　Angry　Tired　Sad　Happy　Excited

_____
_____
_____
_____
_____
_____
_____
_____
_____

What are you grateful for today? _____

"Now more than ever, we need the peace only He can bring. How can we expect peace to exist in the world when we are not individually seeking peace and harmony?...followers of Jesus Christ should set the example for all the world to follow. I plead with you to do all you can to end personal conflicts that are currently raging in your hearts and in your lives." - Russell M. Nelson

DATE: _____

MEMORIES MADE, TOUGH TIMES, & LESSONS LEARNED:

Stressed　Angry　Tired　Sad　Happy　Excited

_____
_____
_____
_____
_____
_____
_____
_____

Prompt of the day:
Teaching Adaptability: Discuss a time you had to adapt your teaching style to better connect with someone. What did you change, and why?

_____
_____
_____
_____

What are you grateful for today? _____

Recognize that your missionary service is an opportunity to deepen your faith and relationship with God. Make personal prayer and scripture study a daily priority. Seek to understand and apply gospel principles in your life. As you exercise faith in Jesus Christ and rely on His Atonement, you'll find the strength and guidance you need to face challenges and grow spiritually. Your increased faith will bring you peace, joy, and a greater capacity to serve others.

DATE: _____

MEMORIES MADE, TOUGH TIMES, & LESSONS LEARNED:   Stressed   Angry   Tired   Sad   Happy   Excited

_____
_____
_____
_____
_____
_____
_____
_____

What are you grateful for today? _____

"This cause will roll on in majesty and power to fill the earth. Doors now closed to the preaching of the gospel will be opened. The Almighty, if necessary, may have to shake the nations to humble them and cause them to listen to the servants of the living God. Whatever is needed will come to pass." - Gordon B. Hinckley

DATE: _____

MEMORIES MADE, TOUGH TIMES, & LESSONS LEARNED:   Stressed   Angry   Tired   Sad   Happy   Excited

_____
_____
_____
_____
_____
_____
_____
_____

Prompt of the day:
Learning from Nonverbal Communication: Share an experience where nonverbal communication was key to understanding or teaching.

_____
_____
_____
_____

What are you grateful for today? _____

Stress manifests in different ways, and being able to recognize the signs can help you address it before it becomes overwhelming. Imagine a spectrum of stress levels, from green (handling everyday stressors well) to yellow (feeling tension and anxiety) to orange (experiencing exhaustion, anger, and a lack of spiritual connection) to red (persistent depression, hopelessness, and feeling overwhelmed). If you find yourself in the orange or red zone, it's important to reach out for support. Your mission president and other leaders are there to help you navigate these challenging times and provide guidance and support.

DATE: _____

MEMORIES MADE, TOUGH TIMES, & LESSONS LEARNED:  Stressed  Angry  Tired  Sad  Happy  Excited

_____
_____
_____
_____
_____
_____
_____
_____

What are you grateful for today? _____

*"Time in the temple will help you to think celestial and to catch a vision of who you really are, who you can become, and the kind of life you can have forever. Regular temple worship will enhance the way you see yourself and how you fit into God's magnificent plan. I promise you that." - Russell M. Nelson*

DATE: _____

MEMORIES MADE, TOUGH TIMES, & LESSONS LEARNED:  Stressed  Angry  Tired  Sad  Happy  Excited

_____
_____
_____
_____
_____
_____
_____

Prompt of the day:
Friendships Formed: Reflect on a friendship you've formed during your mission and how it has impacted you.

_____
_____
_____
_____
_____

What are you grateful for today? _____

Don't be afraid to ask for help when needed. And it's better to reach out early instead of letting the stress build up. No matter what area you need help with, it's seriously great to reach out for resources that are there to help you!

DATE: _____

MEMORIES MADE, TOUGH TIMES, & LESSONS LEARNED:

Stressed  Angry  Tired  Sad  Happy  Excited

_____
_____
_____
_____
_____
_____
_____
_____

What are you grateful for today? _____

"Our Father knows that when we are surrounded by uncertainty and fear, what will help us the very most is to hear His Son. Because when we seek to hear—truly hear—His Son, we will be guided to know what to do in any circumstance." - Russell M. Nelson

DATE: _____

MEMORIES MADE, TOUGH TIMES, & LESSONS LEARNED:

Stressed  Angry  Tired  Sad  Happy  Excited

_____
_____
_____
_____
_____
_____
_____
_____

Prompt of the day:
Appreciating the Beauty of the Mission Area: Write about a moment when the beauty of your mission area struck you profoundly.

_____
_____
_____
_____

What are you grateful for today? _____

Don't let rejection and failure discourage you. Maintain a positive attitude and have faith in the potential success of your labors. Remember that attitude has a lot to do with faith, and faith is contagious. Trust that the Lord will bless you with success as you work hard, stay united with your companion, and believe in the power of your message. When faced with setbacks or disappointments, turn to the Lord for strength and guidance. Focus on the progress you are making, no matter how small, and let your enthusiasm for the gospel carry you through challenging times.

DATE:_____

MEMORIES MADE, TOUGH TIMES, & LESSONS LEARNED:

Stressed    Angry    Tired    Sad    Happy    Excited

_____
_____
_____
_____
_____
_____
_____
_____
_____

What are you grateful for today? _____

"You don't have to wonder about what is true. You do not have to wonder whom you can safely trust. Through personal revelation, you can receive your own witness...Regardless of what others may say or do, no one can ever take away a witness borne to your heart and mind about what is true. I urge you to stretch beyond your current spiritual ability to receive personal revelation." - Russell M. Nelson

DATE:_____

MEMORIES MADE, TOUGH TIMES, & LESSONS LEARNED:

Stressed    Angry    Tired    Sad    Happy    Excited

_____
_____
_____
_____
_____
_____
_____
_____

Prompt of the day:
Missionary Life Lessons: What life lesson has missionary work taught you that you feel will benefit you long after your mission?

_____
_____
_____
_____

What are you grateful for today? _____

Be kind and generous and quick to share! If there's only one thing left, like the last breadstick or the final slice of pie, ask if someone else wants it before grabbing it. This courtesy applies with your companions and others you are eating with. Remember, it's good to think about others, not just yourself. Sometimes, it's okay to take the last bit, but it's always nice to be thoughtful and willing to share. Keep that battle between being a bit selfish and super generous in check, and choose to be considerate and share the last thing!

DATE: _____

MEMORIES MADE, TOUGH TIMES, & LESSONS LEARNED:

Stressed  Angry  Tired  Sad  Happy  Excited

_____
_____
_____
_____
_____
_____
_____
_____

What are you grateful for today? _____

"Entering into a covenant relationship with God binds us to Him in a way that makes everything about life easier. Please do not misunderstand me: I did not say that making covenants makes life easy. In fact, expect opposition, because the adversary does not want you to discover the power of Jesus Christ. But yoking yourself with the Savior means you have access to His strength and redeeming power." - Russell M. Nelson

DATE: _____

MEMORIES MADE, TOUGH TIMES, & LESSONS LEARNED:

Stressed  Angry  Tired  Sad  Happy  Excited

_____
_____
_____
_____
_____
_____
_____
_____

Prompt of the day:

The Role of Physical Fitness in Missionary Work: Reflect on how maintaining physical fitness has impacted your ability to perform missionary work and cope with its demands.

_____
_____
_____
_____
_____

What are you grateful for today? _____

As a missionary, avoid getting sucked into gossip. Speaking negatively about others, including fellow missionaries or those you teach, is hurtful and contrary to the gospel message. Refrain from spreading rumors or opinions, even if it seems entertaining. It's often not your place to discuss others' personal matters. Shut down gossip with phrases like, "I think they're trying their best" or "I know how painful it feels to be talked about." Remember, missionaries who gossip are difficult to trust and can earn negative reputations. If you've experienced the pain of gossip, you understand its consequences. One-sided stories and targeting individuals are harmful. Dwelling on negativity only creates problems and hinders the Spirit. Be the one to stop the cycle; choose Christlike kindness and love over gossip.

DATE: _____

MEMORIES MADE, TOUGH TIMES, & LESSONS LEARNED:

Stressed   Angry   Tired   Sad   Happy   Excited

_____
_____
_____
_____
_____
_____
_____
_____

What are you grateful for today? _____

*"Testimony is to know and to feel, Conversion is to do and to become."*
*- Dallin H. Oaks*

DATE: _____

MEMORIES MADE, TOUGH TIMES, & LESSONS LEARNED:

Stressed   Angry   Tired   Sad   Happy   Excited

_____
_____
_____
_____
_____
_____
_____
_____

Prompt of the day:

Sharing Testimonies: Describe a powerful moment when you shared your testimony. How did it strengthen your faith?

_____
_____
_____
_____

What are you grateful for today? _____

Pray for understanding, guidance, and a positive attitude when facing discouragement. Ask the Lord to help you find the lessons in your challenges and to move forward with faith and purpose. Trust that He will guide you as you seek to overcome obstacles and grow from your experiences. As a missionary, you have the privilege of seeking the Lord's help through prayer whenever you feel doubt, discouraged or unsure. Pour out your heart to Him, expressing your desires to learn and grow, and have faith that He will provide the comfort, direction, and strength you need to press forward with a positive attitude.

DATE: _____

MEMORIES MADE, TOUGH TIMES, & LESSONS LEARNED:

Stressed   Angry   Tired   Sad   Happy   Excited

_____
_____
_____
_____
_____
_____
_____
_____

What are you grateful for today? _____

*"True Christianity is love in action. There is no better way to manifest love for God than to show an unselfish love for your fellow men. This is the spirit of missionary work." - Ezra Taft Benson*

DATE: _____

MEMORIES MADE, TOUGH TIMES, & LESSONS LEARNED:

Stressed   Angry   Tired   Sad   Happy   Excited

_____
_____
_____
_____
_____
_____
_____
_____

Prompt of the day:

Balancing Strictness and Compassion: Share how you balance being strict with rules and showing compassion in your interactions.

_____
_____
_____
_____

What are you grateful for today? _____

Make appreciation a habit. Express gratitude regularly, especially to members, companions, your mission president, those you teach and anyone else that does something nice. Make thanking others a habit, acknowledging the numerous people who go out of their way to help you. Regular expressions of gratitude foster appreciation and increase others' willingness to assist you in the future. The happiest people in this world are those who take time to notice and thank others for the small and simple things they say and do. Be grateful!

DATE: _____

MEMORIES MADE, TOUGH TIMES, & LESSONS LEARNED:

Stressed   Angry   Tired   Sad   Happy   Excited

_____
_____
_____
_____
_____
_____
_____
_____
_____

What are you grateful for today? _____

*"We have never needed positive spiritual momentum more than we do now, to counteract the speed with which evil and the darker signs of the times are intensifying. Positive spiritual momentum will keep us moving forward...Spiritual momentum can help us withstand the relentless, wicked attacks of the adversary and thwart his efforts to erode our personal spiritual foundation." - Russell M. Nelson*

DATE: _____

MEMORIES MADE, TOUGH TIMES, & LESSONS LEARNED:

Stressed   Angry   Tired   Sad   Happy   Excited

_____
_____
_____
_____
_____
_____
_____
_____

Prompt of the day:

The Role of Prayer: Reflect on how your understanding and practice of prayer have evolved during your mission.

_____
_____
_____
_____

What are you grateful for today? _____

Do make yourself available as a resource for members who have questions or need guidance on spiritual matters. If you do not have an answer to their question right away, it is okay to say that! Study up, and allow yourself to learn before responding right away. Don't feel pressured to have all the answers immediately. Be honest about your own learning process and show humility in seeking guidance from the Spirit, scriptures, and church leaders when needed.

DATE: _____

MEMORIES MADE, TOUGH TIMES, & LESSONS LEARNED:     Stressed   Angry   Tired   Sad   Happy   Excited

_____
_____
_____
_____
_____
_____
_____
_____

What are you grateful for today? _____

*"Finally, men captained by Christ will be consumed in Christ. To paraphrase President Harold B. Lee, they set fire in others because they are on fire. Their will is swallowed up in His will (see John 5:30). They do always those things that please the Lord (see John 8:29). Not only would they die for the Lord, but more important they want to live for Him." - Ezra Taft Benson*

DATE: _____

MEMORIES MADE, TOUGH TIMES, & LESSONS LEARNED:     Stressed   Angry   Tired   Sad   Happy   Excited

_____
_____
_____
_____
_____
_____
_____
_____

Prompt of the day:
Unexpected Teaching Methods: Describe an unexpected teaching method you used and its outcome.

_____
_____
_____
_____
_____

What are you grateful for today? _____

Embrace the principle of sacrifice as a missionary: Recognize that your mission is a time of sacred sacrifice, where you put the Lord's work before your own desires. Embrace the opportunity to give of your time, talents, and energy in service to others. Find joy in the knowledge that your sacrifices are helping to build the kingdom of God and bring salvation to His children. As you embrace the principle of sacrifice, you'll develop a deeper love for the Savior and a greater appreciation for the sacrifices He made for you.

DATE: _____

MEMORIES MADE, TOUGH TIMES, & LESSONS LEARNED:

Stressed   Angry   Tired   Sad   Happy   Excited

_____
_____
_____
_____
_____
_____
_____
_____

What are you grateful for today? _____

"So why should we bear frequent and powerful testimony of Christ? Because doing so invites and becomes part of the divine power of testimony borne by God the Father and by the Holy Ghost, a testimony borne on wings of fire to the very hearts of investigators. Such a divine testimony of Christ is the rock upon which every new convert must build. Only this testimony of the atoning Anointed, Victorious One will prevail against the gates of hell." - Jeffrey R. Holland

DATE: _____

MEMORIES MADE, TOUGH TIMES, & LESSONS LEARNED:

Stressed   Angry   Tired   Sad   Happy   Excited

_____
_____
_____
_____
_____
_____
_____
_____

Prompt of the day:

Witnessing Growth in Others: Share a story of witnessing remarkable growth or change in someone you've taught or worked with.

_____
_____
_____
_____
_____

What are you grateful for today? _____

Cultivate a love for all of God's children as a missionary: Develop a deep, Christlike love for every person you encounter during your mission. See them as God sees them, recognizing their inherent worth and divine potential. Treat all people with kindness, respect, and compassion, regardless of their background, beliefs, or challenges. As you cultivate a love for all of God's children, you'll find greater joy in serving and teaching them. Your love will create an atmosphere of trust and acceptance, inviting the Spirit to touch hearts and change lives.

DATE: _____

MEMORIES MADE, TOUGH TIMES, & LESSONS LEARNED:

Stressed   Angry   Tired   Sad   Happy   Excited

_____
_____
_____
_____
_____
_____
_____
_____

What are you grateful for today? _____

*"The Final Judgment is not just an evaluation of a sum total of good and evil acts—what we have done. It is based on the final effect of our acts and thoughts—what we have become. We qualify for eternal life through a process of conversion." - Dallin H. Oaks*

DATE: _____

MEMORIES MADE, TOUGH TIMES, & LESSONS LEARNED:

Stressed   Angry   Tired   Sad   Happy   Excited

_____
_____
_____
_____
_____
_____
_____
_____

Prompt of the day:
Developing Leadership Qualities: Reflect on how your mission has helped develop your leadership qualities.

_____
_____
_____
_____
_____

What are you grateful for today? _____

Be a grateful and friendly passenger. When someone gives you a ride, say hello and chat a bit. Be kind to everyone in the car—no whispering or going silent while staring at your phone or out the window. Always say thank you when you leave. It's important to appreciate those helping you get where you need to be. Using your phone to avoid talking might seem easy, but it's not polite. Make sure to be a friendly and thankful passenger!

DATE: _____

MEMORIES MADE, TOUGH TIMES, & LESSONS LEARNED:

Stressed   Angry   Tired   Sad   Happy   Excited

_____
_____
_____
_____
_____
_____
_____
_____

What are you grateful for today? _____

*"The Book of Mormon is central to this work [of gathering scattered Israel]. It declares the doctrine of the gathering. It causes people to learn about Jesus Christ, to believe His gospel and to join His Church. In fact, if there were no Book of Mormon, the promised gathering of Israel would not occur." - Russell M. Nelson*

DATE: _____

MEMORIES MADE, TOUGH TIMES, & LESSONS LEARNED:

Stressed   Angry   Tired   Sad   Happy   Excited

_____
_____
_____
_____
_____
_____
_____
_____

Prompt of the day:
Finding Joy in Service: How have you found joy in service, even when it's challenging or goes unnoticed?

_____
_____
_____
_____
_____

What are you grateful for today? _____

Serve your companion, even when it is difficult or feels counterintuitive. Acts of service, such as making their bed, sharing a treat, or offering a kind word, can help soften your heart and dissipate feelings of anger or resentment. Remember that you can only control your own actions and attitudes and focus on changing your own heart rather than seeking gratitude or recognition from your companion. Choose to let go of unkind feelings and strive to be happy, even in less-than-ideal circumstances, as this will allow you to feel the influence of the Holy Ghost more strongly in your life and missionary work. As you serve your companion with a sincere heart, you may find that your own perspective shifts and your relationship improves, creating a more positive and spiritually conducive environment for both of you.

DATE: _____

MEMORIES MADE, TOUGH TIMES, & LESSONS LEARNED:

Stressed  Angry  Tired  Sad  Happy  Excited

_____
_____
_____
_____
_____
_____
_____
_____

What are you grateful for today? _____

"We see an ironic . . . trend in the Church. At the very time we are confirming the importance of members in the conversion process, evidence from . . . studies suggests that members are playing a proportionally smaller role in finding people to teach. If our goal is to [bring souls unto Christ], the most productive source is member referrals. . . . We can enlist the help of others and thus multiply the effectiveness of what we do." - Joseph B. Wirthlin

DATE: _____

MEMORIES MADE, TOUGH TIMES, & LESSONS LEARNED:

Stressed  Angry  Tired  Sad  Happy  Excited

_____
_____
_____
_____
_____
_____
_____
_____

Prompt of the day:

The Role of Humor in Coping: Write about how humor has helped you or others cope with the challenges of missionary life.

_____
_____
_____
_____

What are you grateful for today? _____

Find moments of stillness. In his TED talk "The Art of Stillness," Pico Iyer emphasizes the importance of finding quiet moments in our fast-paced world. By slowing down and embracing stillness, missionaries can escape the noise and chaos of daily life, allowing for reflection, recharging, and a clearer understanding of their surroundings and themselves. In an age where everyone is always moving, the real adventure may be found in stopping and being still. Seek moments of stillness to gain insight and peace during your mission.

DATE: _____

MEMORIES MADE, TOUGH TIMES, & LESSONS LEARNED:

Stressed   Angry   Tired   Sad   Happy   Excited

_____
_____
_____
_____
_____
_____
_____

What are you grateful for today? _____

"My dear brothers and sisters, as you choose to let God prevail in your lives, you will experience for yourselves that our God is 'a God of miracles.' As a people, we are His covenant children, and we will be called by His name." - Russell M. Nelson

DATE: _____

MEMORIES MADE, TOUGH TIMES, & LESSONS LEARNED:

Stressed   Angry   Tired   Sad   Happy   Excited

_____
_____
_____
_____
_____
_____

Prompt of the day:

Scripture Character Resonance: Is there a character from the scriptures you particularly resonate with during your mission? Why?

_____
_____
_____
_____
_____

What are you grateful for today? _____

Did you know? Journaling in this and other journals has all kinds of awesome benefits. Forty-plus years of research shows that journaling can boost your mental, emotional, and spiritual well-being as a missionary. Expressing your thoughts, feelings, and experiences on paper can help you process emotions, reduce stress and anxiety, reflect on personal growth, set goals, and cultivate gratitude. Journaling provides a safe space for self-discovery and can improve your writing skills. By taking time each day to record your journey, you'll enhance your overall resilience, memory, and sense of meaning. Embrace the power of positive thinking by focusing on the blessings and tender mercies you experience as a missionary. Keep it up!!

DATE: _____

MEMORIES MADE, TOUGH TIMES, & LESSONS LEARNED:

Stressed   Angry   Tired   Sad   Happy   Excited

_____
_____
_____
_____
_____
_____
_____
_____
_____

What are you grateful for today? _____

"Life is filled with detours and dead ends, trials and challenges of every kind. Each of us has likely had times when distress, anguish, and despair almost consumed us. Yet we are here to have joy? Yes! The answer is a resounding yes!... Joy comes from and because of Him. He is the source of all joy." - Russell M. Nelson

DATE: _____

MEMORIES MADE, TOUGH TIMES, & LESSONS LEARNED:

Stressed   Angry   Tired   Sad   Happy   Excited

_____
_____
_____
_____
_____
_____
_____
_____
_____

Prompt of the day:
Finding Solitude for Reflection: Share how and where you find moments of solitude for personal reflection during your mission.

_____
_____
_____
_____

What are you grateful for today? _____

Myth: Missionaries are always successful in baptizing new members. Reality: Success in missionary work isn't solely measured by baptisms but also by relationships built, service rendered, and personal growth. While baptisms are celebrated, it is important to understand that not everyone will choose baptism. Throughout your mission you will find joy in planting seeds of faith, serving, and growing personally. Do your best to trust God's timing.

DATE: _____

MEMORIES MADE, TOUGH TIMES, & LESSONS LEARNED:

Stressed   Angry   Tired   Sad   Happy   Excited

_____
_____
_____
_____
_____
_____
_____
_____

What are you grateful for today? _____

"I fear that too many have sadly surrendered their agency to the adversary and are saying by their conduct, 'I care more about satisfying my own desires than I do about bearing the Savior's power to bless others." - Russell M. Nelson

DATE: _____

MEMORIES MADE, TOUGH TIMES, & LESSONS LEARNED:

Stressed   Angry   Tired   Sad   Happy   Excited

_____
_____
_____
_____
_____
_____
_____
_____

Prompt of the day:
Missionary Work and Family: How has your mission work influenced your thoughts or feelings about family and future family life?

_____
_____
_____
_____

What are you grateful for today? _____

Focus on developing faith in Jesus Christ and gratitude for His blessings, rather than relying on external measures of success. When faced with rejections or setbacks, pray for a change of heart and increased faith. There are times when raising your expectations leads to more effectiveness and an increase in desire and the Spirit. Recognize and appreciate the daily miracles and blessings in your missionary work, even when things don't go as planned. Trust that Heavenly Father always answers prayers of faith, even if the answers come in unexpected ways.

DATE: _____

MEMORIES MADE, TOUGH TIMES, & LESSONS LEARNED:

| Stressed | Angry | Tired | Sad | Happy | Excited |

_____
_____
_____
_____
_____
_____
_____
_____

What are you grateful for today? _____

*"My dear brothers and sisters, the best is yet to come for those who spend their lives building up others. Today I invite you to examine your discipleship within the context of the way you treat others. I bless you to make any adjustments that may be needed so that your behavior is ennobling, respectful, and representative of a true follower of Jesus Christ." - Russell M. Nelson*

DATE: _____

MEMORIES MADE, TOUGH TIMES, & LESSONS LEARNED:

| Stressed | Angry | Tired | Sad | Happy | Excited |

_____
_____
_____
_____
_____
_____
_____
_____

Prompt of the day:

The Power of Simple Acts of Service: Reflect on a simple act of service that had a profound impact.

_____
_____
_____
_____

What are you grateful for today? _____

Cultivating friendships and companionships demands time and effort. One study from the University of Kansas suggests it takes approximately 40-60 hours for a casual friendship to develop, 80-100 hours to become "friends," and over 200 hours to become close friends. In a world of instant gratification, building strong bonds doesn't follow the same quick pace. To develop lasting connections, invest the necessary time and develop the patience as relationships grow. Start with a couple foundational elements—kindness and gratitude.

DATE: _____

MEMORIES MADE, TOUGH TIMES, & LESSONS LEARNED:

Stressed   Angry   Tired   Sad   Happy   Excited

_____
_____
_____
_____
_____
_____
_____
_____

What are you grateful for today? _____

"My dear brothers and sisters, how we treat each other really matters! How we speak to and about others at home, at church, at work, and online really matters. Today, I am asking us to interact with others in a higher, holier way." - Russell M. Nelson

DATE: _____

MEMORIES MADE, TOUGH TIMES, & LESSONS LEARNED:

Stressed   Angry   Tired   Sad   Happy   Excited

_____
_____
_____
_____
_____
_____
_____
_____

Prompt of the day:
Environmental Adaptation: How have you adapted to the physical environment of your mission area (climate, geography, etc.)?

_____
_____
_____
_____
_____

What are you grateful for today? _____

As a missionary, be fully present in your interactions with others. One of the greatest gifts you can offer is not just your time, but your undivided attention. Whether you are in meetings with other missionaries, members, or teaching those interested in the gospel message, give your complete focus to the people you are with. Treating others with kindness and respect, especially those who are assisting you in your missionary efforts, is crucial. Avoid minimizing their contributions, taking them for granted, or ignoring them. By being fully engaged and attentive, you demonstrate Christlike love and concern for those around you, creating a more meaningful and impactful missionary experience.

DATE: _____

MEMORIES MADE, TOUGH TIMES, & LESSONS LEARNED:

Stressed   Angry   Tired   Sad   Happy   Excited

_____
_____
_____
_____
_____
_____
_____
_____

What are you grateful for today? _____

"When your greatest desire is to let God prevail, to be part of Israel, so many decisions become easier. So many issues become nonissues! You know how best to groom yourself. You know what to watch and read, where to spend your time, and with whom to associate. You know what you want to accomplish. You know the kind of person you really want to become." - Russell M. Nelson

DATE: _____

MEMORIES MADE, TOUGH TIMES, & LESSONS LEARNED:

Stressed   Angry   Tired   Sad   Happy   Excited

_____
_____
_____
_____
_____
_____
_____
_____

Prompt of the day:
Navigating Doubts and Questions: Write about how you navigate your own doubts and questions as well as those of the people you teach.

_____
_____
_____
_____

What are you grateful for today? _____

Celebrate the successes of your companions and those you teach with genuine joy. Share in their happiness without downplaying their achievements or comparing them to your own. Let them shine and relish the moment. Being genuinely happy for others demonstrates emotional and spiritual maturity. Turn any jealousy into admiration and motivation for your own missionary efforts. Celebrating others' spiritual victories brings joy and shows confidence in your testimony. If envy arises, refocus on your own goals and trust in the Lord's plan for you.

DATE: _____

MEMORIES MADE, TOUGH TIMES, & LESSONS LEARNED:

Stressed   Angry   Tired   Sad   Happy   Excited

_____
_____
_____
_____
_____
_____
_____
_____

What are you grateful for today? _____

*"If you look at your life prayerfully, I believe you will see many ways in which the Lord has been guiding you through this time of hardship." - Russell M. Nelson*

DATE: _____

MEMORIES MADE, TOUGH TIMES, & LESSONS LEARNED:

Stressed   Angry   Tired   Sad   Happy   Excited

_____
_____
_____
_____
_____
_____
_____

Prompt of the day:
Spiritual Milestones: Reflect on a recent spiritual milestone or achievement in your mission and what it signifies for you.

_____
_____
_____
_____
_____

What are you grateful for today? _____

Persevere through the hard times and challenges of missionary work, knowing that they are designed to refine your character, strengthen your faith, and shape you into the disciple the Lord knows you can become. When you feel stretched beyond your own capacities, remember that it is often through our trials and weaknesses that we experience the greatest growth and development. Trust that the Lord is molding you into a more effective instrument in His hands, and that He will use your experiences, both positive and negative, to bless your life and the lives of those you serve. As you press forward with faith and determination, you will emerge from your mission a stronger, wiser, and more Christlike individual.

DATE: _____

MEMORIES MADE, TOUGH TIMES, & LESSONS LEARNED:

Stressed   Angry   Tired   Sad   Happy   Excited

_____
_____
_____
_____
_____
_____
_____
_____
_____

What are you grateful for today? _____

"The healing power of the Lord Jesus Christ-whether it removes our burdens or strengthens us to endure and live with them like the Apostle Paul-is available for every affliction in mortality." - Dallin H. Oaks

DATE: _____

MEMORIES MADE, TOUGH TIMES, & LESSONS LEARNED:

Stressed   Angry   Tired   Sad   Happy   Excited

_____
_____
_____
_____
_____
_____
_____
_____

Prompt of the day:

Lessons Learned from Companions: Reflect on a significant lesson learned from one of your companions and how it impacted your mission or personal growth.

_____
_____
_____
_____
_____

What are you grateful for today? _____

As a missionary, strive to emulate Christlike kindness in all your words and actions, especially when interacting with your companion, investigators, and those you serve. Remember that kindness should permeate every aspect of your life, and that by treating others with love and compassion, you can make a significant difference in their lives. When faced with individuals who are rude, obnoxious, or offensive, resist the urge to react negatively and instead choose to respond with love and understanding, following the Savior's example. Pray for the strength to maintain a kind and gentle demeanor, even in challenging situations, and trust that your Christlike approach will soften hearts and open doors for the gospel message.

DATE: _____

MEMORIES MADE, TOUGH TIMES, & LESSONS LEARNED:

Stressed    Angry    Tired    Sad    Happy    Excited

_____
_____
_____
_____
_____
_____
_____
_____

What are you grateful for today? _____

*"Filling our mind with the power of Jesus Christ does not mean that He is the only thought we have. But id does mean that all our thoughts are circumscribed in His love, His life and teachings, and His atoning sacrifice and glorious resurrection." - Neil L. Andersen*

DATE: _____

MEMORIES MADE, TOUGH TIMES, & LESSONS LEARNED:

Stressed    Angry    Tired    Sad    Happy    Excited

_____
_____
_____
_____
_____
_____
_____

Prompt of the day:

Confronting Doubts: How do you confront and deal with doubts, either your own or those of the people you teach?

_____
_____
_____
_____

What are you grateful for today? _____

Embrace the principle of consecration as a missionary: Understand that your mission is a time to consecrate your all to the Lord. Give your heart, might, mind, and strength to His work, holding nothing back. Embrace the opportunity to put God's will before your own, trusting that He will bless and guide you. As you live the principle of consecration, you'll experience a deeper sense of purpose, unity with the Savior, and joy in your missionary service. Your consecrated efforts will invite the Spirit and magnify your impact on those you serve.

DATE: _____

MEMORIES MADE, TOUGH TIMES, & LESSONS LEARNED:

Stressed   Angry   Tired   Sad   Happy   Excited

_____
_____
_____
_____
_____
_____
_____
_____

What are you grateful for today? _____

*"Your choices will not all be between good and evil. Many will be choices between two good options. Not all truths are created equal, so you will need to establish priorities." - Russell M. Nelson*

DATE: _____

MEMORIES MADE, TOUGH TIMES, & LESSONS LEARNED:

Stressed   Angry   Tired   Sad   Happy   Excited

_____
_____
_____
_____
_____
_____
_____
_____

Prompt of the day:
Adapting to Different Learning Styles: Share your experiences adapting your teaching methods to accommodate different learning styles.

_____
_____
_____
_____

What are you grateful for today? _____

Myth: All missionary experiences are the same. Reality: Your missionary experience is unique, influenced by personality, location, companions, and personal challenges. While following a general schedule, day-to-day experiences vary. You might serve in urban areas, while others serve in rural settings. Some have more success finding people to teach, while others focus on service. Each journey is shaped by individual growth, relationships, and the Holy Spirit.

DATE: _____

MEMORIES MADE, TOUGH TIMES, & LESSONS LEARNED:   Stressed   Angry   Tired   Sad   Happy   Excited

_____
_____
_____
_____
_____
_____
_____
_____

What are you grateful for today? _____

"*Mortality is an open-ended, choose-your-own-adventure story. You have commandments, you have covenants, you have inspired prophetic counsel, and you have the gift of the Holy Ghost. That is more than enough to lead you to mortal happiness and eternal joy. Beyond that, don't despair if you make some decisions that are less than perfect. That is how you learn. That's part of the adventure!*" - Dieter F. Uchtdorf

DATE: _____

MEMORIES MADE, TOUGH TIMES, & LESSONS LEARNED:   Stressed   Angry   Tired   Sad   Happy   Excited

_____
_____
_____
_____
_____
_____
_____
_____

Prompt of the day:
Humility Lessons: Share an experience that taught you humility during your mission.

_____
_____
_____
_____

What are you grateful for today? _____

Embrace Carol Dweck's concept of a "growth mindset" by viewing challenges as opportunities for development. Recognize that intelligence and talents can be cultivated through effort, learning, and persistence. Shift from thinking "I can't do this" to "I can't do this yet." Cultivate a love for learning and resilience in the face of setbacks. This approach fosters continuous growth and improvement in all aspects of life.

DATE: _____

MEMORIES MADE, TOUGH TIMES, & LESSONS LEARNED:

Stressed    Angry    Tired    Sad    Happy    Excited

_____
_____
_____
_____
_____
_____
_____
_____

What are you grateful for today? _____

"Our inquiring friends and neighbors not of our faith can also catch the wave. We encourage them to keep all that is good and true in their lives. And we invite them to receive more, especially the glorious truth that through God's eternal plan, families can be together forever." - Russell M. Nelson

DATE: _____

MEMORIES MADE, TOUGH TIMES, & LESSONS LEARNED:

Stressed    Angry    Tired    Sad    Happy    Excited

_____
_____
_____
_____
_____
_____
_____
_____

Prompt of the day:

Embracing New Technologies in Missionary Work: Reflect on how you've embraced new technologies in your missionary work and the impact they've had.

_____
_____
_____
_____
_____

What are you grateful for today? _____

Stay humble: Remember that you are a servant of God and that your mission is not about you. Stay humble and focused on serving others and following God's will. Humility is a key characteristic of a successful missionary, as it allows you to be open to the guidance of the Spirit and the needs of those you serve. Dieter F. Uchtdorf has said, "We don't discover humility by thinking less OF ourselves; we discover humility by thinking less ABOUT ourselves." Cultivate a spirit of humility in all that you do, seeking to emulate the Savior's example of humility and service.

DATE:_____

MEMORIES MADE, TOUGH TIMES, & LESSONS LEARNED:

Stressed　Angry　Tired　Sad　Happy　Excited

_____
_____
_____
_____
_____
_____
_____
_____

What are you grateful for today? _____

*"We do not know the Lord unless and until we think what he thinks, say what he says, and experience what he experiences. In other words, we know God when we become like him." - Bruce R. McConkie*

DATE:_____

MEMORIES MADE, TOUGH TIMES, & LESSONS LEARNED:

Stressed　Angry　Tired　Sad　Happy　Excited

_____
_____
_____
_____
_____
_____
_____

Prompt of the day:
Communication Skills: How have your communication skills continued to develop on your mission, and how do you apply these skills in teaching and everyday interactions?

_____
_____
_____
_____
_____

What are you grateful for today? _____

Be mindful of the spiritual and emotional atmosphere when teaching or interacting with others as a missionary. Consider the situation and the feelings of those present before speaking. Avoid discussing personal challenges or successes that may not be appropriate for the moment. Read the room by recognizing emotions and think about how your words will be received. Practice this awareness to build strong relationships, create a positive teaching environment, and invite the Spirit into your missionary work. Mastering this skill will lead to more effective and empathetic service as a representative of Jesus Christ.

DATE: _____

MEMORIES MADE, TOUGH TIMES, & LESSONS LEARNED:

Stressed  Angry  Tired  Sad  Happy  Excited

_____
_____
_____
_____
_____
_____
_____
_____

What are you grateful for today? _____

"Turbulent times are opportunities for us to thrive spiritually. They are times when our influence can be much more penetrating than in calmer times.... [The] only way to survive spiritually is to be determined to let God prevail in our lives, to learn to hear His voice, and to use our energy to help gather Israel." - Russell M. Nelson

DATE: _____

MEMORIES MADE, TOUGH TIMES, & LESSONS LEARNED:

Stressed  Angry  Tired  Sad  Happy  Excited

_____
_____
_____
_____
_____
_____
_____
_____

Prompt of the day:

The Power of Unified Prayer: Write about a time when unified prayer within your missionary district, zone, or mission had a profound impact.

_____
_____
_____
_____
_____

What are you grateful for today? _____

As a missionary, be mindful of your language and tone in all interactions. Use uplifting, respectful, and appropriate language when speaking with your companions, members, and those you teach. Avoid using slang, making crude jokes, or engaging in sarcasm that could be misinterpreted or cause offense. Remember that as a representative of Jesus Christ, your words should always reflect His love, kindness, and teachings. Choose language that invites the Spirit, uplifts others, and fosters positive relationships. Speak with clarity, sincerity, and gentleness, allowing others to feel the Savior's love through your words and manner of communication.

DATE: _____

MEMORIES MADE, TOUGH TIMES, & LESSONS LEARNED:

Stressed   Angry   Tired   Sad   Happy   Excited

_____
_____
_____
_____
_____
_____
_____
_____

What are you grateful for today? _____

"A missionary who is inspired by the Spirit of the Lord must be led by that Spirit to choose the proper approach to be effective. We must not forget that the Lord Himself provided the Book of Mormon as His chief witness. The Book of Mormon is still our most powerful missionary tool. Let us use it." - Ezra Taft Benson

DATE: _____

MEMORIES MADE, TOUGH TIMES, & LESSONS LEARNED:

Stressed   Angry   Tired   Sad   Happy   Excited

_____
_____
_____
_____
_____
_____
_____
_____

Prompt of the day:
Rest and Rejuvenation: How do you find rest and rejuvenation amidst the demanding schedule of missionary work?

_____
_____
_____
_____

What are you grateful for today? _____

As a missionary, focus on what is truly important and what you can control. Remember that your primary purpose is to invite others to come unto Christ through faith, repentance, baptism, receiving the Holy Ghost, and enduring to the end. While you may face challenges and setbacks, concentrate on your efforts to share the gospel message and love those you serve. You cannot control others' agency or decisions, but you can control your own dedication, obedience, and attitude. Trust in the Lord's plan and timing and find joy in the service you render as His representative.

DATE: _____

MEMORIES MADE, TOUGH TIMES, & LESSONS LEARNED:  Stressed  Angry  Tired  Sad  Happy  Excited

_____
_____
_____
_____
_____
_____
_____
_____

What are you grateful for today? _____

*"The Lord Jesus Christ also observes the eternal principles of the law of consecration. His eternal consecration is essentially himself—his own perfection, his own merits, his own righteousness. In sharing these, his 'earnings,' with us, he raises us to his level, thus making us equal to himself as well as to each other, and making us joint-heirs with him of all that the Father has." - Stephen E. Robinson*

DATE: _____

MEMORIES MADE, TOUGH TIMES, & LESSONS LEARNED:  Stressed  Angry  Tired  Sad  Happy  Excited

_____
_____
_____
_____
_____
_____
_____
_____

Prompt of the day:

Cultivating a Spirit of Gratitude: Share how you cultivate a spirit of gratitude, even in challenging circumstances.

_____
_____
_____
_____

What are you grateful for today? _____

Be aware of the "law of little things" and the "law of least effort." The law of little things simply reminds us that most of what is good in life, from physical and mental health to love and relationships, is strengthened from many "little" things. Small acts of kindness, consistent exercise and eating well, etc. Similarly, the "law of least effort" means it tends to be easier in life to give the least effort possible. It's easier to sleep in than wake up early. It's easier to stay inside rather than go contacting. It's easier to stay quiet instead of opening your mouth and meeting people or talking to members at church. Intentional effort with consistent "little things" will lead to a happier, more fulfilling mission and life.

DATE: _____

MEMORIES MADE, TOUGH TIMES, & LESSONS LEARNED: Stressed  Angry  Tired  Sad  Happy  Excited

_____
_____
_____
_____
_____
_____
_____
_____

What are you grateful for today? _____

*"You can overcome the spiritually and emotionally exhausting plagues of the world, including arrogance, pride, anger, immorality, hatred, greed, jealousy, and fear. Despite the distractions and distortions that swirl around us, you can find true rest—meaning relief and peace—even amid your most vexing problems." - Russell M. Nelson*

DATE: _____

MEMORIES MADE, TOUGH TIMES, & LESSONS LEARNED: Stressed  Angry  Tired  Sad  Happy  Excited

_____
_____
_____
_____
_____
_____
_____
_____

Prompt of the day:
Cultural Adaptation: Describe a moment when you successfully adapted to a cultural norm or practice different from your own.

_____
_____
_____
_____

What are you grateful for today? _____

Practice self-care: Take care of yourself physically, emotionally, and spiritually. Get enough rest, eat well, and take time for activities that rejuvenate you. Missionary work can be demanding, both physically and emotionally, so it's important to prioritize self-care. Make time for activities that nourish your body, mind, and spirit, whether it's exercise, meditation, or simply spending time in nature. Taking care of yourself will not only help you stay healthy and strong but also make you a more effective missionary.

DATE: _____

MEMORIES MADE, TOUGH TIMES, & LESSONS LEARNED:

Stressed    Angry    Tired    Sad    Happy    Excited

_____
_____
_____
_____
_____
_____
_____
_____
_____

What are you grateful for today? _____

"As you think celestial, you will find yourself avoiding anything that robs you of your agency. Any addiction—be it gaming, gambling, debt, drugs, alcohol, anger, pornography, sex, or even food—offends God. Why? Because your obsession becomes your god...Please do not let an obsession rob you of your freedom to follow God's fabulous plan." - Russell M. Nelson

DATE: _____

MEMORIES MADE, TOUGH TIMES, & LESSONS LEARNED:

Stressed    Angry    Tired    Sad    Happy    Excited

_____
_____
_____
_____
_____
_____
_____
_____
_____

Prompt of the day:
Learning from the Children: Share insights or lessons learned from interacting with children during your mission.

_____
_____
_____
_____

What are you grateful for today? _____

Make sure you're doing your laundry regularly! ;) Don't let your clothes pile up in big heaps and then take up the washer and dryer for the day. And get those clothes dried soon to prevent mildew and stink! If you forget, add a bit of vinegar or baking soda to the load and rewash it all before drying. Don't overlook washing sheets and pillowcases to prevent skin issues—and it's gross. Clean clothes and sheets are crucial for better hygiene habits now and in the future. These regular routines will lead to better lifelong habits.

DATE: _____

MEMORIES MADE, TOUGH TIMES, & LESSONS LEARNED:

Stressed   Angry   Tired   Sad   Happy   Excited

_____
_____
_____
_____
_____
_____
_____
_____

What are you grateful for today? _____

"Following Christ is not a casual or occasional practice but a continuous commitment and way of life that applies at all times and in all places." - Dallin H. Oaks

DATE: _____

MEMORIES MADE, TOUGH TIMES, & LESSONS LEARNED:

Stressed   Angry   Tired   Sad   Happy   Excited

_____
_____
_____
_____
_____
_____
_____

Prompt of the day:
Leadership Experiences: Reflect on a leadership role you've taken on during your mission. What lessons have you learned about leading others?

_____
_____
_____
_____
_____

What are you grateful for today? _____

Focus on service: Look for opportunities to serve others, both in your missionary work and in your daily interactions. Service not only blesses the lives of those you serve but also helps you grow in love and compassion. Make service a central part of your mission experience, seeking out ways to help and uplift those around you. Whether it's through a kind word, a listening ear, or a helping hand, your service can make a significant impact on others and bring you closer to the Savior's example of selfless love.

DATE: _____

MEMORIES MADE, TOUGH TIMES, & LESSONS LEARNED:

Stressed    Angry    Tired    Sad    Happy    Excited

_____
_____
_____
_____
_____
_____
_____
_____

What are you grateful for today? _____

*"It is not natural for us to be humble, meek, or willing to submit our wills to God. Yet only by doing so can we be transformed, return to live in the presence of God, and achieve our eternal destiny." - Dale G. Renlund*

DATE: _____

MEMORIES MADE, TOUGH TIMES, & LESSONS LEARNED:

Stressed    Angry    Tired    Sad    Happy    Excited

_____
_____
_____
_____
_____
_____
_____
_____

Prompt of the day:
Navigating Language Barriers in Teaching: Write about creative strategies you've used to navigate language barriers in teaching.

_____
_____
_____
_____
_____

What are you grateful for today? _____

Pay close attention to your personal hygiene and how you present yourself. Consistently practice good habits like showering daily, using deodorant or antiperspirant, brushing your teeth morning and night, flossing, and using mouthwash. Carry breath mints or gum with you to freshen your breath throughout the day. Don't neglect washing your hair regularly, as it can quickly begin to stink. Taking care of basic hygiene tasks should be a top priority for missionaries, as you represent the Church and want to make a positive impression on those you interact with. A clean, well-groomed appearance shows respect for yourself and others.

DATE: _____

MEMORIES MADE, TOUGH TIMES, & LESSONS LEARNED:

Stressed    Angry    Tired    Sad    Happy    Excited

_____
_____
_____
_____
_____
_____
_____
_____

What are you grateful for today? _____

"A strong human spirit with control over appetites of the flesh is master over emotions and passions and not a slave to them. That kind of freedom is as vital to the spirit as oxygen is to the body! Freedom from self-slavery is true liberation!" - Russell M. Nelson

DATE: _____

MEMORIES MADE, TOUGH TIMES, & LESSONS LEARNED:

Stressed    Angry    Tired    Sad    Happy    Excited

_____
_____
_____
_____
_____
_____
_____
_____

Prompt of the day:
Spiritual Resilience: Share a time when your spiritual resilience was tested, and how you strengthened your faith through the challenge.

_____
_____
_____
_____
_____

What are you grateful for today? _____

Be a warrior, not a worrier: Angela Ceberano's TED talk "Be The Warrior Not The Worrier: Fighting Anxiety & Fear" encourages adopting a 'warrior' mindset to tackle anxiety and fear. By facing challenges head-on, setting goals, breaking them into small steps, and regularly stepping out of comfort zones, missionaries can grow stronger and more confident in dealing with life's challenges. Act like a stripling warrior and confront your fears to effectively serve others and navigate the ups and downs of missionary life.

DATE: _____

MEMORIES MADE, TOUGH TIMES, & LESSONS LEARNED:

Stressed  Angry  Tired  Sad  Happy  Excited

_____
_____
_____
_____
_____
_____
_____
_____

What are you grateful for today? _____

*"For Latter-day Saint young men, missionary service is a priesthood responsibility. You young men have been reserved for this time when the promised gathering of Israel is taking place. As you serve missions, you play a pivotal role in this unprecedented event!" - Russell M. Nelson*

DATE: _____

MEMORIES MADE, TOUGH TIMES, & LESSONS LEARNED:

Stressed  Angry  Tired  Sad  Happy  Excited

_____
_____
_____
_____
_____
_____
_____
_____

Prompt of the day:

Dealing with Disappointments in Plans: Share how you deal with disappointments when plans fall through or expectations aren't met.

_____
_____
_____
_____

What are you grateful for today? _____

Embrace the power of the Holy Ghost as a missionary: Recognize the essential role of the Holy Ghost in your missionary work. Strive to live worthy of His constant companionship, listening for His promptings and following His guidance. Teach your investigators to recognize and respond to the Spirit's influence in their lives. As you embrace the power of the Holy Ghost, you'll find greater joy in your missionary service. His presence will bring comfort, insight, and a deeper witness of the truths you teach.

DATE: _____

MEMORIES MADE, TOUGH TIMES, & LESSONS LEARNED:

Stressed    Angry    Tired    Sad    Happy    Excited

_____
_____
_____
_____
_____
_____
_____
_____

What are you grateful for today? _____

"Let Him know through your prayers and your actions that you are serious about overcoming the world. Ask Him to enlighten your mind and send the help you need. Each day, record the thoughts that come to you as you pray; then follow through diligently." - Russell M. Nelson

DATE: _____

MEMORIES MADE, TOUGH TIMES, & LESSONS LEARNED:

Stressed    Angry    Tired    Sad    Happy    Excited

_____
_____
_____
_____
_____
_____
_____

Prompt of the day:
Missionary Community: How does being part of the missionary community support and inspire you in your service?

_____
_____
_____
_____

What are you grateful for today? _____

Cultivate a spirit of optimism as a missionary: Approach your missionary service with a positive, optimistic outlook. Choose to focus on the good in each day, even amidst challenges and setbacks. Look for the potential in people and situations, trusting in God's ability to bring about miracles. As you cultivate a spirit of optimism, you'll find greater resilience, enthusiasm, and joy in your work. Your positive attitude will be contagious, uplifting those around you and creating an environment where the Spirit can thrive.

DATE: _____

MEMORIES MADE, TOUGH TIMES, & LESSONS LEARNED:

Stressed    Angry    Tired    Sad    Happy    Excited

_____
_____
_____
_____
_____
_____
_____
_____

What are you grateful for today? _____

"When you make choices, I invite you to take the long view—an eternal view. Put Jesus Christ first because your eternal life is dependent upon your faith in Him and in His Atonement. It is also dependent upon your obedience to His laws. Obedience paves the way for a joyful life for you today and a grand, eternal reward tomorrow." - Russell M. Nelson

DATE: _____

MEMORIES MADE, TOUGH TIMES, & LESSONS LEARNED:

Stressed    Angry    Tired    Sad    Happy    Excited

_____
_____
_____
_____
_____
_____
_____
_____

Prompt of the day:
The Role of Discipline in Missionary Life: Reflect on how discipline plays a role in your daily missionary life and its impact.

_____
_____
_____
_____

What are you grateful for today? _____

Do show support and respect for local church leaders. Collaborate with them and seek their guidance in working within the community. Ask them questions when needed and be sure to have scheduled meetings with them as well, this will help the work move forward! Don't disregard or undermine the authority of local church leaders. Work in harmony with them and follow their counsel to ensure a united effort.

DATE: _____

MEMORIES MADE, TOUGH TIMES, & LESSONS LEARNED:

Stressed    Angry    Tired    Sad    Happy    Excited

_____
_____
_____
_____
_____
_____
_____
_____

What are you grateful for today? _____

"When we share the gospel as members or full-time missionaries, our friends and investigators need to feel our convictions and testimonies about the Atonement of Jesus Christ. Yes, we are teaching a deep concept, but we should also be sharing a deep conviction about that powerful doctrine." - Neal A. Maxwell

DATE: _____

MEMORIES MADE, TOUGH TIMES, & LESSONS LEARNED:

Stressed    Angry    Tired    Sad    Happy    Excited

_____
_____
_____
_____
_____
_____
_____

Prompt of the day:
Self-Reliance Skills: What self-reliance skills have you developed on your mission, and how do you see them being useful in the future?

_____
_____
_____
_____
_____

What are you grateful for today? _____

Be open to and embrace feedback. Though hearing criticism isn't enjoyable, it helps you improve—if you're open to it. When those who love and care for you offer feedback, listen and consider their good intentions—whether it's about missionary work or different approaches for door contacting. Weigh their input and decide if changes would benefit you. This is especially true of your leaders! Humbling yourself and being open and accepting of feedback will take you far in life. You may not always choose to change, but being open to and accepting feedback promotes growth.

DATE: _____

MEMORIES MADE, TOUGH TIMES, & LESSONS LEARNED:

Stressed   Angry   Tired   Sad   Happy   Excited

_____
_____
_____
_____
_____
_____
_____
_____

What are you grateful for today? _____

*"...in coming days, it will not be possible to survive spiritually without the guiding, directing, comforting, and constant influence of the Holy Ghost." - Russell M. Nelson*

DATE: _____

MEMORIES MADE, TOUGH TIMES, & LESSONS LEARNED:

Stressed   Angry   Tired   Sad   Happy   Excited

_____
_____
_____
_____
_____
_____
_____
_____

Prompt of the day:
Spiritual Moments in Nature: Write about a time when you felt close to God while in nature during your mission.

_____
_____
_____
_____
_____

What are you grateful for today? _____

Find deep meaning in your missionary service, even when faced with challenges and difficulties. Just as a mother giving birth or a marathon runner pushes through pain for a greater purpose, you can find profound significance in your efforts to bring souls to Christ, even when the journey is not always enjoyable. Dedicate your strengths and talents to this higher cause, recognizing that true meaning comes from serving others and inviting them to come unto the Savior. As you search for meaning in your daily missionary work, you'll discover a sense of fulfillment and satisfaction that surpasses temporary happiness.

DATE: _____

MEMORIES MADE, TOUGH TIMES, & LESSONS LEARNED:

Stressed    Angry    Tired    Sad    Happy    Excited

_____
_____
_____
_____
_____
_____
_____
_____

What are you grateful for today? _____

*"The power of the Atonement makes repentance possible and quells the despair caused by sin; it also strengthens us to see, do, and become good in ways that we could never recognize or accomplish with our limited mortal capacity." - David A. Bednar*

DATE: _____

MEMORIES MADE, TOUGH TIMES, & LESSONS LEARNED:

Stressed    Angry    Tired    Sad    Happy    Excited

_____
_____
_____
_____
_____
_____
_____
_____

Prompt of the day:
Teaching Revelations: Describe a revelation or insight you received while teaching that changed your approach or understanding.

_____
_____
_____
_____

What are you grateful for today? _____

Embrace the unexpected and be open to change. Your missionary experiences will be unique, and not everything will go as planned. Cultivate a positive attitude, exercise faith in the Lord, and trust that all experiences, even challenging ones, can be for your good and growth. When faced with unexpected obstacles or setbacks, remember that the Lord is aware of you and that He will use these experiences to shape you into the missionary and person He knows you can become. Embrace the journey with humility, gratitude, and a willingness to learn.

DATE: _____

MEMORIES MADE, TOUGH TIMES, & LESSONS LEARNED:

Stressed   Angry   Tired   Sad   Happy   Excited

_____
_____
_____
_____
_____
_____
_____
_____

What are you grateful for today? _____

*"It requires all the atonement of Christ, the mercy of the Father, the pity of angels and the grace of the Lord Jesus Christ to be with us always, and then to do the very best we possibly can, to get rid of this sin within us." - Brigham Young*

DATE: _____

MEMORIES MADE, TOUGH TIMES, & LESSONS LEARNED:

Stressed   Angry   Tired   Sad   Happy   Excited

_____
_____
_____
_____
_____
_____
_____
_____

Prompt of the day:
Learning from the Life of Christ: Reflect on how the life of Christ influences your daily actions and decisions on your mission.

_____
_____
_____
_____

What are you grateful for today? _____

Do live the gospel principles in your daily actions. Being a good example can be more powerful than words in teaching and inspiring others. Remember, oftentimes missionaries are being watched by others, be sure to reflect Christ in all that you do and say! Don't expect perfection from yourself or others. Missionaries are human and make mistakes. Learn from your experiences and strive to improve, but don't be too hard on yourself or others when things don't go perfectly!

DATE: _____

MEMORIES MADE, TOUGH TIMES, & LESSONS LEARNED:

Stressed  Angry  Tired  Sad  Happy  Excited

_____
_____
_____
_____
_____
_____
_____
_____

What are you grateful for today? _____

*"Returning to the covenant path does not mean that life will be easy. This path is rigorous and at times will feel like a steep climb. This ascent, however, is designed to test and teach us, refine our natures, and help us to become saints. It is the only path that leads to exaltation." - Russell M. Nelson*

DATE: _____

MEMORIES MADE, TOUGH TIMES, & LESSONS LEARNED:

Stressed  Angry  Tired  Sad  Happy  Excited

_____
_____
_____
_____
_____
_____
_____
_____

Prompt of the day:
Personal Sacrifices: Reflect on the personal sacrifices you've made to serve your mission and how these sacrifices have shaped your experience.

_____
_____
_____
_____

What are you grateful for today? _____

The law of attraction – you attract what you are. People tend to receive what they put out into the world. Want others to be more kind? Start with being more kind. Dislike drama? Refrain from being drawn into and contributing to it. Want more positivity? Be more positive and happier. Want a companion who is more uplifting? Turn outward and start lifting them. Small changes can lead to significant improvements in yourself and your surroundings. Remember, the only person you can change is yourself. If you're not happy with your companion, area, members or other circumstances, consider altering the energy you're putting into the world.

DATE: _____

MEMORIES MADE, TOUGH TIMES, & LESSONS LEARNED:

Stressed   Angry   Tired   Sad   Happy   Excited

_____
_____
_____
_____
_____
_____
_____
_____

What are you grateful for today? _____

"Jesus Christ can lighten our load. Jesus Christ can lift our burdens. Jesus Christ provides a way for us to be relieved of the weight of sin. Jesus Christ is our relief." - Camille N. Johnson

DATE: _____

MEMORIES MADE, TOUGH TIMES, & LESSONS LEARNED:

Stressed   Angry   Tired   Sad   Happy   Excited

_____
_____
_____
_____
_____
_____
_____
_____

Prompt of the day:
Lessons from Your Mission President's Wife: Share some lessons you have learned from your mission president's wife:

_____
_____
_____
_____
_____

What are you grateful for today? _____

Remember that bearing one another's burdens is a powerful representation of the Atonement of Jesus Christ. By seeking to lift the burdens of others, you align yourself with the Savior and His mission. When you help someone who is struggling, you are symbolically taking upon yourself a portion of their pain and sorrow, just as Christ did for all of us in the Garden of Gethsemane and on the cross. This selfless service not only blesses the lives of those you serve but also helps you develop greater love, empathy, and Christlike attributes.

DATE: _____

MEMORIES MADE, TOUGH TIMES, & LESSONS LEARNED:

Stressed   Angry   Tired   Sad   Happy   Excited

_____
_____
_____
_____
_____
_____
_____
_____

What are you grateful for today? _____

*"If you are serious about helping to gather Israel and about building relationships that will last throughout the eternities, now is the time to lay aside bitterness. Now is the time to cease insisting that it is your way or no way...Now is the time to bury your weapons of war. If your verbal arsenal is filled with insults and accusations, now is the time to put them away. You will arise as a spiritually strong man or woman of Christ." - Russell M. Nelson*

DATE: _____

MEMORIES MADE, TOUGH TIMES, & LESSONS LEARNED:

Stressed   Angry   Tired   Sad   Happy   Excited

_____
_____
_____
_____
_____
_____
_____
_____

Prompt of the day:
Learning from Elders and Leaders: Share something valuable you've learned from a companion, leader, or president.

_____
_____
_____
_____

What are you grateful for today? _____

Develop a plan to address the sources of your discouragement, focusing on problem-solving rather than worrying. Shift your thinking from the emotional to the logical and spiritual, and marshal your resources to create a strategy for moving forward. Break your plan down into small, manageable goals that will help you progress one step at a time. As a missionary, you may face discouragement in various aspects of your work, such as finding new investigators, helping others progress towards baptism, or overcoming personal weaknesses. By creating a prayerful, practical plan to tackle these challenges, you can replace worry with purposeful action and begin to see progress in your efforts.

DATE: _____

MEMORIES MADE, TOUGH TIMES, & LESSONS LEARNED:

Stressed    Angry    Tired    Sad    Happy    Excited

_____
_____
_____
_____
_____
_____
_____
_____

What are you grateful for today? _____

"Repentance is not an event; it is a process. It is the key to happiness and peace of mind. When coupled with faith, repentance opens our access to the power of the Atonement of Jesus Christ." - Russell M. Nelson

DATE: _____

MEMORIES MADE, TOUGH TIMES, & LESSONS LEARNED:

Stressed    Angry    Tired    Sad    Happy    Excited

_____
_____
_____
_____
_____
_____
_____
_____

Prompt of the day:
Witnessing Personal Transformations: Write about witnessing the personal transformation of someone you've taught or worked with closely.

_____
_____
_____
_____
_____

What are you grateful for today? _____

Work smarter and harder in your missionary efforts. Be creative in finding people to teach, under the guidance of your mission president. Remember that the Lord's work doesn't always have to be difficult to be considered valuable. Look for fun and non-threatening ways to share the gospel, such as organizing activities for youth to invite their friends. Seek inspiration to know how to best use your time and talents to further the work, and be willing to try new approaches when prompted. Balance your efforts between finding, teaching, and strengthening members, and trust that your diligence will yield fruit.

DATE: _____

MEMORIES MADE, TOUGH TIMES, & LESSONS LEARNED:

Stressed · Angry · Tired · Sad · Happy · Excited

_____
_____
_____
_____
_____
_____
_____
_____

What are you grateful for today? _____

*"Each day, ours is the challenge to access the power of the Atonement so that we can truly change, become more Christlike and qualify for the gift of exaltation and live eternally with God, Jesus Christ and our families." - Russell M. Nelson*

DATE: _____

MEMORIES MADE, TOUGH TIMES, & LESSONS LEARNED:

Stressed · Angry · Tired · Sad · Happy · Excited

_____
_____
_____
_____
_____
_____
_____
_____

Prompt of the day:
Nature and God's Creations: Write about a time when nature or your surroundings on your mission reminded you of God's creations and love.

_____
_____
_____
_____

What are you grateful for today? _____

Establish a safety code word with your companion to discreetly signal feeling unsafe or a need to leave a situation. Agree on a word or phrase like "fish" that can be said casually to communicate discomfort. Plan how you will promptly remove yourselves when the code is used. As missionaries, your safety should be the top priority. This predetermined code provides a way to notify your companion without causing a scene when circumstances don't feel right. It allows you an excuse to extract yourselves from challenging or concerning environments. This code serves as a signal that you need help or need an excuse to get out of challenging situations.

DATE: _____

MEMORIES MADE, TOUGH TIMES, & LESSONS LEARNED:

Stressed    Angry    Tired    Sad    Happy    Excited

_____
_____
_____
_____
_____
_____
_____
_____

What are you grateful for today? _____

"Positive spiritual momentum increases as we worship in the temple and grow in our understanding of the magnificent breadth and depth of the blessings we receive there. I plead with you to counter worldly ways by focusing on the eternal blessings of the temple. Your time there brings blessings for eternity." - Russell M. Nelson

DATE: _____

MEMORIES MADE, TOUGH TIMES, & LESSONS LEARNED:

Stressed    Angry    Tired    Sad    Happy    Excited

_____
_____
_____
_____
_____
_____
_____
_____

Prompt of the day:
The Challenge of Keeping Personal Faith Strong: Reflect on the challenges of keeping your personal faith strong while focusing on the faith of others.

_____
_____
_____
_____

What are you grateful for today? _____

When teaching those of different faiths, show respect for their religious beliefs and practices. Avoid disparaging their traditions or speaking negatively about their experiences. Instead, focus on sharing the message of the Restoration with love, understanding, and clarity. Encourage them to hold fast to the truths they already possess while introducing additional light and knowledge. Invite them to pray and seek personal revelation, allowing the Holy Ghost to testify of the truthfulness of your message. Through respectful dialogue and a spirit of love, you can create an environment where the Spirit can touch hearts and minds.

DATE: _____

MEMORIES MADE, TOUGH TIMES, & LESSONS LEARNED:

Stressed   Angry   Tired   Sad   Happy   Excited

_____
_____
_____
_____
_____
_____
_____
_____

What are you grateful for today? _____

*"Keep studying the scriptures, keep doing the things that build your faith in Jesus Christ and then notice the wise choices you are naturally drawn to make." - Russell M. Nelson*

DATE: _____

MEMORIES MADE, TOUGH TIMES, & LESSONS LEARNED:

Stressed   Angry   Tired   Sad   Happy   Excited

_____
_____
_____
_____
_____
_____
_____

Prompt of the day:
Deepening Scripture Understanding: How has your mission deepened your understanding and appreciation of the scriptures?

_____
_____
_____
_____

What are you grateful for today? _____

Master the art of actively listening with compassion as you teach and interact. Fully engage with the others when speaking by facing them, putting your phone away, maintaining eye contact, and nodding with affirmative responses like "uh huh." Avoid interrupting, prematurely judging, or planning your response. Stay focused, ask questions, and paraphrase to ensure understanding. In a world lacking good listeners, this invaluable skill will set you apart as a missionary. Effective listening fosters trust, shows respect, and enhances your ability to minister. Though difficult at times, honing this practice strengthens connections and spiritual communication. Strive to be a genuine, attentive listener.

DATE: _____

MEMORIES MADE, TOUGH TIMES, & LESSONS LEARNED:

Stressed    Angry    Tired    Sad    Happy    Excited

_____
_____
_____
_____
_____
_____
_____
_____

What are you grateful for today? _____

"Desires dictate our priorities, priorities shape our choices, and choices determine our actions." - Dallin H. Oaks

DATE: _____

MEMORIES MADE, TOUGH TIMES, & LESSONS LEARNED:

Stressed    Angry    Tired    Sad    Happy    Excited

_____
_____
_____
_____
_____
_____
_____
_____

Prompt of the day:
Adapting to Food and Dietary Changes: Share your experiences and adjustments to local food and dietary practices.

_____
_____
_____
_____
_____

What are you grateful for today? _____

Build a sense of belonging in your missionary community: Foster a sense of belonging and connection with your fellow missionaries, local members, and investigators. Participate in district and zone activities, attend ward events, and look for ways to serve and support others. As you build relationships and contribute to your missionary community, you'll feel a greater sense of purpose and fulfillment. Remember that you are part of a worldwide family of Saints, united in the goal of bringing others to Christ.

DATE: _____

MEMORIES MADE, TOUGH TIMES, & LESSONS LEARNED:

Stressed   Angry   Tired   Sad   Happy   Excited

_____
_____
_____
_____
_____
_____
_____

What are you grateful for today? _____

*"Obedience brings success; exact obedience brings miracles."* - Russell M. Nelson

DATE: _____

MEMORIES MADE, TOUGH TIMES, & LESSONS LEARNED:

Stressed   Angry   Tired   Sad   Happy   Excited

_____
_____
_____
_____
_____
_____

Prompt of the day:
Impact of Missionary Work: Reflect on how you believe your missionary work has made an impact, however small it may seem.

_____
_____
_____
_____

What are you grateful for today? _____

One of the beautiful life-changing miracles that Jesus performed was healing the sight of those who were blind. With the touch of his hand or even a spoken word, He miraculously restored the vision of those who could not see. One of the blessings in the initiatory ordinance is being blessed with eyes to see clearly and discern truth from error. Jesus can help you see clearly—your companion, those you teach, and others differently. To see what He sees. We can see past mortal flaws and failures. He can change our hearts and our eyes to feel and see differently. Pray for eyes to see clearly.

DATE: _____

MEMORIES MADE, TOUGH TIMES, & LESSONS LEARNED:

Stressed    Angry    Tired    Sad    Happy    Excited

_____
_____
_____
_____
_____
_____
_____
_____

What are you grateful for today? _____

*"Please know this: if everything and everyone else in the world whom you trust should fail, Jesus Christ and His Church will never fail you...He will not forsake His covenants, His promises, or His love for His people. He works miracles today, and He will work miracles tomorrow. Faith in Jesus Christ is the greatest power available to us in this life. All things are possible to them that believe." - Russell M. Nelson*

DATE: _____

MEMORIES MADE, TOUGH TIMES, & LESSONS LEARNED:

Stressed    Angry    Tired    Sad    Happy    Excited

_____
_____
_____
_____
_____
_____
_____
_____

Prompt of the day:

Building Confidence in Speaking: Write about how you've built confidence in speaking and teaching during your mission.

_____
_____
_____
_____
_____

What are you grateful for today? _____

Celebrate both small wins and great victories: Acknowledge and celebrate the small successes you experience each day. Recognizing these moments will help you stay motivated and positive throughout your mission. Missionary work is full of challenges, so it's important to celebrate the small wins along the way. Whether it's a successful lesson, a positive interaction with someone you're teaching, or a personal achievement, take the time to acknowledge and celebrate these moments. Doing so will not only boost your morale but also help you stay focused on the positive aspects of your mission. And when the great victories come, look upward and give God the glory.

DATE: _____

MEMORIES MADE, TOUGH TIMES, & LESSONS LEARNED:

Stressed  Angry  Tired  Sad  Happy  Excited

_____
_____
_____
_____
_____
_____
_____
_____

What are you grateful for today? _____

"Write down in a secure place the important things you learn from the Spirit. You will find that as you write down precious impressions, often more will come. Also, the knowledge you gain will be available throughout your life. Always, day or night, wherever you are, whatever you are doing, seek to recognize and respond to the direction of the Spirit." - Richard G. Scott

DATE: _____

MEMORIES MADE, TOUGH TIMES, & LESSONS LEARNED:

Stressed  Angry  Tired  Sad  Happy  Excited

_____
_____
_____
_____
_____
_____
_____
_____

Prompt of the day:

Future Goals Inspired by Mission: How has your mission experience influenced your goals for the future, both personal and professional?

_____
_____
_____
_____

What are you grateful for today? _____

Measure your success as a missionary by your willingness to repent, your determination to keep working, and your efforts to bring souls to Christ. Remember that you cannot control others' choices, but you can control the kind of missionary you choose to be. Seek to develop the attributes and behaviors of a successful missionary as outlined in Preach My Gospel, and trust that as you do your best to be an instrument in the Lord's hands, He will be pleased with your service and you will feel at peace with your efforts.

DATE: _____

MEMORIES MADE, TOUGH TIMES, & LESSONS LEARNED:

Stressed    Angry    Tired    Sad    Happy    Excited

_____
_____
_____
_____
_____
_____
_____
_____

What are you grateful for today? _____

*"God's plan is in place. He is at the helm, and His great and powerful ship flows toward salvation and exaltation. Remember that we cannot get there by jumping out of the boat and trying to swim there by ourselves." - M. Russell Ballard*

DATE: _____

MEMORIES MADE, TOUGH TIMES, & LESSONS LEARNED:

Stressed    Angry    Tired    Sad    Happy    Excited

_____
_____
_____
_____
_____
_____
_____
_____

Prompt of the day:
Reflecting on Historical and Sacred Sites: If you've visited historical or sacred sites during your mission, reflect on those experiences.

_____
_____
_____
_____

What are you grateful for today? _____

Do take the opportunity to share personal moments of spiritual reflection or testimony when appropriate. These heartfelt insights can foster deeper spiritual connections with those you teach and serve. Allow moments of silence to settle in, creating space for the Spirit to work in powerful ways. Your personal experiences and convictions can touch hearts and inspire others in their own faith development.

DATE: _____

MEMORIES MADE, TOUGH TIMES, & LESSONS LEARNED:

Stressed   Angry   Tired   Sad   Happy   Excited

_____
_____
_____
_____
_____
_____
_____
_____

What are you grateful for today? _____

"As the work expands at a rate that many have described as 'unbelievable,' we should recall a remarkable admonition given by the Lord through the Prophet Joseph Smith on 11 September 1831 to the elders of the Church assembled at the Morley Farm near Kirtland, Ohio. There the Master simply said: 'Wherefore, be not weary in well-doing, for ye are laying the foundation of a great work. And out of small things proceedeth that which is great.' (D&C 64:33.)" – Russell M. Nelson

DATE: _____

MEMORIES MADE, TOUGH TIMES, & LESSONS LEARNED:

Stressed   Angry   Tired   Sad   Happy   Excited

_____
_____
_____
_____
_____
_____
_____
_____

Prompt of the day:

Fostering Unity: Share an experience where you worked to foster unity within your missionary district, zone, or with the community you serve.

_____
_____
_____
_____
_____

What are you grateful for today? _____

In this chapter of your life, wear that badge with honor and humility. Make the remaining time you have the best you can, and that means going all-in and pleading for help. Allow yourself to feel and be influenced. Choose to be changed. And Christ will change your heart, but only if you give it to Him completely, withholding nothing, giving everything.

DATE: _____

MEMORIES MADE, TOUGH TIMES, & LESSONS LEARNED:

Stressed   Angry   Tired   Sad   Happy   Excited

_____
_____
_____
_____
_____
_____
_____
_____

What are you grateful for today? _____

"My beloved brothers and sisters, what has been accomplished thus far in this dispensation communicating gospel messages through social media channels is a good beginning—but only a small trickle. I now extend to you the invitation to help transform the trickle into a flood. Beginning at this place on this day, I exhort you to sweep the earth with messages filled with righteousness and truth—messages that are authentic, edifying, and praiseworthy—and literally to sweep the earth as with a flood." - David A. Bednar

DATE: _____

MEMORIES MADE, TOUGH TIMES, & LESSONS LEARNED:

Stressed   Angry   Tired   Sad   Happy   Excited

_____
_____
_____
_____
_____
_____
_____
_____

Prompt of the day:

Coping with Extreme Weather: Share how you cope with and adapt to extreme weather conditions during your mission.

_____
_____
_____
_____
_____

What are you grateful for today? _____

Seek professional help when needed. If stress becomes overwhelming or interferes with daily life during your mission, consider seeking help from a mental health professional. Talk to your mission nurse or mission president. Counseling services can offer support and strategies for managing stress effectively. Remember, seeking help is a sign of strength, not weakness. By taking care of your mental health, you can better serve others and make the most of your mission experience. It's okay to ask for help!

DATE: _____

MEMORIES MADE, TOUGH TIMES, & LESSONS LEARNED:  Stressed   Angry   Tired   Sad   Happy   Excited

_____
_____
_____
_____
_____
_____
_____
_____

What are you grateful for today? _____

*"Individual worthiness to enter the Lord's house requires much individual spiritual preparation. But with the Lord's help, nothing is impossible... Individual worthiness requires a total conversion of mind and heart to be more like the Lord, to be an honest citizen, to be a better example, and to be a holier person." - Russell M. Nelson*

DATE: _____

MEMORIES MADE, TOUGH TIMES, & LESSONS LEARNED:  Stressed   Angry   Tired   Sad   Happy   Excited

_____
_____
_____
_____
_____
_____
_____

Prompt of the day:
Patience in Progress: Reflect on a situation where you had to exercise patience, either with yourself, your companion, or someone you're teaching.

_____
_____
_____
_____
_____
_____

What are you grateful for today? _____

There may will be times when you feel discouraged or overwhelmed. What is the solution? Come Unto Christ. He beckons us to come and receive healing. And hope. And help. If we need a new heart, we give it to the ONLY one who can change it – Jesus. Then stay positive, lean on your faith, and remember why you chose to serve a mission. Turn outward and focus on the blessings and opportunities of missionary work, and trust that your efforts are making a difference. Cultivate a mindset of resilience and determination, knowing that challenges are temporary and can be overcome with faith and perseverance. Surround yourself with positive influences and seek out activities that bring you joy and peace. Elder Jeffrey R. Holland once said, "The solutions to life's problems are always gospel solutions." Jesus is the solution.

DATE:_____

MEMORIES MADE, TOUGH TIMES, & LESSONS LEARNED:

Stressed   Angry   Tired   Sad   Happy   Excited

_____
_____
_____
_____
_____
_____
_____
_____

What are you grateful for today? _____

*"I plead with you to make time for the Lord! Make your own spiritual foundation firm and able to stand the test of time by doing those things that allow the Holy Ghost to be with you always." - Russell M. Nelson*

DATE:_____

MEMORIES MADE, TOUGH TIMES, & LESSONS LEARNED:

Stressed   Angry   Tired   Sad   Happy   Excited

_____
_____
_____
_____
_____
_____
_____
_____

Prompt of the day:

The Importance of Personal Testimony: Reflect on the importance of personal testimony in your teaching and daily interactions.

_____
_____
_____
_____
_____

What are you grateful for today? _____

Cultivate a love for the scriptures as a missionary: Develop a deep love and appreciation for the scriptures during your mission. Make time each day to study the word of God, pondering its messages and applying its teachings to your life. Share your favorite scriptures with your companion, investigators, and members. As you immerse yourself in the scriptures, you'll find wisdom, comfort, and inspiration. Your growing love for the word of God will bring you joy and strengthen your testimony of the gospel.

DATE: _____

MEMORIES MADE, TOUGH TIMES, & LESSONS LEARNED:

Stressed    Angry    Tired    Sad    Happy    Excited

_____
_____
_____
_____
_____
_____
_____
_____

What are you grateful for today? _____

*"Few things will accelerate your spiritual momentum more than realizing the Lord is helping you to move a mountain in your life."* - *Russell M. Nelson*

DATE: _____

MEMORIES MADE, TOUGH TIMES, & LESSONS LEARNED:

Stressed    Angry    Tired    Sad    Happy    Excited

_____
_____
_____
_____
_____
_____
_____

Prompt of the day:
Living Gospel Principles: How has living the gospel principles more fully during your mission changed you?

_____
_____
_____
_____

What are you grateful for today? _____

Rejoice in God's relentless love. Rejoice in the knowledge that God's love for you is constant and unwavering. He is continually working to help you grow and return to Him. Trust in His plan for you, knowing that He will provide the experiences and resources you need to progress on your spiritual journey. Let go of guilt and self-disappointment, and instead delight in the love and grace of God. He loves you. He has always loved you. And He will do all that He can to bring you home. And He will use you to bring His other children, your brothers and sisters, home again as well. His love is beautiful.

DATE: _____

MEMORIES MADE, TOUGH TIMES, & LESSONS LEARNED:

Stressed    Angry    Tired    Sad    Happy    Excited

_____
_____
_____
_____
_____
_____
_____
_____

What are you grateful for today? _____

"You must be your first convert regarding this great message of the restored gospel. Everything you will want for the people with whom you share the gospel, Heavenly Father wants for you...Remember this truth: Everything in the conversion process must happen to you before it can happen to them – everything." - Jeffrey R. Holland

DATE: _____

MEMORIES MADE, TOUGH TIMES, & LESSONS LEARNED:

Stressed    Angry    Tired    Sad    Happy    Excited

_____
_____
_____
_____
_____
_____
_____
_____

Prompt of the day:
Balancing Enthusiasm and Realism: Write about how you balance enthusiasm for your mission with realism about challenges and setbacks.

_____
_____
_____
_____

What are you grateful for today? _____

Find happiness in obedience as a missionary: Discover the joy that comes from being obedient to mission rules and the promptings of the Spirit. Recognize that obedience is an expression of your love for God and your commitment to His work. As you strive to be exactly obedient, you'll invite the companionship of the Holy Ghost and qualify for divine blessings. Remember that obedience brings peace, protection, and spiritual power. Embrace the happiness that comes from living a life of integrity and devotion.

DATE: _____

MEMORIES MADE, TOUGH TIMES, & LESSONS LEARNED:  Stressed  Angry  Tired  Sad  Happy  Excited

_____
_____
_____
_____
_____
_____
_____
_____

What are you grateful for today? _____

"In the school of mortality, the tutor is often pain and tribulation, but the lessons are meant to refine and bless us and strengthen us, not destroy us." - Robert D. Hales

DATE: _____

MEMORIES MADE, TOUGH TIMES, & LESSONS LEARNED:  Stressed  Angry  Tired  Sad  Happy  Excited

_____
_____
_____
_____
_____
_____
_____

Prompt of the day:
Overcoming Fears: Share a fear you've had to overcome on your mission and how you did it.

_____
_____
_____
_____

What are you grateful for today? _____

There will be times when you become irritated with others, including companions, members, and those you teach and interact with. It is normal! But be slow to anger. Anger blinds us to any other position but our own. We can't see their side, and even worse, we don't care. Our ability to have compassion and even have the Spirit diminishes. One of the most challenging aspects of relationships in this life includes anger. Here is the truth: It is possible to be stressed, irritated, frustrated, disappointed, and even angry...and still be KIND. Please understand that irritations are invitations to see differently, to act differently, to love differently. Replace irritation with compassion and charity, replace accusations with humility, replace frustration with an invitation for understanding. Watching our temper, tongue, and tone of voice is so critical. And when we blow it, we apologize and ask for forgiveness.

DATE: _____

MEMORIES MADE, TOUGH TIMES, & LESSONS LEARNED:

Stressed    Angry    Tired    Sad    Happy    Excited

_____
_____
_____
_____
_____
_____
_____
_____
_____

What are you grateful for today? _____

*"Pour out your heart to God. Ask Him if these things are true. Make time to study His words. Really study! If you truly love your family and if you desire to be exalted with them throughout eternity, pay the price now— through serious study and fervent prayer—to know these eternal truths and then to abide by them." - Russell M. Nelson*

DATE: _____

MEMORIES MADE, TOUGH TIMES, & LESSONS LEARNED:

Stressed    Angry    Tired    Sad    Happy    Excited

_____
_____
_____
_____
_____
_____
_____
_____

Prompt of the day:

Missionary Work and Personal Boundaries: Write about establishing and maintaining personal boundaries during your mission.

_____
_____
_____
_____

What are you grateful for today? _____

When working with a companion who struggles with obedience, strive to see them through the eyes of the Savior and to respond with love, patience, and understanding. Remember that they, like you, are a work in progress, and that their challenges with obedience may stem from personal struggles, past experiences, or a lack of understanding. Rather than passing judgment or harboring resentment, pray for the ability to see your companion as the Lord sees them, and for the wisdom to know how to best support and encourage them in their efforts to grow and improve. As you consistently exemplify obedience in your own actions and decisions, you will create an environment of trust, accountability, and mutual support that will invite the Spirit and help your companion to make positive changes.

DATE: _____

MEMORIES MADE, TOUGH TIMES, & LESSONS LEARNED:  Stressed  Angry  Tired  Sad  Happy  Excited

_____
_____
_____
_____
_____
_____
_____
_____

What are you grateful for today? _____

"Now, my dear young friends, missionary work is not easy. In fact, it is often quite difficult, but the Lord is the greatest paymaster in the world. Dedicated missionary service is one of life's most fulfilling experiences. This is in large measure because of the divine agency which flows so richly from the Lord to His humble and obedient servants to bless the lives of others. I know this because I have seen it manifested in the lives of thousands and have felt it in my own life." - James E. Faust

DATE: _____

MEMORIES MADE, TOUGH TIMES, & LESSONS LEARNED:  Stressed  Angry  Tired  Sad  Happy  Excited

_____
_____
_____
_____
_____
_____
_____
_____

Prompt of the day:

Adapting to Life Without Modern Conveniences: Write about adapting to life without certain modern conveniences and how it has changed your perspective on daily living.

_____
_____
_____
_____

What are you grateful for today? _____

As a missionary, be willing to apologize and make amends when necessary. If you make a mistake, offend someone, or fall short of your commitments, take responsibility for your actions and apologize sincerely. Seek forgiveness from those you have wronged and strive to rectify the situation. Look for ways to make amends and demonstrate your desire to improve. Use these experiences as opportunities to learn, grow, and develop Christlike attributes. By showing humility, remorse, and a genuine willingness to change, you can strengthen your relationships with your companions, those you teach, and the Lord. Remember, extending and seeking forgiveness are essential aspects of the gospel and can help you become a more effective instrument in God's hands.

DATE: _____

MEMORIES MADE, TOUGH TIMES, & LESSONS LEARNED:

Stressed    Angry    Tired    Sad    Happy    Excited

_____
_____
_____
_____
_____
_____
_____
_____

What are you grateful for today? _____

*"The nearer we get to our Heavenly Father, the more we are disposed to look with compassion on perishing souls." - Joseph Smith*

DATE: _____

MEMORIES MADE, TOUGH TIMES, & LESSONS LEARNED:

Stressed    Angry    Tired    Sad    Happy    Excited

_____
_____
_____
_____
_____
_____
_____
_____

Prompt of the day:
Learning to Trust in Divine Timing: Reflect on a time when you learned to trust in divine timing, even when it was difficult.

_____
_____
_____
_____
_____

What are you grateful for today? _____

Use humor to relieve stress. Missionary life can be stressful, but humor is a great way to lighten the mood. When you laugh with your companion or those you teach, it releases feel-good chemicals that reduce stress and strengthen your connections. Seeing things in a humorous light can break the cycle of worry and help you feel more positive and hopeful. Remember to find appropriate ways to bring laughter into your day and share joy with others.

DATE: _____

MEMORIES MADE, TOUGH TIMES, & LESSONS LEARNED:

Stressed    Angry    Tired    Sad    Happy    Excited

_____
_____
_____
_____
_____
_____
_____
_____

What are you grateful for today? _____

*"No missionary that ever lived failed to influence the lives of many for the better regardless of the number of converts he may have gained." - James M. Dunn*

DATE: _____

MEMORIES MADE, TOUGH TIMES, & LESSONS LEARNED:

Stressed    Angry    Tired    Sad    Happy    Excited

_____
_____
_____
_____
_____
_____
_____
_____

Prompt of the day:
Influence of Prayer in Teaching: How has prayer influenced your teaching and interactions on your mission?

_____
_____
_____
_____

What are you grateful for today? _____

Maintain integrity in your missionary service. Give your full attention to the work you've been called to do. Resist distractions like scrolling through your phone or engaging in personal activities during proselyting hours. If uncertain, clarify expectations with your mission president, just so it's clear what you can and can't do during your missionary service. It's tempting to take shortcuts when unsupervised, but being a missionary requires active dedication. Before accepting your call, understand the expectations and commit to fulfilling all requirements. Your integrity and diligence will bring blessings to yourself and those you serve.

DATE: _____

MEMORIES MADE, TOUGH TIMES, & LESSONS LEARNED:

Stressed   Angry   Tired   Sad   Happy   Excited

_____
_____
_____
_____
_____
_____
_____
_____

What are you grateful for today? _____

*"God's objective should be our objective. He wants His children to choose to return to Him, prepared, qualified, endowed, sealed, and faithful to covenants made in holy temples." - Russell M. Nelson*

DATE: _____

MEMORIES MADE, TOUGH TIMES, & LESSONS LEARNED:

Stressed   Angry   Tired   Sad   Happy   Excited

_____
_____
_____
_____
_____
_____
_____

Prompt of the day:
The Role of a Senior Couple as Mentors: Write about a senior couple in your mission who have been mentors to you and the impact they've had.

_____
_____
_____
_____
_____

What are you grateful for today? _____

Don't ever forget the eternal truth that God does not give up on His children. The scriptures are full of examples of the Lord extending His arm and hand to us. Here are a few: "directed continually by the Hand of the Lord," "deliverance by the hand of the Lord," "he stretches forth his hands unto them all the day long," "the arms of mercy were extended towards them, and they would not," "I remember His merciful arm which He extended towards me," "O ye fair ones, how could ye have rejected that Jesus, who stood with open arms to receive you." And in 3 Nephi 9 the people hear the Lord's voice in the darkness: "Behold, mine arm of mercy is extended towards you, and whosoever will come, him will I receive; and blessed are those who come unto me. Behold, I am Jesus Christ." (3 Ne 9:14). Study these and other scriptures about Jesus' loving kindness He extends with His arms and hands "all the day long."

DATE: _____

MEMORIES MADE, TOUGH TIMES, & LESSONS LEARNED:

Stressed   Angry   Tired   Sad   Happy   Excited

_____
_____
_____
_____
_____
_____
_____
_____

What are you grateful for today? _____

"One of the most evident signs that we are drawing closer to the Savior and becoming more like Him is the loving, patience, and kind way which we treat our fellow beings, whatever the circumstances."
- Ulisses Soares

DATE: _____

MEMORIES MADE, TOUGH TIMES, & LESSONS LEARNED:

Stressed   Angry   Tired   Sad   Happy   Excited

_____
_____
_____
_____
_____
_____
_____
_____

Prompt of the day:
Adapting to Mission Life: Describe your initial adaptation to mission life and how you've settled into your role.

_____
_____
_____
_____
_____

What are you grateful for today? _____

As you faithfully respond to the call to spread the gospel and share His message, you can promise that Christ will bind up their broken hearts, dry their tears, and set them and their families free. This is the missionary promise and message to the world. Assure them that as they center their lives on the Savior and His Atonement, they will find healing, peace, and deliverance from their dark and difficult days and lonely nights. The Atonement of Jesus Christ not only provides salvation and redemption for those you teach but also brings comfort, strength, and freedom to you and your loved ones as you serve the Lord with all your heart, might, mind, and strength.

DATE: _____

MEMORIES MADE, TOUGH TIMES, & LESSONS LEARNED:

Stressed   Angry   Tired   Sad   Happy   Excited

_____
_____
_____
_____
_____
_____
_____
_____

What are you grateful for today? _____

"My brothers and sisters, I plead with you to make time for the Lord! Make your own spiritual foundation firm and able to stand the test of time by doing those things that allow the Holy Ghost to be with you always." - Russell M. Nelson

DATE: _____

MEMORIES MADE, TOUGH TIMES, & LESSONS LEARNED:

Stressed   Angry   Tired   Sad   Happy   Excited

_____
_____
_____
_____
_____
_____
_____
_____

Prompt of the day:
Dealing with Burnout: Share your strategies for dealing with feelings of burnout and maintaining your energy and spirit.

_____
_____
_____
_____

What are you grateful for today? _____

Be patient and trust in the Lord's timing, both in your personal growth and in the progress of those you teach. Missionary work rarely follows a tidy little timeline, and it's easy to become discouraged when things don't happen as quickly as we hope. But remember that the Lord sees the bigger picture and knows what is best for each of His children. Instead of focusing on numbers (baptisms and lessons taught), focus on Jesus and on planting seeds of faith in the hearts of others. Trust that as you diligently strive to do your part, the Lord will help those seeds to sprout and grow in His own due time. When you feel impatient or discouraged, turn to the Savior and seek His peace and perspective. Remember that His work will not fail, and that He is guiding your efforts as you strive to align your will with His.

DATE: _____

MEMORIES MADE, TOUGH TIMES, & LESSONS LEARNED:  Stressed  Angry  Tired  Sad  Happy  Excited

_____
_____
_____
_____
_____
_____
_____
_____

What are you grateful for today? _____

"The gathering of Israel is the most important work taking place on earth today. One crucial element of this gathering is preparing a people who are able, ready, and worthy to receive the Lord when He comes again, a people who have already chosen Jesus Christ over this fallen world, a people who rejoice in their agency to live the higher, holier laws of Jesus Christ." - Russell M. Nelson

DATE: _____

MEMORIES MADE, TOUGH TIMES, & LESSONS LEARNED:  Stressed  Angry  Tired  Sad  Happy  Excited

_____
_____
_____
_____
_____
_____
_____

Prompt of the day:
Spiritual Guidance in Daily Tasks: Share how you've seen spiritual guidance in even the small, daily tasks of your mission.

_____
_____
_____
_____

What are you grateful for today? _____

Find joy in your eternal identity as a missionary: Remember that your mission is a time to deepen your understanding of your eternal identity as a child of God. Recognize that you are engaged in a divine work, with eternal consequences for yourself and others. Find joy in the knowledge that you are a beloved son or daughter of Heavenly Father, with a unique role to play in His plan. As you anchor your sense of self in your eternal identity, you'll find greater purpose, peace, and joy in your missionary service.

DATE: _____

MEMORIES MADE, TOUGH TIMES, & LESSONS LEARNED:

Stressed    Angry    Tired    Sad    Happy    Excited

_____
_____
_____
_____
_____
_____
_____
_____

What are you grateful for today? _____

*"It matters not that giants of tribulation torment you. Your prayerful access to help is just as real as when David battled his Goliath (see 1 Samuel 17)." - Russell M. Nelson*

DATE: _____

MEMORIES MADE, TOUGH TIMES, & LESSONS LEARNED:

Stressed    Angry    Tired    Sad    Happy    Excited

_____
_____
_____
_____
_____
_____
_____
_____

Prompt of the day:
Missionary Work's Impact on Family Back Home: Reflect on how your missionary work has impacted your family back home, based on their communications.

_____
_____
_____
_____

What are you grateful for today? _____

Prioritize presence over phone distractions. DON'T IGNORE THIS ONE! When you're with others, give them your all-in attention! Quit scrolling, looking at your watch, dozing off when you're tired. Be in the present moment with who you are with and what you are doing rather than wondering about your next appointment or meeting. Be sure to put your phone on silent or disable notifications. Being fully present with others will deepen connections and strengthen relationships and invite the Spirit. If you are expecting an important text or call, give others a heads up. Embrace the habit of being fully present for more meaningful relationships and experiences.

DATE: _____

MEMORIES MADE, TOUGH TIMES, & LESSONS LEARNED:

Stressed   Angry   Tired   Sad   Happy   Excited

_____
_____
_____
_____
_____
_____
_____
_____

What are you grateful for today? _____

"Repentance is the key to avoiding misery inflicted by traps of the adversary. The Lord does not expect perfection from us at this point in our eternal progression. But He does expect us to become increasingly pure. Daily repentance is the pathway to purity, and purity brings power. Personal purity can make us powerful tools in the hands of God." - Russell M. Nelson

DATE: _____

MEMORIES MADE, TOUGH TIMES, & LESSONS LEARNED:

Stressed   Angry   Tired   Sad   Happy   Excited

_____
_____
_____
_____
_____
_____
_____
_____

Prompt of the day:

Expressions of Faith: How have you seen expressions of faith that have moved or inspired you, either in yourself or others?

_____
_____
_____
_____

What are you grateful for today? _____

Cultivate a love for service as a missionary: Develop a genuine love for serving others during your mission. Look for opportunities to help, support, and bless those around you, whether through planned service projects or spontaneous acts of kindness. As you focus on serving others, you'll experience the joy that comes from following Christ's example of selfless love. Remember that your mission is not just about teaching the gospel, but about living it through acts of service and compassion.

DATE: _____

MEMORIES MADE, TOUGH TIMES, & LESSONS LEARNED:

Stressed  Angry  Tired  Sad  Happy  Excited

_____
_____
_____
_____
_____
_____
_____
_____
_____

What are you grateful for today? _____

"I promise that as you prayerfully study the Book of Mormon every day, you will make better decisions—every day. I promise that as you ponder what you study, the windows of heaven will open, and you will receive answers to your own questions and direction for your own life. I promise that as you daily immerse yourself in the Book of Mormon, you can be immunized against the evils of the day." - Russell M. Nelson

DATE: _____

MEMORIES MADE, TOUGH TIMES, & LESSONS LEARNED:

Stressed  Angry  Tired  Sad  Happy  Excited

_____
_____
_____
_____
_____
_____
_____
_____

Prompt of the day:
Growth Through Teaching: Write about how teaching others has contributed to your own personal growth and understanding.

_____
_____
_____
_____

What are you grateful for today? _____

As a missionary, maintain the confidentiality of those you teach and serve. Respect their privacy by keeping personal information shared with you in confidence. This includes their struggles, doubts, and personal experiences. Building trust through confidentiality is essential for creating an environment where others feel safe to open their hearts and receive the gospel message. However, if someone shares information that raises serious concerns about their safety or well-being, consult with your mission president to ensure appropriate steps are taken to help the individual. Remember, your role as a missionary is to be a trustworthy and compassionate listener, fostering relationships built on trust and Christlike love.

DATE: _____

MEMORIES MADE, TOUGH TIMES, & LESSONS LEARNED:

Stressed    Angry    Tired    Sad    Happy    Excited

_____
_____
_____
_____
_____
_____
_____
_____

What are you grateful for today? _____

*"I suppose there would never be an apostate, there would never be a crime, if people remembered, really remembered, the things they had covenanted at the water's edge or at the sacrament table and in the temple." - Spencer W. Kimball*

DATE: _____

MEMORIES MADE, TOUGH TIMES, & LESSONS LEARNED:

Stressed    Angry    Tired    Sad    Happy    Excited

_____
_____
_____
_____
_____
_____
_____

Prompt of the day:

Adapting to Unexpected Roles: Write about a time when you had to take on an unexpected role or responsibility during your mission and how you adapted.

_____
_____
_____
_____

What are you grateful for today? _____

Missionary work involves a wide range of demands, from physical tasks to emotional challenges to intellectual pursuits. To meet these demands, it's important to proactively build resources that can support you. This might include developing a routine of personal prayer and scripture study, relying on the guidance of the Holy Ghost, and seeking support from your mission companions and leaders. By fortifying yourself spiritually, you'll be better equipped to handle the challenges of missionary work and find joy in your service.

DATE: _____

MEMORIES MADE, TOUGH TIMES, & LESSONS LEARNED:

Stressed   Angry   Tired   Sad   Happy   Excited

_____
_____
_____
_____
_____
_____
_____
_____

What are you grateful for today? _____

"Use the Book of Mormon to help people have spiritual experiences, especially a witness from the Holy Ghost that the book itself is the word of God. When you teach the gospel using the Book of Mormon, your teaching will resonate with power and clarity in the heart and mind." - Elder D. Todd Christofferson

DATE: _____

MEMORIES MADE, TOUGH TIMES, & LESSONS LEARNED:

Stressed   Angry   Tired   Sad   Happy   Excited

_____
_____
_____
_____
_____
_____
_____
_____

Prompt of the day:

Handling Language and Cultural Faux Pas: Share an experience of handling a language or cultural faux pas with grace and learning.

_____
_____
_____
_____

What are you grateful for today? _____

Be a friend to yourself. As a missionary, remember that perfection isn't expected. Focus on the good you do and treat your feelings with respect. Don't compare yourself to others who may seem more capable. Your feelings matter, so listen to them. Learn from mistakes and let them go, ensuring your expectations for yourself are reasonable. Treat yourself with kindness and understanding, just as you would a dear friend. By being a friend to yourself, you'll be better equipped to manage stress and serve others effectively. Embrace your unique talents and use them to make a difference.

DATE: _____

MEMORIES MADE, TOUGH TIMES, & LESSONS LEARNED:

Stressed    Angry    Tired    Sad    Happy    Excited

_____
_____
_____
_____
_____
_____
_____
_____

What are you grateful for today? _____

"When you are confronted with a dilemma, think celestial! When tested by temptation, think celestial! When life or loved ones let you down, think celestial! When someone dies prematurely, think celestial. When someone lingers with a devastating illness, think celestial. When the pressures of life crowd in upon you, think celestial!" - Russell M. Nelson

DATE: _____

MEMORIES MADE, TOUGH TIMES, & LESSONS LEARNED:

Stressed    Angry    Tired    Sad    Happy    Excited

_____
_____
_____
_____
_____
_____
_____
_____

Prompt of the day:
Building Trust: How do you approach building trust with those you teach and serve?

_____
_____
_____
_____
_____

What are you grateful for today? _____

Stand tall and be grateful that Jesus Christ, the only perfect being to walk the earth, intimately understands your sorrows, struggles, and afflictions as a missionary. When you face rejection, loneliness, or disappointment, remember that He too was despised, betrayed, and ultimately sacrificed for the very people He came to save. Draw strength from His example of unwavering love, compassion, and dedication in the face of adversity. Find solace in the knowledge that He is with you always, and that He will never leave you comfortless. There are literal angels surrounding you on every doorstep. As you strive to follow in His footsteps and emulate His character, you will discover a deeper sense of purpose, peace, and joy in your missionary labors. You are never alone in this great work.

DATE: _____

MEMORIES MADE, TOUGH TIMES, & LESSONS LEARNED:

Stressed   Angry   Tired   Sad   Happy   Excited

_____
_____
_____
_____
_____
_____
_____
_____
_____

What are you grateful for today? _____

"It was meant to be that life would be a challenge. To suffer some anxiety, some depression, even some failure is normal. If you have a good, miserable day once in a while—or several in a row—stand steady and face them. Things will straighten out. There is great purpose in our struggle in life." - Boyd K. Packer

DATE: _____

MEMORIES MADE, TOUGH TIMES, & LESSONS LEARNED:

Stressed   Angry   Tired   Sad   Happy   Excited

_____
_____
_____
_____
_____
_____
_____
_____

Prompt of the day:

Reflections on the Power of Prayer: Reflect on a specific experience that highlighted the power of prayer in your mission.

_____
_____
_____
_____

What are you grateful for today? _____

Take the opportunity to build relationships with people of other faiths in the community. Engage in respectful dialogue, seek to understand their beliefs, and find common ground. Interfaith understanding can enrich your mission and foster a spirit of unity and compassion. These relationships can broaden your perspective and create a more inclusive community.

DATE: _____

MEMORIES MADE, TOUGH TIMES, & LESSONS LEARNED:

Stressed  Angry  Tired  Sad  Happy  Excited

_____
_____
_____
_____
_____
_____
_____
_____

What are you grateful for today? _____

"Charity is having patience with someone who has let us down; it is resisting the impulse to become offended easily. It is accepting weaknesses and shortcomings. It is accepting people as they truly are. It is looking beyond physical appearances to attributes that will not dim through time. It is resisting the impulse to categorize others." - Thomas S. Monson

DATE: _____

MEMORIES MADE, TOUGH TIMES, & LESSONS LEARNED:

Stressed  Angry  Tired  Sad  Happy  Excited

_____
_____
_____
_____
_____
_____
_____
_____

Prompt of the day:
Gratitude for the Mission Experience: Write about what you're most grateful for regarding your mission experience.

_____
_____
_____
_____

What are you grateful for today? _____

Remember that ultimate judgment belongs to the Lord. When you find yourself upset or disagreeing with someone's actions, resist the urge to make assumptions about their character. Instead, remind yourself that everyone is doing their best and that the Savior's Atonement has the power to heal and redeem all of us. Focus on aligning your own life with your covenants and allow others the space to do the same without criticism or judgment. As a missionary, your role is to invite others to come unto Christ, not to determine their worthiness or progress. Trust in the Lord's wisdom and mercy, and leave the final judgment in His hands.

DATE: _____

MEMORIES MADE, TOUGH TIMES, & LESSONS LEARNED:  Stressed  Angry  Tired  Sad  Happy  Excited

_____
_____
_____
_____
_____
_____
_____
_____

What are you grateful for today? _____

*"Young men, prepare to serve as missionaries. Going on a mission teaches you to live the law of consecration. It may be the only time in your life when you can give to the Lord all your time, talents, and resources. In return, the Lord will bless you with His Spirit to be with you. He will be close to you and strengthen you." - Robert D. Hales*

DATE: _____

MEMORIES MADE, TOUGH TIMES, & LESSONS LEARNED:  Stressed  Angry  Tired  Sad  Happy  Excited

_____
_____
_____
_____
_____
_____
_____
_____

Prompt of the day:
Embracing the Journey: Write about embracing the journey of your mission, with all its unpredictability and opportunities for growth.

_____
_____
_____
_____

What are you grateful for today? _____

Find joy in the Atonement of Jesus Christ as a missionary: Deepen your understanding and appreciation of the Atonement of Jesus Christ during your mission. Recognize that His sacrifice is the ultimate source of hope, healing, and joy for yourself and those you teach. Rely on the Savior's grace and mercy as you strive to overcome weaknesses and become more like Him. As you find joy in the Atonement, you'll be better able to help others experience its transformative power in their own lives.

DATE: _____

MEMORIES MADE, TOUGH TIMES, & LESSONS LEARNED:

Stressed    Angry    Tired    Sad    Happy    Excited

_____
_____
_____
_____
_____
_____
_____
_____

What are you grateful for today? _____

*"Dear young friends, you are each vital to the Lord. He has held you in reserve until now to help gather Israel. Your decision to serve a mission, whether a proselyting or a service mission, will bless you and many others." - Russell M. Nelson*

DATE: _____

MEMORIES MADE, TOUGH TIMES, & LESSONS LEARNED:

Stressed    Angry    Tired    Sad    Happy    Excited

_____
_____
_____
_____
_____
_____
_____

Prompt of the day:
Handling Homesickness: Share strategies or thoughts that have helped you handle homesickness or longing for familiar comforts.

_____
_____
_____
_____

What are you grateful for today? _____

Be aware that many of God's children suffer silently and alone. Make an effort to reassure those who are struggling that they are not alone, and that God, angels, and fellow members of the Church are with them. Many people feel isolated and hopeless when facing difficult challenges, and they may be reluctant to reach out for help. As a missionary, you can be proactive in offering support and encouragement, letting them know that they are loved and valued. Help them recognize the resources available to them, both spiritually and temporally, and encourage them to seek the help they need.

DATE: _____

MEMORIES MADE, TOUGH TIMES, & LESSONS LEARNED:

Stressed    Angry    Tired    Sad    Happy    Excited

_____
_____
_____
_____
_____
_____
_____
_____

What are you grateful for today? _____

"As we seek to be disciples of Jesus Christ, our efforts to hear Him need to be ever more intentional. It takes conscious and consistent effort to fill our daily lives with His words, His teachings, His truths." - Russell M. Nelson

DATE: _____

MEMORIES MADE, TOUGH TIMES, & LESSONS LEARNED:

Stressed    Angry    Tired    Sad    Happy    Excited

_____
_____
_____
_____
_____
_____
_____
_____

Prompt of the day:
The Impact of Community Service: Reflect on a community service activity that left a lasting impact on you and those you served.

_____
_____
_____
_____

What are you grateful for today? _____

Actively seek out and engage in mission-appropriate activities that help you manage stress, maintain a positive outlook, and draw closer to the Savior. Take time each day to pray meaningfully and frequently, study the scriptures, and ponder on the gospel truths you are learning and teaching. Write uplifting letters or emails to family and friends, sharing your experiences and testimony. Have open and honest conversations with your companion and mission leaders about your struggles and successes. Participate in wholesome recreational activities, such as playing uplifting music, creating artwork, or writing in this journal. As you make these stress-relieving practices a regular part of your missionary life, you will find renewed strength, peace, and enthusiasm for this awesome life-changing work!

DATE: _____

MEMORIES MADE, TOUGH TIMES, & LESSONS LEARNED:

Stressed  Angry  Tired  Sad  Happy  Excited

_____
_____
_____
_____
_____
_____
_____
_____

What are you grateful for today? _____

*"You and I, today and always, are to bear witness of Jesus Christ and declare the message of the Restoration....Missionary work is a manifestation of our spiritual identity and heritage." - David A. Bednar*

DATE: _____

MEMORIES MADE, TOUGH TIMES, & LESSONS LEARNED:

Stressed  Angry  Tired  Sad  Happy  Excited

_____
_____
_____
_____
_____
_____
_____

Prompt of the day:
Moments of Clarity: Describe a moment of clarity or profound peace you experienced, and what it taught you.

_____
_____
_____
_____
_____

What are you grateful for today? _____

Do include members in planning and activities. Their insights and participation can lead to more effective and inclusive efforts. Don't plan everything on your own or assume you know what's best for the community. Value the input and participation of local members.

DATE: _____

MEMORIES MADE, TOUGH TIMES, & LESSONS LEARNED:

Stressed   Angry   Tired   Sad   Happy   Excited

_____
_____
_____
_____
_____
_____
_____
_____

What are you grateful for today? _____

*"Love for the Lord, love for His servants the missionaries. Missionary work is a work of love and trust, and it has to be done on that basis." - Gordon B. Hinckley*

DATE: _____

MEMORIES MADE, TOUGH TIMES, & LESSONS LEARNED:

Stressed   Angry   Tired   Sad   Happy   Excited

_____
_____
_____
_____
_____
_____
_____
_____

Prompt of the day:
Learning from Local Church Leaders: Share insights or lessons learned from local church leaders and how they've influenced your mission.

_____
_____
_____
_____

What are you grateful for today?

Use your weekly companionship inventory as a loving and constructive tool to identify areas for improvement and to set goals for becoming better missionaries together. Approach these discussions with humility, openness, and a genuine desire to grow. Be willing to listen to your companion's insights and feedback, even if they come across as criticism or complaints, and be courageous in sharing your own thoughts and concerns. Remember that the purpose of companionship inventory is not to criticize or demean, but rather to build each other up, enhance understanding, and to work together in harmony. As you do so, you will find that your companionship will be strengthened, and your effectiveness as missionaries will increase. Above all, have compassion and pray for charity.

DATE: _____

MEMORIES MADE, TOUGH TIMES, & LESSONS LEARNED:

Stressed    Angry    Tired    Sad    Happy    Excited

_____
_____
_____
_____
_____
_____
_____
_____

What are you grateful for today? _____

"No matter how hard we work, no matter how much we obey, no matter how many good things we do in this life, it would not be enough were it not for Jesus Christ and His loving grace. On our own we cannot earn the kingdom of God, no matter what we do." - M. Russell Ballard

DATE: _____

MEMORIES MADE, TOUGH TIMES, & LESSONS LEARNED:

Stressed    Angry    Tired    Sad    Happy    Excited

_____
_____
_____
_____
_____
_____
_____

Prompt of the day:

Spiritual Routine: How have you established a spiritual routine during your mission, and how does it help you?

_____
_____
_____
_____

What are you grateful for today? _____

Bear frequent and powerful testimony of Christ as Savior, Redeemer, and Atoning Lamb of God. Doing so invokes the power of God the Father and the Holy Ghost, touching the hearts of investigators and building their faith upon the rock of Christ. Your testimony will bring an echo of truth to the investigators, reminding them of the pre-mortal life where they heard the plan of salvation and the role of Jesus Christ. As you testify of the Savior and your Heavenly Father, the Holy Ghost will bear record of Him, helping investigators build their foundation on Christ.

DATE: _____

MEMORIES MADE, TOUGH TIMES, & LESSONS LEARNED:

Stressed   Angry   Tired   Sad   Happy   Excited

_____
_____
_____
_____
_____
_____
_____
_____

What are you grateful for today? _____

"Nothing invites the Spirit more than fixing your focus on Jesus Christ. Talk of Christ, rejoice in Christ, feast upon the words of Christ, and press forward with steadfastness in Christ. Make your Sabbath a delight as you worship Him, partake of the sacrament, and keep His day holy...please make time for the Lord in His holy house. Nothing will strengthen your spiritual foundation like temple service and temple worship." - Russell M. Nelson

DATE: _____

MEMORIES MADE, TOUGH TIMES, & LESSONS LEARNED:

Stressed   Angry   Tired   Sad   Happy   Excited

_____
_____
_____
_____
_____
_____
_____
_____

Prompt of the day:

The Role of Patience in Personal Growth: Reflect on how patience has played a role in your personal growth during your mission.

_____
_____
_____
_____
_____

What are you grateful for today? _____

Do be willing to adapt your plans throughout the day. Missionaries often plan their day in the morning, to find that at the end of the day, it did not go according to the plan. Remember, if the spirit is involved in your planning, the day will go how the Lord needs it to go. Review your day with the Lord in prayer each night personally, and with your companion. Be open to change. Don't rigidly stick to your plans when circumstances change or when the Spirit prompts you otherwise. Be flexible and trust that the Lord is guiding your efforts, even when things don't go as expected.

DATE: _____

MEMORIES MADE, TOUGH TIMES, & LESSONS LEARNED:

Stressed    Angry    Tired    Sad    Happy    Excited

_____
_____
_____
_____
_____
_____
_____
_____

What are you grateful for today? _____

*"Generally speaking, the most miserable people I know are those who are obsessed with themselves; the happiest people I know are those who lose themselves in the service of others...By and large, I have come to see that if we complain about life, it is because we are thinking only of ourselves." - Gordon B. Hinckley*

DATE: _____

MEMORIES MADE, TOUGH TIMES, & LESSONS LEARNED:

Stressed    Angry    Tired    Sad    Happy    Excited

_____
_____
_____
_____
_____
_____
_____

Prompt of the day:

Missionary Work's Impact on Family: Reflect on how your missionary work has impacted your family or loved ones, based on communications from home.

_____
_____
_____
_____

What are you grateful for today? _____

Cultivate a spirit of humility as a missionary: Develop a deep sense of humility as you serve the Lord. Recognize that your talents, abilities, and successes are gifts from God, given to bless others. Be willing to learn from your companions, your leaders, and those you teach. Seek to serve without pride or desire for recognition, focusing instead on glorifying God and building His kingdom. As you cultivate a spirit of humility, you'll find greater peace, unity, and joy in your missionary work.

DATE: _____

MEMORIES MADE, TOUGH TIMES, & LESSONS LEARNED:

Stressed　Angry　Tired　Sad　Happy　Excited

_____
_____
_____
_____
_____
_____
_____
_____
_____

What are you grateful for today? _____

*"Obedience allows God's blessings to flow without constraint. He will bless His obedient children with freedom from bondage and misery. And He will bless them with more light." - Russell M. Nelson*

DATE: _____

MEMORIES MADE, TOUGH TIMES, & LESSONS LEARNED:

Stressed　Angry　Tired　Sad　Happy　Excited

_____
_____
_____
_____
_____
_____
_____
_____
_____

Prompt of the day:
Adapting to Missionary Life's Rhythms: Write about adapting to the rhythms of missionary life and finding your own pace within it.

_____
_____
_____
_____
_____

What are you grateful for today? _____

Enhance your missionary success by mastering conversation. Use a simple formula: make an observation and ask a question. Comment on shared experiences or something you notice about the person. Although initiating a discussion can be challenging, the relief and rewards are significant. Being the catalyst for a great conversation not only brings people together but also allows you to share the gospel message. Genuine connections are sought by everyone, and the ability to start meaningful conversations can open doors to teaching opportunities. Despite the initial difficulty, the value of being brave enough to start a conversation is worth it as a missionary!

DATE: _____

MEMORIES MADE, TOUGH TIMES, & LESSONS LEARNED:

| Stressed | Angry | Tired | Sad | Happy | Excited |
|----------|-------|-------|-----|-------|---------|

_____
_____
_____
_____
_____
_____
_____

What are you grateful for today? _____

*"The gospel of Jesus Christ challenges us to become converted. It teaches us what we should do, and it provides us opportunities to become what our Heavenly Father desires us to become. The full measure of this conversion to men and women of God happens best through our labors in His vineyard." - Dallin H. Oaks*

DATE: _____

MEMORIES MADE, TOUGH TIMES, & LESSONS LEARNED:

| Stressed | Angry | Tired | Sad | Happy | Excited |
|----------|-------|-------|-----|-------|---------|

_____
_____
_____
_____
_____
_____
_____

Prompt of the day:
Staying Motivated: What keeps you motivated during challenging times in your mission?

_____
_____
_____
_____

What are you grateful for today? _____

Do show respect for local customs and culture: Try to learn about and respect the local customs, traditions, and culture. This shows your respect for the members' heritage and can minimize cultural misunderstandings. Don't impose your own cultural norms or make judgments about local practices. Embrace the opportunity to learn and appreciate how cool the culture is!

DATE: _____

MEMORIES MADE, TOUGH TIMES, & LESSONS LEARNED:

Stressed   Angry   Tired   Sad   Happy   Excited

_____
_____
_____
_____
_____
_____
_____
_____

What are you grateful for today?
_____

"So the fact of the matter is investigators are not only hearing our testimony of Christ, but they are hearing echoes of other, earlier testimonies, including their own testimony of Him, for they were on the side of the faithful who kept their first estate and earned the privilege of a second estate. We must always remember that these investigators, every man, woman, and child, were among the valiant who once overcame Satan by the power of their testimony of Christ! So, when they hear others bear that witness of Christ's saving mission, it has a familiar feeling; it brings an echo of truth they themselves already know." - Jeffrey R. Holland

DATE: _____

MEMORIES MADE, TOUGH TIMES, & LESSONS LEARNED:

Stressed   Angry   Tired   Sad   Happy   Excited

_____
_____
_____
_____
_____
_____
_____
_____

Prompt of the day:
Personal Reflections on Sacrifice: Share your personal reflections on the concept of sacrifice and how it has become meaningful to you during your mission.

_____
_____
_____
_____
_____

What are you grateful for today? _____

Lose yourself in service as a missionary: Instead of focusing solely on your own happiness, immerse yourself in serving others. Look for ways to lift, support, and minister to your companions, investigators, and members. As you lose yourself in the work of the Lord, you'll find a deeper sense of joy and satisfaction. Remember that true happiness comes from living a Christ-centered life of service and sacrifice. Embrace the opportunity to forget yourself and focus on the needs of others.

DATE: _____

MEMORIES MADE, TOUGH TIMES, & LESSONS LEARNED:

Stressed   Angry   Tired   Sad   Happy   Excited

_____
_____
_____
_____
_____
_____
_____
_____
_____

What are you grateful for today? _____

*"I am very grateful for each man who bears the holy priesthood. You are the hope of our Redeemer, who desires 'that every man might speak in the name of God the Lord, even the Savior of the world' (D&C 1:20). He wants all of His ordained sons to represent Him, to speak for Him, to act for Him and to bless the lives of God's children throughout the world, to the end 'that faith also might increase in [all] the earth' (D&C 1:21)." - Russell M. Nelson*

DATE: _____

MEMORIES MADE, TOUGH TIMES, & LESSONS LEARNED:

Stressed   Angry   Tired   Sad   Happy   Excited

_____
_____
_____
_____
_____
_____
_____
_____
_____

Prompt of the day:

Maintaining Health: How do you maintain your physical and mental health during the rigorous demands of missionary work?

_____
_____
_____
_____
_____

What are you grateful for today? _____

Recognize that your companions, like you, are beloved sons of God with their own unique background, experiences, and personalities. Despite any differences you may have, focus on your shared desire to serve the Lord and bring others unto Christ. Remember that your companion has been called by the same authority as you have, and that together, you form a powerful partnership in the work of salvation. Strive to see your companion through the eyes of the Savior, and treat them with the same love, patience, and understanding that He would extend to them. You may never be best friends, but strive for unity and peace so you can both have the Spirit to be with you.

DATE: _____

MEMORIES MADE, TOUGH TIMES, & LESSONS LEARNED:

Stressed   Angry   Tired   Sad   Happy   Excited

_____
_____
_____
_____
_____
_____
_____
_____

What are you grateful for today? _____

*"The gospel messages you share will be accepted more readily if your Christlike example is evident in the ongoing pattern of your posts."* - David A. Bednar

DATE: _____

MEMORIES MADE, TOUGH TIMES, & LESSONS LEARNED:

Stressed   Angry   Tired   Sad   Happy   Excited

_____
_____
_____
_____
_____
_____
_____
_____

Prompt of the day:
The Joy of Small Victories: Reflect on the joy and significance of small victories in your daily missionary work.

_____
_____
_____
_____
_____

What are you grateful for today? _____

Practice patience. Do you get bugged easily? When companions or others chew with their mouth open? Lick their fingers? Annoying laugh? Most of us get bothered by little things. If you can bring it up with the person in a kind or humorous way and then chat about it, give it a try. If it's something they can't help (snoring!?), practice patience or get some earplugs. Chances are you will work and/or live with someone who bugs you. Learn patience and practice kindness throughout your mission. Remember people are more important than problems.

DATE: _____

MEMORIES MADE, TOUGH TIMES, & LESSONS LEARNED:

Stressed    Angry    Tired    Sad    Happy    Excited

_____
_____
_____
_____
_____
_____
_____
_____

What are you grateful for today? _____

*"You're the most prayed for people on the face of the earth. I really believe that. I do not believe, collectively speaking, that there is any body of people that's any collective circle of individuals are prayed for on the face of the earth than the LDS missionaries." - Jeffrey R. Holland*

DATE: _____

MEMORIES MADE, TOUGH TIMES, & LESSONS LEARNED:

Stressed    Angry    Tired    Sad    Happy    Excited

_____
_____
_____
_____
_____
_____
_____

Prompt of the day:
Adapting Spiritual Messages: Share an experience where you had to adapt a spiritual message to better resonate with your audience.

_____
_____
_____
_____

What are you grateful for today? _____

Develop the ability to confidently discuss your interests and hobbies when meeting new people. One of the common introductory questions is "What do you like to do?" or "Tell me about yourself." Avoid replying with "I don't know" or "Nothing, I'm pretty boring." You don't need to be an expert to enjoy an activity. If you're unsure about your interests, be open to trying new things. Your pastimes help define your personality and make you more relatable and interesting. Don't be afraid to share enthusiastically about what you find fun or fulfilling, even if it's unique. And feel free to explore new interests - your passions can evolve over time. Prepare to engage in genuine conversation about who you are.

DATE: _____

MEMORIES MADE, TOUGH TIMES, & LESSONS LEARNED:

Stressed    Angry    Tired    Sad    Happy    Excited

_____
_____
_____
_____
_____
_____
_____
_____

What are you grateful for today? _____

"Whatever questions or problems you have, the answer is always found in the life and teachings of Jesus Christ. Learn more about His Atonement, His love, His mercy, His doctrine and His restored gospel of healing and progression. Turn to Him! Follow Him!" - Russell M. Nelson

DATE: _____

MEMORIES MADE, TOUGH TIMES, & LESSONS LEARNED:

Stressed    Angry    Tired    Sad    Happy    Excited

_____
_____
_____
_____
_____
_____
_____
_____

Prompt of the day:
Learning from Rejections: Write about what you've learned from rejections during your teaching and how it has shaped your approach.

_____
_____
_____
_____
_____

What are you grateful for today? _____

Seek confirmation from the Lord that your plan to overcome discouragement is a good one. Pray for His guidance and support as you work to implement your plan and make necessary changes in your life. Trust that He will help you move beyond the failures or challenges that have caused your discouragement. As a missionary, you have the right to receive personal revelation for your own life and work. As you develop a plan to overcome discouragement, take it to the Lord in prayer and ask for His confirmation and guidance. Have faith that He will inspire you with any necessary adjustments and will provide the strength and support you need to succeed.

DATE: _____

MEMORIES MADE, TOUGH TIMES, & LESSONS LEARNED:   Stressed   Angry   Tired   Sad   Happy   Excited

_____
_____
_____
_____
_____
_____
_____
_____

What are you grateful for today? _____

*"I am convinced that missionary work is not easy because salvation is not a cheap experience. Salvation never was easy. We are The Church of Jesus Christ, this is the truth, and He is our Great Eternal Head. How could we believe it would be easy for us when it was never, ever easy for Him?" - Elder Jeffrey R. Holland*

DATE: _____

MEMORIES MADE, TOUGH TIMES, & LESSONS LEARNED:   Stressed   Angry   Tired   Sad   Happy   Excited

_____
_____
_____
_____
_____
_____
_____
_____

Prompt of the day:

Learning from Failures: Reflect on a moment that felt like a failure and what you learned from the experience.

_____
_____
_____
_____

What are you grateful for today? _____

Next time you're in line at the store, or getting gas, or at a restaurant, notice the people around you and the quick judgements and conclusions you're tempted to make. Catch yourself judging unfairly and rewind the scene in your mind. Instead, see this person as a child of God who is loved and hoped for. See them as a person who awaits a Patriarchal Blessing. Remember they cheered in the premortal existence when they heard the Plan of Happiness. Ask a silent prayer to see if your path was meant to cross theirs today, to help them and bring them light, truth, and joy. Then open your mouth.

DATE: _____

MEMORIES MADE, TOUGH TIMES, & LESSONS LEARNED:

Stressed　Angry　Tired　Sad　Happy　Excited

_____
_____
_____
_____
_____
_____
_____
_____

What are you grateful for today? _____

"Our goal should be to live life in radical amazement... get up in the morning and look at the world in a way that takes nothing for granted. Everything is phenomenal; everything is incredible; never treat life casually. To be spiritual is to be amazed." - Abraham Joshua Heschel

DATE: _____

MEMORIES MADE, TOUGH TIMES, & LESSONS LEARNED:

Stressed　Angry　Tired　Sad　Happy　Excited

_____
_____
_____
_____
_____
_____
_____

Prompt of the day:
The Role of Faith in Overcoming Challenges: Reflect on a challenge you faced where your faith played a crucial role in overcoming it.

_____
_____
_____
_____

What are you grateful for today? _____

Pray for others by name. Create your own prayer roll of those you are teaching and others who need blessings. Take your list to God. Plead that the windows of heaven will be opened and blessings be poured out upon those you love and serve. Add names to your list. Spend time on your knees. Have a prayer in your heart throughout the day. When your companion is teaching, pray for them in your heart. When someone is speaking in a sacrament meeting, pray for them. Pray that the Spirit will guide them and that your heart will be open to the Spirit. Come with questions and pray for guidance and answers. Then be still and notice the nudges and follow the feelings. Joseph Smith didn't just go into the grove of trees to know, but to know what to DO. Answers come with action.

DATE: _____

MEMORIES MADE, TOUGH TIMES, & LESSONS LEARNED:

Stressed   Angry   Tired   Sad   Happy   Excited

_____
_____
_____
_____
_____
_____
_____
_____

What are you grateful for today? _____

*"To have the continuous companionship of the Holy Ghost is the most precious possession we can have in mortality" - Dallin H. Oaks*

DATE: _____

MEMORIES MADE, TOUGH TIMES, & LESSONS LEARNED:

Stressed   Angry   Tired   Sad   Happy   Excited

_____
_____
_____
_____
_____
_____
_____
_____

Prompt of the day:
Unexpected Blessings: Write about an unexpected blessing or positive outcome that arose from a difficult situation.

_____
_____
_____
_____
_____

What are you grateful for today? _____

When God sends you a message, a nudge, a feeling, a prompting, commit to turning towards that bid for connection and act. There may be times when you are tempted to ignore a prompting, thinking it's just your own thoughts. It may feel inconvenient or odd. Act on it anyway. Follow the feelings you get. The promptings of the Spirit will never lead you to be disobedient. The Spirit will guide you. Sometimes it is subtle. Other times it is clear and direct. Commit early on to act on those promptings. Every. Single. One. Even if nothing comes of the prompting. You may never see the results of those actions in this life. But God sees the bigger picture. When He places you on a path, sometimes only He knows why. Go anyway. Every time.

DATE: _____

MEMORIES MADE, TOUGH TIMES, & LESSONS LEARNED:

Stressed   Angry   Tired   Sad   Happy   Excited

_____
_____
_____
_____
_____
_____
_____
_____

What are you grateful for today? _____

"As you shift your focus away from worldly distractions, some things that seem important to you now will recede in priority. You will need to say no to some things, even though they may seem harmless. As you embark upon and continue this lifelong process of consecrating your life to the Lord, the changes in your perspective, feelings, and spiritual strength will amaze you!" - Russell M. Nelson

DATE: _____

MEMORIES MADE, TOUGH TIMES, & LESSONS LEARNED:

Stressed   Angry   Tired   Sad   Happy   Excited

_____
_____
_____
_____
_____
_____
_____

Prompt of the day:

Missionary Work as a Learning Experience: Share your view on missionary work as a learning experience, highlighting both challenges and growth.

_____
_____
_____
_____
_____

What are you grateful for today? _____

Respect what others love. You don't have to like everything, but avoid putting down their interests, even as a joke. Criticizing someone's passion creates disconnection. If a companion loves golf, or collecting sea shells, no need to call it stupid. If another missionary is from a place you didn't enjoy, don't rattle off its flaws. If someone you're teaching likes a restaurant, don't say it's gross. Those kinds of comments turn people off immediately. Instead, stay quiet or ask what they love about it. Differing opinions are okay, but expressing disgust for others' loves hurts feelings. Approach their interests with curiosity, not judgment.

DATE: _____

MEMORIES MADE, TOUGH TIMES, & LESSONS LEARNED:

Stressed   Angry   Tired   Sad   Happy   Excited

_____
_____
_____
_____
_____
_____
_____
_____

What are you grateful for today? _____

*"...our ultimate security comes as we yoke ourselves to Heavenly Father and Jesus Christ! Life without God is a life filled with fear. Life with God is a life filled with peace. This is because spiritual blessings come to the faithful. Receiving personal revelation is one of the greatest of those blessings." - Russell M. Nelson*

DATE: _____

MEMORIES MADE, TOUGH TIMES, & LESSONS LEARNED:

Stressed   Angry   Tired   Sad   Happy   Excited

_____
_____
_____
_____
_____
_____
_____
_____

Prompt of the day:

Community Service Impact: Reflect on a community service project and its impact on both the community and your own spiritual and personal growth.

_____
_____
_____
_____
_____

What are you grateful for today? _____

This mission was never about you. You need Him more than ever before. He's there, I promise. He's anxious to bless you and is blessing you more than you know. The tests of faith in the mission field may be there because He may be waiting until you're ready to hear the answers. And waiting until you are ready to ACT on His answers. Because once He reaches down and gives you a heavenly hug, your life will never be the same. Everything you watch or listen to will change. Are you ready for that? Because what He touches changes. Are you willing to pay the price and act on the answer? If you're not sure, He may not be willing to give you everything you're asking if you're not willing to give up everything and follow Him based on His answer. Don't just pray to know, pray to know what to DO. That's what Joseph Smith did in the grove of trees. He will hear and answer your prayers as well.

DATE: _____

MEMORIES MADE, TOUGH TIMES, & LESSONS LEARNED:

Stressed   Angry   Tired   Sad   Happy   Excited

_____
_____
_____
_____
_____
_____
_____
_____

What are you grateful for today? _____

"Sometimes ... we find that even when we do our best to serve the Lord, we still suffer. You may know someone who faces these most challenging of circumstances: consider the missionary who sacrifices to go on a mission, then develops a terrible illness that leaves him or her severely disabled or in chronic pain. ... The key is to remember that faith and obedience are still the answers—even when things go wrong, perhaps especially when things go wrong." - David E. Sorensen

DATE: _____

MEMORIES MADE, TOUGH TIMES, & LESSONS LEARNED:

Stressed   Angry   Tired   Sad   Happy   Excited

_____
_____
_____
_____
_____
_____
_____
_____

Prompt of the day:

Reflecting on Personal Changes: Write about the personal changes you've noticed in yourself since starting your mission. How have you grown or shifted in your beliefs, attitudes, or behaviors?

_____
_____
_____

What are you grateful for today? _____

Cultivate confidence in the Lord and in your identity as a child of God and in your own place on the path of discipleship. When you feel secure in God's love for you and your efforts to follow Him, you will be less prone to judge others unfairly or compare yourself to them. Strive to see yourself and others through the Lord's eyes, and trust that His view is the only one that truly matters. As you focus more on Jesus and less worrying about yourself and your own growth, you will find greater peace and satisfaction in your missionary service, and you will be better equipped to help others do the same.

DATE: _____

MEMORIES MADE, TOUGH TIMES, & LESSONS LEARNED:

Stressed · Angry · Tired · Sad · Happy · Excited

_____
_____
_____
_____
_____
_____
_____
_____

What are you grateful for today? _____

"When you choose to follow Christ, you choose to be changed. . . . The Lord works from the inside out. The world works from the outside in. The world would take people out of the slums. Christ takes the slums out of people, and then they take themselves out of the slums. The world would mold men by changing their environment. Christ changes men, who then change their environment. The world would shape human behavior, but Christ can change human nature." - Ezra Taft Benson

DATE: _____

MEMORIES MADE, TOUGH TIMES, & LESSONS LEARNED:

Stressed · Angry · Tired · Sad · Happy · Excited

_____
_____
_____
_____
_____
_____
_____

Prompt of the day:

Evolving Perspectives: How have your perspectives on faith, service, and the gospel evolved during your mission?

_____
_____
_____
_____

What are you grateful for today? _____

Do focus on building genuine relationships with those you serve. Take the time to get to know them as individuals, understanding their stories, struggles, and aspirations. Support them in their spiritual journeys, regardless of their stage of faith or readiness for conversion. Don't focus solely on conversion. While it is an important goal, remember to truly connect with your friends and keep in contact with them even after your mission. Your sincere care and friendship can make a lasting impact. They are not just your "key indicators" for the week!

DATE: _____

MEMORIES MADE, TOUGH TIMES, & LESSONS LEARNED:

Stressed    Angry    Tired    Sad    Happy    Excited

_____
_____
_____
_____
_____
_____
_____
_____

What are you grateful for today? _____

*"During these perilous times of which the Apostle Paul prophesied, Satan is no longer even trying to hide his attacks on God's plan. Emboldened evil abounds. Therefore, the only way to survive spiritually is to be determined to let God prevail in our lives, to learn to hear His voice, and to use our energy to help gather Israel." - Russell M. Nelson*

DATE: _____

MEMORIES MADE, TOUGH TIMES, & LESSONS LEARNED:

Stressed    Angry    Tired    Sad    Happy    Excited

_____
_____
_____
_____
_____
_____
_____
_____

Prompt of the day:
Embracing New Roles: Reflect on a new role or responsibility you've taken on during your mission. How has it challenged and developed you?

_____
_____
_____
_____

What are you grateful for today? _____

When teaching the gospel, be respectful of all questions. Never mock investigators with remarks like "You don't know that?" or "How can you not understand?" If someone asks, they genuinely want to learn. Respond kindly and listen patiently. People gain knowledge at different rates; your prior understanding doesn't mean others had the same opportunity. Allow them to learn without feeling foolish. As a missionary, foster a respectful environment where all feel comfortable seeking truth. Remember, everyone faces moments of uncertainty, so guide them with Christlike love and understanding.

DATE: _____

MEMORIES MADE, TOUGH TIMES, & LESSONS LEARNED:

Stressed   Angry   Tired   Sad   Happy   Excited

_____
_____
_____
_____
_____
_____
_____

What are you grateful for today? _____

*"My dear brothers and sisters, I testify that the Book of Mormon is truly the word of God. It contains the answers to life's most compelling questions. It teaches the doctrine of Christ. It expands and clarifies many of the 'plain and precious' truths that were lost through centuries of time and numerous translations of the Bible." - Russell M. Nelson*

DATE: _____

MEMORIES MADE, TOUGH TIMES, & LESSONS LEARNED:

Stressed   Angry   Tired   Sad   Happy   Excited

_____
_____
_____
_____
_____
_____
_____

Prompt of the day:

Spiritual Leadership: Reflect on a moment when you felt you were a spiritual leader. What qualities did you embody?

_____
_____
_____
_____
_____
_____

What are you grateful for today? _____

When someone rejects your message or invitation to learn more about the gospel, remember that their decision is not a reflection of your worth or effectiveness as a missionary. Recognize that each person has the God-given gift of .agency, and that their choice to accept or reject the truth is ultimately between them and the Lord. Rather than dwelling on the disappointment of rejection, focus on the seeds of faith that you have planted and trust that they may still take root and grow in the future. Continue to pray for those who have turned you away, and leave the door open for future opportunities to share your testimony and extend the love of the Savior.

DATE: _____

MEMORIES MADE, TOUGH TIMES, & LESSONS LEARNED:

Stressed   Angry   Tired   Sad   Happy   Excited

_____
_____
_____
_____
_____
_____
_____
_____

What are you grateful for today? _____

"My plea to you this morning is to find rest from the intensity, uncertainty, and anguish of this world by overcoming the world through your covenants with God. Let Him know through your prayers and your actions that you are serious about overcoming the world. Ask Him to enlighten your mind and send the help you need." - Russell M. Nelson

DATE: _____

MEMORIES MADE, TOUGH TIMES, & LESSONS LEARNED:

Stressed   Angry   Tired   Sad   Happy   Excited

_____
_____
_____
_____
_____
_____
_____
_____

Prompt of the day:
Impact of Daily Devotionals: Share how daily devotionals or spiritual studies have impacted your missionary work and personal spirituality.

_____
_____
_____
_____

What are you grateful for today? _____

Take action to overcome anxiety. When you feel anxious about teaching or other missionary tasks, remember that taking action can help defeat those feelings. Focus on what you can do right now, even if it's small. Knock on one more door, share a brief testimony, or say a prayer. Small actions create momentum and help you move forward. Don't let worry hinder your work; trust in the Lord and take steps to serve.

DATE: _____

MEMORIES MADE, TOUGH TIMES, & LESSONS LEARNED:

Stressed   Angry   Tired   Sad   Happy   Excited

_____
_____
_____
_____
_____
_____
_____
_____

What are you grateful for today? _____

"Dear brothers and sisters, I grieve for those who leave the Church because they feel membership requires too much of them. They have not yet discovered that making and keeping covenants actually makes life easier! Each person who makes covenants in baptismal fonts and in temples—and keeps them—has increased access to the power of Jesus Christ. Please ponder that stunning truth!" - Russell M. Nelson

DATE: _____

MEMORIES MADE, TOUGH TIMES, & LESSONS LEARNED:

Stressed   Angry   Tired   Sad   Happy   Excited

_____
_____
_____
_____
_____
_____
_____
_____

Prompt of the day:

Cultivating Your Testimony: Reflect on the evolution of your testimony during your mission. How has it been challenged, strengthened, and deepened through your experiences?

_____
_____
_____

What are you grateful for today? _____

When faced with a companion who struggles with obedience, lead by example and let your actions speak louder than words. Consistently strive to follow the mission rules and schedules, and pray for guidance and patience as you navigate this challenge. Remember that your role is not to condemn or lecture your companion, but rather to love and support them in their own personal growth. Seek inspiration through prayer and scripture study on how to best help your companion overcome their struggles, and trust that the Lord will guide you in your efforts to be a positive influence. If needed, talk to your mission president about your concerns.

DATE: _____

MEMORIES MADE, TOUGH TIMES, & LESSONS LEARNED:

Stressed  Angry  Tired  Sad  Happy  Excited

_____
_____
_____
_____
_____
_____
_____
_____

What are you grateful for today? _____

"I pray that you will . . . love everything He did, everywhere He went, everything He said, and everything He is. I would walk on hot lava, I would drink broken glass to find one more word, one more phrase, one more doctrine, any parable that anyone could give me of the life of Christ the living Son of the living God. The doctrine of Christ means everything to me as a result of [my feelings] for the author of the doctrine of Christ." - Jeffrey R. Holland

DATE: _____

MEMORIES MADE, TOUGH TIMES, & LESSONS LEARNED:

Stressed  Angry  Tired  Sad  Happy  Excited

_____
_____
_____
_____
_____
_____
_____

Prompt of the day:
Experiencing Divine Interventions: Write about a moment you felt was a divine intervention or a clear answer to prayers during your mission.

_____
_____
_____
_____
_____

What are you grateful for today? _____

Achieving your goals is less about technical know-how, which is only about 10%, and more about how you interact with others, making up over 90% of success. While liking, caring, and listening to people are important, the true essence lies in your own character. It all begins with who you are at your core. Your personal qualities, virtues, and values set the foundation for effective people skills, which in turn, drive your ability to reach your objectives. Review your values and virtues that you (hopefully) completed in the beginning of this journal. Assess how you're doing. Are you living true to your core four?

DATE: _____

MEMORIES MADE, TOUGH TIMES, & LESSONS LEARNED:

Stressed    Angry    Tired    Sad    Happy    Excited

_____
_____
_____
_____
_____
_____
_____
_____

What are you grateful for today? _____

*"Part of the gathering of Israel, and a very important part, is the charge for us as a people to be worthy and willing to help prepare the world for the Second Coming of the Lord." - Russell M. Nelson*

DATE: _____

MEMORIES MADE, TOUGH TIMES, & LESSONS LEARNED:

Stressed    Angry    Tired    Sad    Happy    Excited

_____
_____
_____
_____
_____
_____
_____
_____

Prompt of the day:
Receiving and Giving Support: Write about a time you received support from someone unexpectedly or when you provided support to someone in need.

_____
_____
_____
_____
_____

What are you grateful for today? _____

Stress. To share or not to share? Is complaining or sharing your stress with others helpful? It depends! Some research suggests when we complain to just "get it off our chests" then it may not be helpful. Like a scab, when we continue to dig and poke at a wound, it tends to make things worse when we complain about stress, causing more stress and worry. However, sharing your stress and complaints with others may be helpful in some situations if the person is helpful in processing the situation, helps you see different perspectives, helps you find the positive and/or helps you think about what you can do about it moving forward. The goal is to move past the complaint to processing what to do next or how to respond.

DATE: _____

MEMORIES MADE, TOUGH TIMES, & LESSONS LEARNED:

Stressed    Angry    Tired    Sad    Happy    Excited

_____
_____
_____
_____
_____
_____
_____
_____
_____

What are you grateful for today? _____

*"You will remember that I have invited the youth of The Church of Jesus Christ of Latter-day Saints to enlist in the Lord's youth battalion to participate in the greatest cause on earth today—the gathering of Israel. I issued this invitation to our youth because they are unusually gifted in reaching out to others and sharing what they believe in a convincing fashion." - Russell M. Nelson*

DATE: _____

MEMORIES MADE, TOUGH TIMES, & LESSONS LEARNED:

Stressed    Angry    Tired    Sad    Happy    Excited

_____
_____
_____
_____
_____
_____
_____
_____
_____

Prompt of the day:

Cultural Insights and Understanding: Reflect on a cultural insight you've gained that has deepened your understanding and empathy for the people you serve.

_____
_____
_____
_____
_____

What are you grateful for today? _____

Do take the time to genuinely get to know the local members, showing interest in their lives, families, and personal stories. Building strong, sincere relationships can enhance trust and cooperation. Let them speak! Don't dominate conversations or make assumptions about their experiences. Listen attentively and show genuine interest in understanding their perspectives and challenges. Members are the best!

DATE: _____

MEMORIES MADE, TOUGH TIMES, & LESSONS LEARNED:   Stressed   Angry   Tired   Sad   Happy   Excited

_____
_____
_____
_____
_____
_____
_____
_____

What are you grateful for today? _____

*"Youth of the Church, the world is in need of your help. There are feet to steady, hands to grasp, minds to encourage, hearts to inspire, and souls to save. The harvest truly is great. Let there be no mistake about it; the missionary opportunity of a lifetime is yours. The blessings of eternity await you. Yours is the privilege to be, not spectators, but participants on the stage of service to others." - Thomas S. Monson*

DATE: _____

MEMORIES MADE, TOUGH TIMES, & LESSONS LEARNED:   Stressed   Angry   Tired   Sad   Happy   Excited

_____
_____
_____
_____
_____
_____
_____
_____

Prompt of the day:

Daily Acts of Faith: Reflect on the small, daily acts of faith that you perform or witness and their cumulative impact.

_____
_____
_____
_____
_____

What are you grateful for today? _____

Embrace the refining process of missionary service: Recognize that the challenges and struggles of missionary life are opportunities for growth and refinement. Embrace the process of becoming more like Christ through your service. When faced with difficulties, seek to learn and develop Christlike attributes such as patience, humility, and perseverance. Trust that God is shaping you into the person He wants you to become. As you embrace the refining process, you'll find joy in your personal growth and in becoming a more effective instrument in the Lord's hands.

DATE: _____

MEMORIES MADE, TOUGH TIMES, & LESSONS LEARNED: 

Stressed   Angry   Tired   Sad   Happy   Excited

_____
_____
_____
_____
_____
_____
_____
_____

What are you grateful for today? _____

"Mend a quarrel. Seek out a forgotten friend. Dismiss suspicion and replace it with trust. Write a letter. Give a soft answer...Manifest your loyalty in word and deed. Keep a promise. Forgo a grudge. Forgive an enemy. Apologize. Try to understand. Examine your demands on others. Think first of someone else. Be kind. Be gentle. Laugh a little more. Express your gratitude...pleasure in the beauty and wonder of the earth. Speak your love and then speak it again." - Howard W. Hunter

DATE: _____

MEMORIES MADE, TOUGH TIMES, & LESSONS LEARNED: 

Stressed   Angry   Tired   Sad   Happy   Excited

_____
_____
_____
_____
_____
_____
_____
_____

Prompt of the day:

The Influence of Local Members: Write about the influence and support of local church members on your mission. How have they contributed to your experience?

_____
_____
_____
_____

What are you grateful for today? _____

Find strength and comfort in your testimony and knowledge that the Savior's Atonement has the power to carry you through the trials and difficulties of missionary work, just as it carries those you teach towards eternal life. When you feel overwhelmed, discouraged, or inadequate, remember that Jesus Christ has already borne the weight of your burdens and that He stands ready to help you overcome every obstacle. Turn to Him in prayer and plead for His grace and enabling power to be with you. Trust that as you rely on His Atonement and strive to do His will, He will magnify your efforts, heal your wounds, and give you the strength to endure and succeed.

DATE: _____

MEMORIES MADE, TOUGH TIMES, & LESSONS LEARNED:

Stressed   Angry   Tired   Sad   Happy   Excited

_____
_____
_____
_____
_____
_____
_____
_____

What are you grateful for today? _____

*"The God of heaven and earth will help us overcome discouragement and whatever obstacles we encounter if we look to Him, follow the promptings of the Holy Ghost and just keep going with faith." - Carl B. Cook*

DATE: _____

MEMORIES MADE, TOUGH TIMES, & LESSONS LEARNED:

Stressed   Angry   Tired   Sad   Happy   Excited

_____
_____
_____
_____
_____
_____
_____
_____

Prompt of the day:
Adjusting to a New Companion: Share your experience and feelings when adjusting to a new companion and how you worked to build a harmonious relationship.

_____
_____
_____
_____

What are you grateful for today? _____

Seek support from loved ones. Your companion, fellow missionaries, and family back home can provide strength during tough times. When stress starts to build, reach out to those who help you feel loved and hopeful. Share your feelings and listen to their advice. Avoid those who bring you down when you're already stressed. Remember, you're not alone in this work. Lean on your support system and face challenges together with faith. United in the gospel, you can overcome any obstacle.

DATE: _____

MEMORIES MADE, TOUGH TIMES, & LESSONS LEARNED:

Stressed    Angry    Tired    Sad    Happy    Excited

_____
_____
_____
_____
_____
_____
_____
_____

What are you grateful for today? _____

"There are few things in life that bring as much joy as the joy that comes from assisting another improve his or her life. That joy is increased when those efforts help someone understand the teachings of the Savior and that person decides to obey them, is converted, and joins His Church." - Richard G. Scott

DATE: _____

MEMORIES MADE, TOUGH TIMES, & LESSONS LEARNED:

Stressed    Angry    Tired    Sad    Happy    Excited

_____
_____
_____
_____
_____
_____
_____
_____

Prompt of the day:
Overcoming Discouragement: Share strategies or experiences that have helped you overcome discouragement in your missionary work.

_____
_____
_____
_____

What are you grateful for today? _____

As you interact with new converts who may be struggling with the transition into the Church, remember to show empathy and understanding. Your own experiences adjusting to mission life can help you relate to their challenges. Offer them support and encouragement, just as you would want during your own challenging times. By extending patience and personal ministry to these individuals, you can help them feel welcome and supported as they navigate this new chapter in their lives. Your kindness and compassion can make a big difference in their lives and help them feel loved and accepted in their new faith community.

DATE: _____

MEMORIES MADE, TOUGH TIMES, & LESSONS LEARNED:

Stressed    Angry    Tired    Sad    Happy    Excited

_____
_____
_____
_____
_____
_____
_____
_____

What are you grateful for today? _____

*"The truth is that it is much more exhausting to seek happiness where you can never find it! However, when you yoke yourself to Jesus Christ and do the spiritual work required to overcome the world, He, and He alone, does have the power to lift you above the pull of this world." - Russell M. Nelson*

DATE: _____

MEMORIES MADE, TOUGH TIMES, & LESSONS LEARNED:

Stressed    Angry    Tired    Sad    Happy    Excited

_____
_____
_____
_____
_____
_____
_____

Prompt of the day:

Teaching Through Example: Describe a situation where you felt you taught more through your actions and example than through words.

_____
_____
_____
_____

What are you grateful for today? _____

Be inclusive and make room for others. Whether at church, on P-day, or zone conference, if someone approaches the group, be sure to smile, greet them, and make room. Create space. It takes guts to approach a group and try to fit in, especially when you're new to an area, so help others feel included by inviting them in and introducing them. Inclusivity means the world to those feeling like they're on the outside. Choose to be remembered for your kindness rather than your greatness. Choose to make others feel more comfortable and accepted. There's always room for one more.

DATE: _____

MEMORIES MADE, TOUGH TIMES, & LESSONS LEARNED:

Stressed   Angry   Tired   Sad   Happy   Excited

_____
_____
_____
_____
_____
_____
_____
_____

What are you grateful for today? _____

"Preach My Gospel was written so that the missionaries would immerse themselves in the scriptures, in the gospel itself, thereby enabling them to give strong gospel lessons oriented to the need of the investigator and the wide variety of circumstances the missionary would find." - Jeffrey R. Holland

DATE: _____

MEMORIES MADE, TOUGH TIMES, & LESSONS LEARNED:

Stressed   Angry   Tired   Sad   Happy   Excited

_____
_____
_____
_____
_____
_____
_____

Prompt of the day:
Building Lasting Faith: Reflect on how you've worked to build lasting faith, both in Jesus Christ and in those you teach.

_____
_____
_____
_____

What are you grateful for today? _____

Myth: Missionaries must already be proficient teachers and speakers. Reality: Many missionaries develop teaching and public speaking skills during their mission, benefiting from training, practice, and real-world experience. A willingness to learn and grow in these areas can lead to personal and professional development.

DATE: _____

MEMORIES MADE, TOUGH TIMES, & LESSONS LEARNED:

Stressed  Angry  Tired  Sad  Happy  Excited

_____
_____
_____
_____
_____
_____
_____

What are you grateful for today? _____

*"Just when all seems to be going right, challenges often come in multiple doses applied simultaneously. When those trials are not consequences of your disobedience, they are evidence that the Lord feels you are prepared to grow more...To get you from where you are to where He wants you to be requires a lot of stretching, and that generally entails discomfort and pain."* - Richard G. Scott

DATE: _____

MEMORIES MADE, TOUGH TIMES, & LESSONS LEARNED:

Stressed  Angry  Tired  Sad  Happy  Excited

_____
_____
_____
_____
_____
_____
_____
_____

Prompt of the day:
Witnessing Change: Write about witnessing a change in someone you've been teaching or interacting with. How did it affect you?

_____
_____
_____
_____

What are you grateful for today? _____

Your physical health significantly impacts your emotional well-being. It's been said that moving your body moves your brain (okay, and spirit!?). Ensuring you eat a balanced diet, get enough restful sleep, and engage in regular physical activity can positively influence mood regulation, energy levels, and overall emotional resilience. Taking care of your body is a showing God you are grateful for this gift, and it lays a foundation for emotional well-being. When your body feels good, it's easier for your mind and spirit to follow suit (and you'll fall asleep less often during teaching moments when it's warm…).

DATE: _____

MEMORIES MADE, TOUGH TIMES, & LESSONS LEARNED:

Stressed   Angry   Tired   Sad   Happy   Excited

_____
_____
_____
_____
_____
_____
_____
_____

What are you grateful for today? _____

"Our Savior and Redeemer, Jesus Christ, will perform some of His mightiest works between now and when He comes again. We will see miraculous indications that God the Father and His Son, Jesus Christ, preside over this Church in majesty and glory. But in coming days, it will not be possible to survive spiritually without the guiding, directing, comforting, and constant influence of the Holy Ghost." - Russell M. Nelson

DATE: _____

MEMORIES MADE, TOUGH TIMES, & LESSONS LEARNED:

Stressed   Angry   Tired   Sad   Happy   Excited

_____
_____
_____
_____
_____
_____
_____

Prompt of the day:
Navigating Differences with Companions: Write about navigating differences with a companion and finding common ground or resolutions.

_____
_____
_____
_____
_____
_____

What are you grateful for today? _____

Remember that the first principle of the gospel is faith in the Lord Jesus Christ specifically. Avoid referring to just "faith" in general. The purpose of faith is to act on God's will, not try to change it. When you teach about faith, consistently include the phrase "in the Lord Jesus Christ." This makes it clear where we should direct our faith and trust. It also reminds us that faith is not just positive thinking or wishful hoping, but a spiritual power grounded in our Savior. Strive to develop this Christ-centered faith yourself.

DATE: _____

MEMORIES MADE, TOUGH TIMES, & LESSONS LEARNED:  Stressed  Angry  Tired  Sad  Happy  Excited

_____
_____
_____
_____
_____
_____
_____
_____

What are you grateful for today? _____

"When a man understands the majesty and power of a righteous, seeking, endowed Latter-day Saint woman, is it any wonder that he feels like standing when she enters the room?" - Russell M. Nelson

DATE: _____

MEMORIES MADE, TOUGH TIMES, & LESSONS LEARNED:  Stressed  Angry  Tired  Sad  Happy  Excited

_____
_____
_____
_____
_____
_____
_____

Prompt of the day:
Reflections on Obedience: Reflect on your understanding and practice of obedience in missionary work and its impact on your mission.

_____
_____
_____
_____

What are you grateful for today? _____

Place your hope in Jesus Christ and His promises that He will never leave you or forsake you. Even in the midst of great challenges, this hope can bring peace and keep you from being overwhelmed. When the burdens of missionary work and ministering to others feel heavy, turn to the Savior and trust in His unfailing love and support. Remember His words: "Come unto me, all ye that labour and are heavy laden, and I will give you rest" (Matthew 11:28). Let His hope fill your heart and give you the strength to press forward, knowing that He is with you every step of the way.

DATE: _____

MEMORIES MADE, TOUGH TIMES, & LESSONS LEARNED:

Stressed    Angry    Tired    Sad    Happy    Excited

_____
_____
_____
_____
_____
_____
_____
_____

What are you grateful for today? _____

"Missionary work is a manifestation of our spiritual identity and heritage. We were foreordained in the premortal existence and born into mortality to fulfill the covenant and promise God made to Abraham. We are here upon the earth at this time to magnify the priesthood and to preach the gospel. That is who we are, and that is why we are here - today and always." - David A. Bednar

DATE: _____

MEMORIES MADE, TOUGH TIMES, & LESSONS LEARNED:

Stressed    Angry    Tired    Sad    Happy    Excited

_____
_____
_____
_____
_____
_____
_____
_____

Prompt of the day:

Finding Joy in the Gospel: Share a moment when you found profound joy in the gospel or in sharing it with others.

_____
_____
_____
_____

What are you grateful for today? _____

Improve self-awareness. Make time to regularly reflect on your thoughts, emotions, and actions. Before speaking your mind, pause and think about the situation and what you are about to do. Seek feedback from others and be open to others' suggestions. Journaling (in this!) can aid in understanding patterns and triggers. Cultivate a mindset of curiosity about yourself and your reactions. Clarify your core values and ensure your actions align with them. Developing self-awareness is an ongoing prayerful journey that involves introspection and a genuine desire for personal understanding.

DATE: _____

MEMORIES MADE, TOUGH TIMES, & LESSONS LEARNED:

Stressed    Angry    Tired    Sad    Happy    Excited

_____
_____
_____
_____
_____
_____
_____
_____

What are you grateful for today? _____

*"Let us do the best we can, and if we make a mistake once, seven times, or seventy times seven in a day, and are honest in our confessions, we shall be forgiven freely. As we expect to obtain mercy, so let us have mercy upon each other." - Brigham Young*

DATE: _____

MEMORIES MADE, TOUGH TIMES, & LESSONS LEARNED:

Stressed    Angry    Tired    Sad    Happy    Excited

_____
_____
_____
_____
_____
_____
_____
_____

Prompt of the day:
Handling Criticism: Share an experience of receiving criticism or negative feedback and how you dealt with it constructively.

_____
_____
_____
_____

What are you grateful for today? _____

Make Jesus Christ the center of EVERYTHING you teach, and always testify of Him. He lives and leads His Church today. As you humbly and earnestly seek His will, you will experience miracles and revelation. Bear witness that the gospel is true and divine as you teach it to others. Remember that through repentance, Christ can work His healing miracle in your life, giving you strength, hope, love, and understanding.

DATE: _____

MEMORIES MADE, TOUGH TIMES, & LESSONS LEARNED:

Stressed   Angry   Tired   Sad   Happy   Excited

_____
_____
_____
_____
_____
_____
_____
_____

What are you grateful for today? _____

"Sweet serenity is found in fervent prayer. Then, we forget ourselves and remember the reaching hands of the Savior, who said, 'Come unto me, all ye that are heavy laden, and I will give you rest.' As our burdens are shared with Him, they do become lighter." - Russell M. Nelson

DATE: _____

MEMORIES MADE, TOUGH TIMES, & LESSONS LEARNED:

Stressed   Angry   Tired   Sad   Happy   Excited

_____
_____
_____
_____
_____
_____
_____
_____

Prompt of the day:
The Role of Silence in Spirituality: Reflect on the role of silence in your spiritual life and how it has impacted your mission experience.

_____
_____
_____
_____
_____

What are you grateful for today? _____

Phone manners matter. While many of us have grown accustomed to casual texting, voice calls require basic courtesies. Answer with a polite "hello" and conclude the conversation with "good-bye." Speak clearly and minimize background noise or distractions so you can actively listen to the other person. It's frustrating when you're speaking and can tell the other party is distracted or not fully engaged. Put forth your complete attention during phone interactions to show respect. These simple practices elevate your professionalism and consideration for others. Exemplifying good phone manners helps create a positive impression and facilitates clear communication in your vital missionary efforts. The greatest gift you can give the person you are talking with is your all-in attention.

DATE: _____

MEMORIES MADE, TOUGH TIMES, & LESSONS LEARNED:

Stressed   Angry   Tired   Sad   Happy   Excited

_____
_____
_____
_____
_____
_____
_____
_____

What are you grateful for today? _____

*"The reward for keeping covenants with God is heavenly power—power that strengthens us to withstand our trials, temptations, and heartaches better. This power eases our way. Those who live the higher laws of Jesus Christ have access to His higher power. Thus, covenant keepers are entitled to a special kind of rest that comes to them through their covenantal relationship with God." - Russell M. Nelson*

DATE: _____

MEMORIES MADE, TOUGH TIMES, & LESSONS LEARNED:

Stressed   Angry   Tired   Sad   Happy   Excited

_____
_____
_____
_____
_____
_____
_____

Prompt of the day:

Spiritual Promptings: Share a time when you followed a spiritual prompting and the outcome of that decision.

_____
_____
_____
_____
_____

What are you grateful for today? _____

Find humor and laughter in missionary life: Embrace moments of lightheartedness and joy during your mission. Look for opportunities to share a clean joke, a funny story, or a humorous observation with your companion and those you teach. Laughter can ease tension, create connections, and make your missionary experience more enjoyable. Remember to be appropriate and sensitive in your humor, but don't be afraid to find reasons to smile and laugh. A cheerful disposition can make your message more inviting and your service more fulfilling.

DATE: _____

MEMORIES MADE, TOUGH TIMES, & LESSONS LEARNED:   Stressed   Angry   Tired   Sad   Happy   Excited

_____
_____
_____
_____
_____
_____
_____
_____

What are you grateful for today? _____

*"Because of the Savior's Atonement, His gospel provides an invitation to keep changing, growing, and becoming more pure. It is a gospel of hope, of healing, and of progress. Thus, the gospel is a message of joy!"* - Russell M. Nelson

DATE: _____

MEMORIES MADE, TOUGH TIMES, & LESSONS LEARNED:   Stressed   Angry   Tired   Sad   Happy   Excited

_____
_____
_____
_____
_____
_____
_____

Prompt of the day:
Personal and Spiritual Reflections at Night: Write about your thoughts and reflections during quiet nights on your mission. How do these moments of solitude affect you?

_____
_____
_____
_____

What are you grateful for today? _____

Live with integrity by keeping your commitments and covenants. Integrity is a foundation of good character and is necessary to enjoy God's presence. Avoid compromising your integrity, as it can wound your eternal self. Remember that covenants are sacred promises, and excusing or covering up sins can lead to losing the Spirit and being left to yourself. Strengthen your integrity to resist the devil's attacks on your weak spots.

DATE: _____

MEMORIES MADE, TOUGH TIMES, & LESSONS LEARNED:

Stressed   Angry   Tired   Sad   Happy   Excited

_____
_____
_____
_____
_____
_____
_____
_____

What are you grateful for today? _____

*"I bless you to be filled with the peace of the Lord Jesus Christ. His peace is beyond all mortal understanding. I bless you with an increased desire and ability to obey the laws of God. I promise that as you do, you will be showered with blessings, including greater courage, increased personal revelation, sweeter harmony in your homes, and joy even amid uncertainty." - Russell M. Nelson*

DATE: _____

MEMORIES MADE, TOUGH TIMES, & LESSONS LEARNED:

Stressed   Angry   Tired   Sad   Happy   Excited

_____
_____
_____
_____
_____
_____
_____
_____

Prompt of the day:
Celebrating Successes: Reflect on a recent success or victory, no matter how small, and how it felt.

_____
_____
_____
_____

What are you grateful for today? _____

Embrace the unexpected and be willing to adapt to changing circumstances. Missionary life is full of surprises, and your ability to go with the flow will make your experience more enjoyable and less stressful. Remember that flexibility also applies to your plans and expectations. Sometimes, things won't go as planned, but being adaptable will allow you to find new opportunities and blessings in unexpected places. Trust in the Lord's timing and plan for you, knowing that He is guiding you and is guiding you to those He loves. He wants us ALL home again. Think celestial and trust Him.

DATE: _____

MEMORIES MADE, TOUGH TIMES, & LESSONS LEARNED:

Stressed   Angry   Tired   Sad   Happy   Excited

_____
_____
_____
_____
_____
_____
_____
_____

What are you grateful for today? _____

*"One of the greatest sermons ever pronounced on missionary work is this simple thought attributed to Saint Francis of Assisi: 'Preach the gospel at all times and if necessary, use words.' Opportunities to do so are all around us. Do not miss them by waiting too long on the road to Damascus." - Dieter F. Uchtdorf*

DATE: _____

MEMORIES MADE, TOUGH TIMES, & LESSONS LEARNED:

Stressed   Angry   Tired   Sad   Happy   Excited

_____
_____
_____
_____
_____
_____
_____
_____

Prompt of the day:

Witnessing the Gospel's Impact: Share a story where you witnessed the gospel making a tangible impact on an individual or community.

_____
_____
_____
_____

What are you grateful for today? _____

Embrace new experiences for growth as a missionary. This is a unique time to try different approaches to teaching the gospel (while following mission rules and staying safe), discover your talents, and explore new ways to serve. Accept being a beginner and learn from each experience. You have ample opportunities to practice new skills. Embrace mistakes as crucial for growth. Don't feel pressured to have everything figured out. Pray for the Spirit and find what works best for you and those you teach through experience, so be brave and try new things. Set a goal to attempt something new during your mission—you might discover a more effective way to share the gospel message!

DATE: _____

MEMORIES MADE, TOUGH TIMES, & LESSONS LEARNED:

Stressed   Angry   Tired   Sad   Happy   Excited

_____
_____
_____
_____
_____
_____
_____
_____

What are you grateful for today? _____

"The long-standing objective of the Church is to assist all members to increase their faith in our Lord Jesus Christ and in His Atonement, to assist them in making and keeping their covenants with God, and to strengthen and seal their families.... Why do we need such resilient faith? Because difficult days are ahead. Rarely in the future will it be easy or popular to be a faithful Latter-day Saint." - Russell M. Nelson

DATE: _____

MEMORIES MADE, TOUGH TIMES, & LESSONS LEARNED:

Stressed   Angry   Tired   Sad   Happy   Excited

_____
_____
_____
_____
_____
_____
_____
_____

Prompt of the day:

The Role of Dreams and Goals: Share how your dreams and goals have evolved since starting your mission and how they align with your experiences.

_____
_____
_____
_____

What are you grateful for today? _____

Embrace the language learning process. If you're learning a new language, immerse yourself in it fully. Embrace the challenges of language learning as opportunities to grow. Practice regularly, engage with native speakers as much as possible, and be patient with yourself. Understand that fluency takes time, and every effort you make, no matter how small, contributes to your progress. Celebrate your progress, no matter how small, and remember that language learning is a journey, not a destination.

DATE: _____

MEMORIES MADE, TOUGH TIMES, & LESSONS LEARNED:

Stressed  Angry  Tired  Sad  Happy  Excited

_____
_____
_____
_____
_____
_____
_____
_____

What are you grateful for today? _____

*"True doctrine, understood, changes attitudes and behavior. The study of the doctrines of the gospel will improve behavior quicker than a study of behavior will improve behavior....That is why we stress so forcefully the study of the doctrines of the gospel"* - Boyd K. Packer

DATE: _____

MEMORIES MADE, TOUGH TIMES, & LESSONS LEARNED:

Stressed  Angry  Tired  Sad  Happy  Excited

_____
_____
_____
_____
_____
_____
_____
_____

Prompt of the day:
Cherished Companionship Moments: Reflect on a cherished moment with a companion that strengthened your bond and enhanced your mission experience.

_____
_____
_____
_____

What are you grateful for today? _____

Be patient with yourself and the process of overcoming discouragement. Recognize that growth and change often happen gradually, and focus on making small improvements each day. Trust in the Lord's timing and have faith that as you continue to work and pray, you will see progress and find the happiness you seek. As a missionary, it's easy to become impatient with yourself or the work when you don't see immediate results. However, remember that the Lord's work often moves forward at a different pace than we expect. Be patient with yourself and the process, celebrating each small victory and trusting that the Lord is guiding your path. As you persist in faith, you will see His hand in your life and work.

DATE: _____

MEMORIES MADE, TOUGH TIMES, & LESSONS LEARNED:

Stressed   Angry   Tired   Sad   Happy   Excited

_____
_____
_____
_____
_____
_____
_____
_____
_____

What are you grateful for today? _____

*"Our main task is to declare the gospel and do it effectively. We are not obligated to answer every objection. Every man eventually is backed up to the wall of faith, and there he must make his stand." - Ezra Taft Benson*

DATE: _____

MEMORIES MADE, TOUGH TIMES, & LESSONS LEARNED:

Stressed   Angry   Tired   Sad   Happy   Excited

_____
_____
_____
_____
_____
_____
_____
_____

Prompt of the day:

Learning from Local Religious Practices: Share insights gained from observing or participating in local religious practices outside your own faith tradition.

_____
_____
_____
_____

What are you grateful for today? _____

Embrace the adventure of missionary service: Approach your mission with a spirit of adventure and enthusiasm. Embrace the opportunity to explore new places, meet new people, and have unique experiences. Find joy in the diversity of God's children and in the beauty of His creations. As you embrace the adventure of missionary service, you'll develop a greater appreciation for the world around you and for the privilege of being a gospel messenger.

DATE: _____

MEMORIES MADE, TOUGH TIMES, & LESSONS LEARNED:

Stressed    Angry    Tired    Sad    Happy    Excited

_____
_____
_____
_____
_____
_____
_____
_____

What are you grateful for today? _____

"My dear brothers and sisters, so many wonderful things are ahead. In coming days, we will see the greatest manifestations of the Savior's power that the world has ever seen. Between now and the time He returns 'with power and great glory,' He will bestow countless privileges, blessings, and miracles upon the faithful." - Russell M. Nelson

DATE: _____

MEMORIES MADE, TOUGH TIMES, & LESSONS LEARNED:

Stressed    Angry    Tired    Sad    Happy    Excited

_____
_____
_____
_____
_____
_____
_____
_____

Prompt of the day:

Adapting to Unexpected Changes: Write about a time when you had to adapt to an unexpected change or challenge during your mission. How did you handle it?

_____
_____
_____
_____
_____

What are you grateful for today? _____

Respond to rejection with love and forgiveness. Choose to develop Christlike charity toward those who may reject you or your message. Maintaining a positive attitude and avoiding negative feelings will help your spiritual progress and your ability to effectively serve others. Strive to develop Christlike love and compassion for those who reject you. Pray for them, seek to understand their perspective, and forgive them for any offense. Responding with charity will bring greater peace and happiness into your life and set a powerful example of the Savior's love and teachings.

DATE: _____

MEMORIES MADE, TOUGH TIMES, & LESSONS LEARNED:

Stressed  Angry  Tired  Sad  Happy  Excited

_____
_____
_____
_____
_____
_____
_____
_____

What are you grateful for today? _____

*"Remember that this work is not yours and mine alone. It is the Lord's work, and when we are on the Lord's errand, we are entitled to the Lord's help. Remember that the Lord will shape the back to bear the burden placed upon it." - Thomas S. Monson*

DATE: _____

MEMORIES MADE, TOUGH TIMES, & LESSONS LEARNED:

Stressed  Angry  Tired  Sad  Happy  Excited

_____
_____
_____
_____
_____
_____
_____
_____

Prompt of the day:
Learning from the People You Serve: Write about something significant you've learned from the people you're serving.

_____
_____
_____
_____

What are you grateful for today? _____

Make a conscious effort to find joy and beauty in the unique aspects of your mission area, even as you face the challenges and rigors of missionary work. Take time on p-days to explore your area, cultural landmarks, and recreational opportunities that your area has to offer, within mission rules. Make time for the fun stuff and change it up instead of basketball every week at the church. Seek to build relationships with local members and investigators, and participate in ward and community events that allow you to immerse yourself in the richness of the local culture. As you do so, you will develop a deeper appreciation for the people and place you have been called to serve, and you will find renewed energy, enthusiasm, and purpose in your missionary labors.

DATE: _____

MEMORIES MADE, TOUGH TIMES, & LESSONS LEARNED:

Stressed    Angry    Tired    Sad    Happy    Excited

_____
_____
_____
_____
_____
_____
_____
_____
_____

What are you grateful for today? _____

*"There is not a single condition of life that is entirely unnecessary; there is not one hour's experience but what is beneficial to all those who make it their study, and aim to improve upon the experience they gain." - Brigham Young*

DATE: _____

MEMORIES MADE, TOUGH TIMES, & LESSONS LEARNED:

Stressed    Angry    Tired    Sad    Happy    Excited

_____
_____
_____
_____
_____
_____
_____
_____

Prompt of the day:
The Power of Forgiveness: Reflect on an experience of forgiveness, either offering or receiving it, during your mission and its impact.

_____
_____
_____
_____
_____

What are you grateful for today? _____

What is the most important question in this life? President Ezra Taft Benson said, "A man can ask no more important question in his life than that which Paul asked: 'Lord, what wilt thou have me to do?' A man can take no greater action than to pursue a course that will bring to him the answer to that question and then to carry out that answer. What would the Lord Jesus Christ have us do?" As you face challenges in the mission field or have struggles to find answers to your own prayers and seeking for guidance, sometimes you will feel and other times you will find answers you are seeking. Be patient. Be still. Listen and feel. Then go and do!

DATE: _____

MEMORIES MADE, TOUGH TIMES, & LESSONS LEARNED:

Stressed   Angry   Tired   Sad   Happy   Excited

_____
_____
_____
_____
_____
_____
_____
_____

What are you grateful for today? _____

*"Missionaries try with every capacity-prayer, fasting, and testifying-to help individuals embrace the truth. A mission teaches one to be led by the Spirit, to understand our purpose for being on earth and how to accomplish it." - Richard G. Scott*

DATE: _____

MEMORIES MADE, TOUGH TIMES, & LESSONS LEARNED:

Stressed   Angry   Tired   Sad   Happy   Excited

_____
_____
_____
_____
_____
_____
_____
_____

Prompt of the day:
Mentoring Others: If you've had the chance to mentor or guide other missionaries, reflect on that experience and what it taught you.

_____
_____
_____
_____
_____
_____

What are you grateful for today? _____

Embrace the principle of obedience with exactness as a missionary: Strive to be obedient to mission rules, gospel principles, and the promptings of the Spirit with exactness. Recognize that obedience is an expression of your love for God and your commitment to His work. Embrace the blessings and protection that come from living a life of exactness. As you find joy in obedience, you'll experience greater spiritual power, personal growth, and effectiveness in your missionary service. Your example of exactness will also inspire others to live with greater faith and dedication.

DATE: _____

MEMORIES MADE, TOUGH TIMES, & LESSONS LEARNED:

Stressed    Angry    Tired    Sad    Happy    Excited

_____
_____
_____
_____
_____
_____
_____
_____

What are you grateful for today? _____

*"Do not be discouraged on account of the greatness of the work; only be humble and faithful. . . . He who scattered Israel has promised to gather them; therefore inasmuch as you are to be instrumental in this great work, He will endow you with power, wisdom, might, and intelligence, and every qualification necessary." - Joseph Smith*

DATE: _____

MEMORIES MADE, TOUGH TIMES, & LESSONS LEARNED:

Stressed    Angry    Tired    Sad    Happy    Excited

_____
_____
_____
_____
_____
_____
_____

Prompt of the day:

Gratitude for Divine Guidance: Share moments of gratitude for divine guidance and how it has directed your path during your mission.

_____
_____
_____
_____
_____

What are you grateful for today? _____

When you invite people to attend Church meetings, talk with them ahead of time about what to expect. Emphasize that the focus of sacrament meeting is on Jesus Christ and explain that they can feel the same Spirit in Church meetings as they experience when being taught by you. Explain the significance of the sacrament ordinance and its connection to the Atonement of Jesus Christ and renewing of baptismal covenants. Help investigators understand the prayers, hymns, and talks associated with the sacrament, so they can have a meaningful, Christ-centered experience when attending church. A spiritual sacrament meeting can be a powerful tool in helping investigators progress towards baptism and conversion.

DATE: _____

MEMORIES MADE, TOUGH TIMES, & LESSONS LEARNED:  Stressed  Angry  Tired  Sad  Happy  Excited

_____
_____
_____
_____
_____
_____
_____
_____

What are you grateful for today? _____

"Everything good in life – every potential blessing of eternal significance – begins with faith. Allowing God to prevail in our lives begins with faith that He is willing to guide us. True repentance begins with faith that Jesus Christ has the power to cleanse, heal, and strengthen us." - Russell M. Nelson

DATE: _____

MEMORIES MADE, TOUGH TIMES, & LESSONS LEARNED:  Stressed  Angry  Tired  Sad  Happy  Excited

_____
_____
_____
_____
_____
_____
_____
_____

Prompt of the day:
Self-Care Practices: Share the self-care practices you've found essential during your mission and why they're important.

_____
_____
_____
_____
_____

What are you grateful for today? _____

Do celebrate the successes and achievements of local members, your companionship, or that of other missionaries, whether personal, professional, or spiritual. Recognition can be very encouraging. Don't compare others' successes to your own or belittle your own achievements. Everyone's journey is unique, and every success, no matter how small, is worth celebrating. Ccelllllllebrate good times, come on!

DATE: _____

MEMORIES MADE, TOUGH TIMES, & LESSONS LEARNED:

Stressed   Angry   Tired   Sad   Happy   Excited

_____
_____
_____
_____
_____
_____
_____
_____

What are you grateful for today? _____

"*The commandments from God we obey and the inspired counsel from Church leaders we follow principally focus upon obtaining the companionship of the Spirit. Fundamentally, all gospel teachings and activities are centered on coming unto Christ by receiving the Holy Ghost in our lives*" - David A. Bednar

DATE: _____

MEMORIES MADE, TOUGH TIMES, & LESSONS LEARNED:

Stressed   Angry   Tired   Sad   Happy   Excited

_____
_____
_____
_____
_____
_____
_____

Prompt of the day:

Learning from a Special Family: Write about a special family you have met on your mission and describe what makes them so special?

_____
_____
_____
_____

What are you grateful for today? _____

Help investigators understand that the two most fundamental things they must do prior to baptism are to have faith in the Lord Jesus Christ and repent of their sins. These are the first principles of the gospel, followed by baptism and receiving the gift of the Holy Ghost. While commitments like reading the Book of Mormon, praying, and attending church are important, the primary focus should be on helping investigators develop faith in Christ and repent. Teach them that baptism is an outward expression of their inward commitment to follow the Savior and rely on His atoning sacrifice.

DATE: _____

MEMORIES MADE, TOUGH TIMES, & LESSONS LEARNED:

Stressed   Angry   Tired   Sad   Happy   Excited

_____
_____
_____
_____
_____
_____
_____
_____

What are you grateful for today? _____

"With the power of the holy apostleship vested in me, I bless you in your quest to overcome this world. I bless you to increase your faith in Jesus Christ and learn better how to draw upon His power. I bless you to be able to discern truth from error. I bless you to care more about the things of God than the things of this world. I bless you to see the needs of those around you and strengthen those you love." - Russell M. Nelson

DATE: _____

MEMORIES MADE, TOUGH TIMES, & LESSONS LEARNED:

Stressed   Angry   Tired   Sad   Happy   Excited

_____
_____
_____
_____
_____
_____
_____
_____

Prompt of the day:

Spiritual Resolutions: Write about any spiritual resolutions you've made during your mission and your progress on them.

_____
_____
_____
_____

What are you grateful for today? _____

Understand that obedience is a key principle of missionary work. Follow the rules and guidelines set forth by the Church and your mission president—even if they seem strange or are different from your friends in other missions. Obedience demonstrates your love and commitment to the Lord and His work. Trust that by being obedient, you will be blessed with greater strength, guidance, and protection throughout your mission. Elder Renlund stated, "Obedience is our choice. The Savior made this clear. As stated in the Joseph Smith Translation of Luke 14:28, Jesus directed, 'Wherefore, settle this in your hearts, that ye will do the things which I shall teach, and command you.' As we do so, our spiritual stability will be greatly enhanced."

DATE: _____

MEMORIES MADE, TOUGH TIMES, & LESSONS LEARNED:

Stressed   Angry   Tired   Sad   Happy   Excited

_____
_____
_____
_____
_____
_____
_____
_____
_____

What are you grateful for today? _____

"When you are faced with temptation—even if the temptation comes when you are exhausted or feeling alone or misunderstood—imagine the courage you can muster as you choose to let God prevail in your life and as you plead with Him to strengthen you." - Russell M. Nelson

DATE: _____

MEMORIES MADE, TOUGH TIMES, & LESSONS LEARNED:

Stressed   Angry   Tired   Sad   Happy   Excited

_____
_____
_____
_____
_____
_____
_____
_____
_____

Prompt of the day:
The Comfort of Familiar Rituals: Reflect on the comfort and stability that familiar rituals bring to your missionary life.

_____
_____
_____
_____
_____

What are you grateful for today? _____

Develop Christlike love for those you serve as a missionary: Strive to develop a deep, Christlike love for the people you serve. See them as God sees them, recognizing their divine potential and infinite worth. Seek to understand their struggles, their hopes, and their dreams. Serve them with compassion, patience, and kindness, even when it is difficult. As you develop this pure love of Christ, you'll find greater joy and fulfillment in your missionary work. Your love will touch hearts and invite others to come unto the Savior.

DATE: _____

MEMORIES MADE, TOUGH TIMES, & LESSONS LEARNED:  Stressed  Angry  Tired  Sad  Happy  Excited

_____
_____
_____
_____
_____
_____
_____
_____

What are you grateful for today? _____

*"God never closes one door before us but he opens another beside us, and many of us in looking back can see now a door he closed that we thought then was a denial, and discover another that he opened, which we know now was the real answer." - Merl B. Grover*

DATE: _____

MEMORIES MADE, TOUGH TIMES, & LESSONS LEARNED:  Stressed  Angry  Tired  Sad  Happy  Excited

_____
_____
_____
_____
_____
_____
_____

Prompt of the day:
Adapting to Setbacks: Reflect on how you adapt to and grow from setbacks in your mission work.

_____
_____
_____
_____

What are you grateful for today? _____

It's important to recognize that stress is a normal and expected part of missionary service. Throughout your mission, you'll likely experience different levels of stress, from the excitement and nervousness of the initial weeks to moments when challenges seem overwhelming. Learning to manage stress effectively is a crucial skill that will serve you well not just on your mission, but throughout your life. It's about finding healthy ways to cope with stress, maintaining perspective, and recognizing that stress is a natural response to new and challenging situations. By embracing stress as a normal part of your missionary experience, you can learn to navigate it more effectively and use it as an opportunity for growth.

DATE: _____

MEMORIES MADE, TOUGH TIMES, & LESSONS LEARNED:

Stressed   Angry   Tired   Sad   Happy   Excited

_____
_____
_____
_____
_____
_____
_____
_____

What are you grateful for today? _____

*"Understand that it's not your job to convert people. That is the role of the Holy Ghost. Your role is to share what is in your heart and live consistent with your beliefs." - Dieter F. Uchtdorf*

DATE: _____

MEMORIES MADE, TOUGH TIMES, & LESSONS LEARNED:

Stressed   Angry   Tired   Sad   Happy   Excited

_____
_____
_____
_____
_____
_____
_____
_____

Prompt of the day:
Personal Reflections on Leadership: Share your personal reflections on leadership based on your experiences and observations during your mission.

_____
_____
_____
_____
_____

What are you grateful for today? _____

As a missionary, finding a sense of belonging within your missionary cohort can greatly contribute to your overall well-being and success. Cultivate meaningful relationships with your companions, district members, and other missionaries by showing acceptance, support, and genuine interest in their lives. Seek out commonalities, such as shared goals, interests, and experiences, to foster a sense of unity and camaraderie. Recognize that you matter to your fellow missionaries and that your contributions are valued. By finding your missionary tribe and actively participating in this supportive community, you'll experience a greater sense of purpose, fulfillment, and resilience throughout your service.

DATE: _____

MEMORIES MADE, TOUGH TIMES, & LESSONS LEARNED:

Stressed   Angry   Tired   Sad   Happy   Excited

_____
_____
_____
_____
_____
_____
_____
_____

What are you grateful for today? _____

*"The Savior's compassion in the face of our imperfections draws us toward Him and motivates us in our repeated struggles to repent and emulate Him." – Dale G. Renlund*

DATE: _____

MEMORIES MADE, TOUGH TIMES, & LESSONS LEARNED:

Stressed   Angry   Tired   Sad   Happy   Excited

_____
_____
_____
_____
_____
_____
_____
_____

Prompt of the day:
Coping with Change: Write about how you cope with constant changes, such as new areas, companions, or challenges.

_____
_____
_____
_____
_____

What are you grateful for today? _____

Testify that Jesus Christ lives and that the triumph of the gospel is centered on His Resurrection. The good news of the gospel is change is possible! He is the Savior of the world, the Shepherd of our souls, and through His Atonement, all can be lifted up unto eternal life. Bear witness that because He lives, we too will live again. Share your conviction that He overcame death and hell, and through His sacrifice, we can be cleansed from our sins and return to the presence of our Heavenly Father. The Resurrection of Christ is the ultimate proof of His divinity and the reality of His atoning sacrifice.

DATE: _____

MEMORIES MADE, TOUGH TIMES, & LESSONS LEARNED:

Stressed   Angry   Tired   Sad   Happy   Excited

_____
_____
_____
_____
_____
_____
_____
_____

What are you grateful for today? _____

"Each of God's children deserves the opportunity to hear and accept the healing, redeeming message of Jesus Christ. No other message is more vital to our happiness—now and forever. No other message is more filled with hope. No other message can eliminate contention in our society." - Russell M. Nelson

DATE: _____

MEMORIES MADE, TOUGH TIMES, & LESSONS LEARNED:

Stressed   Angry   Tired   Sad   Happy   Excited

_____
_____
_____
_____
_____
_____
_____

Prompt of the day:
The Impact of Kindness: Write about a small act of kindness you received or witnessed during your mission and its impact.

_____
_____
_____
_____
_____

What are you grateful for today? _____

When faced with the stresses of missionary life, it can be comforting to turn to the Savior Jesus Christ and His Atonement for strength and guidance. Trust in His ability to heal and uplift you, knowing that He understands your struggles and is always there to support you. When missionary work feels burdensome, take time to pray, study the scriptures, and seek the guidance of the Holy Ghost. Then be still and notice the nudges and follow the feelings. Through His grace, you can find peace and strength to overcome any challenge. Remember, you are not alone in your mission. The Savior is with you every step of the way, ready to support and guide you through your trials and triumphs.

DATE: _____

MEMORIES MADE, TOUGH TIMES, & LESSONS LEARNED:

Stressed   Angry   Tired   Sad   Happy   Excited

_____
_____
_____
_____
_____
_____
_____
_____

What are you grateful for today? _____

*"The decision to serve a mission will shape the spiritual destiny of the missionary, his or her spouse, and their posterity for generations to come. A desire to serve is a natural outcome of one's conversion, worthiness, and preparation." - Russell M. Nelson*

DATE: _____

MEMORIES MADE, TOUGH TIMES, & LESSONS LEARNED:

Stressed   Angry   Tired   Sad   Happy   Excited

_____
_____
_____
_____
_____
_____
_____

Prompt of the day:

Maintaining Personal Identity: Reflect on how you maintain your personal identity and interests while fully engaging in your mission.

_____
_____
_____
_____

What are you grateful for today? _____

Focus on meaningful tasks. As a missionary, you may face many distractions. Focus on the most important tasks, like studying the scriptures, sharing the gospel, and serving others. Prioritize your time and attention on what matters most in your missionary work. Take breaks when needed, practice meditation or prayer, and avoid multitasking. By being deliberate about where you direct your attention, you can improve your focus and be more productive in your service to the Lord.

DATE: _____

MEMORIES MADE, TOUGH TIMES, & LESSONS LEARNED:

Stressed   Angry   Tired   Sad   Happy   Excited

_____
_____
_____
_____
_____
_____
_____
_____

What are you grateful for today? _____

"When you reach up for the Lord's power in your life with the same intensity that a drowning person has when grasping and gasping for air, power from Jesus Christ will be yours. When the Savior knows you truly want to reach up to Him—when He can feel that the greatest desire of your heart is to draw His power into your life—you will be led by the Holy Ghost to know exactly what you should do." - Russell M. Nelson

DATE: _____

MEMORIES MADE, TOUGH TIMES, & LESSONS LEARNED:

Stressed   Angry   Tired   Sad   Happy   Excited

_____
_____
_____
_____
_____
_____
_____
_____

Prompt of the day:

Embracing Individuality in Teaching: Reflect on how you embrace and incorporate your individuality into your teaching methods.

_____
_____
_____
_____

What are you grateful for today? _____

Study the scriptures, especially the Book of Mormon, to become familiar with passages that teach and testify of Christ's redeeming mission. The Book of Mormon is an unparalleled testament of Jesus Christ and His messianic message, with prophets like Nephi, Jacob, King Benjamin, and Lehi powerfully declaring the importance of the Atonement of Jesus Christ. As you study and teach from the Book of Mormon, you will change lives, including your own, by focusing on the Savior's atoning sacrifice and its central role in God's plan of salvation. We included book chapters on the Atonement of Jesus Christ in the beginning pages of the Book of Mormon. Study those and others that relate to Jesus.

DATE: _____

MEMORIES MADE, TOUGH TIMES, & LESSONS LEARNED:

Stressed    Angry    Tired    Sad    Happy    Excited

_____
_____
_____
_____
_____
_____
_____
_____

What are you grateful for today? _____

"Missionary work is work....You will not be measured by the number of baptisms you have. You will be measured by the amount of work you do. . . . You may go to many doorsteps without having the exultation, the satisfaction of having someone listen to you, but you will have been a success judged by the amount of work that you do." - Boyd K. Packer

DATE: _____

MEMORIES MADE, TOUGH TIMES, & LESSONS LEARNED:

Stressed    Angry    Tired    Sad    Happy    Excited

_____
_____
_____
_____
_____
_____
_____
_____

Prompt of the day:

Influence of Nature on Spirituality: Describe how the natural environment of your mission area has influenced your spirituality or provided solace.

_____
_____
_____
_____

What are you grateful for today? _____

Watch your words! Saying "no offense" or "not to be rude" doesn't guarantee your words won't hurt. If you're thinking about using these phrases, maybe it's best not to say anything. Just because you hope someone won't be offended doesn't mean they won't be. If you need to say it, share with love in the right place and right time. Think twice before using those tricky phrases, and make sure what you're saying is important and can be shared with kindness!

DATE: _____

MEMORIES MADE, TOUGH TIMES, & LESSONS LEARNED:

| Stressed | Angry | Tired | Sad | Happy | Excited |
|----------|-------|-------|-----|-------|---------|

_____
_____
_____
_____
_____
_____
_____
_____

What are you grateful for today? _____

*"Please remember that 'the real success of a mission is not measured on a chart - it is etched in your heart and the hearts of those whose lives are eternally changed because of you." - Dennis B. Neuenschwander*

DATE: _____

MEMORIES MADE, TOUGH TIMES, & LESSONS LEARNED:

| Stressed | Angry | Tired | Sad | Happy | Excited |
|----------|-------|-------|-----|-------|---------|

_____
_____
_____
_____
_____
_____
_____

Prompt of the day:
The Journey of Faith: Write about your journey of faith during your mission, including moments of doubt, reaffirmation, and growth.

_____
_____
_____
_____
_____

What are you grateful for today? _____

Serve with a spirit of love and compassion as a missionary: Approach your missionary service with a heart filled with love and compassion. Remember that every person you meet is a beloved child of God, deserving of kindness and respect. Seek to understand their challenges, hopes, and dreams. Serve them with sincerity and empathy, striving to meet their spiritual and temporal needs. As you serve with Christlike love, you'll experience the joy that comes from blessing the lives of others and bringing them closer to the Savior.

DATE: _____

MEMORIES MADE, TOUGH TIMES, & LESSONS LEARNED:  Stressed  Angry  Tired  Sad  Happy  Excited

_____
_____
_____
_____
_____
_____
_____
_____

What are you grateful for today? _____

*"To be a successful missionary one must have the Spirit of the Lord. We are also taught that the Spirit will not dwell in unclean tabernacles. Therefore, one of the first things a missionary must do to gain spirituality is to make sure his own personal life is in order." - Ezra Taft Benson*

DATE: _____

MEMORIES MADE, TOUGH TIMES, & LESSONS LEARNED:  Stressed  Angry  Tired  Sad  Happy  Excited

_____
_____
_____
_____
_____
_____
_____
_____

Prompt of the day:
Impactful Scriptures: Share scriptures that have become particularly impactful to you during your mission and why.

_____
_____
_____
_____

What are you grateful for today? _____

Take action against anxiety. When you worry excessively about the future, it hinders your ability to serve in the present. Combat anxiety by taking action. Set a small goal, like sharing a brief testimony or studying a chapter in Preach My Gospel. Small victories create momentum and help you move forward. Don't let fear paralyze you; trust in the Lord and take steps to serve. By acting in faith, you'll overcome anxiety and find greater purpose in your mission.

DATE: _____

MEMORIES MADE, TOUGH TIMES, & LESSONS LEARNED:  Stressed  Angry  Tired  Sad  Happy  Excited

_____
_____
_____
_____
_____
_____
_____
_____

What are you grateful for today? _____

*"Perhaps it is time that we humble ourselves and overcome the obstacles to faith, and then become converted as Peter did. Why go through life with two candlepower when more than four hundred watts are available? The tasks are so great! How can we possibly take the gospel to all the world and redeem the dead at the same time? I don't know, but the power and energy to do so must and will come by faith in the Lord Jesus Christ." - John K. Carmack*

DATE: _____

MEMORIES MADE, TOUGH TIMES, & LESSONS LEARNED:  Stressed  Angry  Tired  Sad  Happy  Excited

_____
_____
_____
_____
_____
_____
_____
_____

Prompt of the day:
The Value of Hard Work: Reflect on the value of hard work in missionary efforts and personal development.

_____
_____
_____
_____

What are you grateful for today? _____

In his book, The Power of Habit, Charles Duhigg refers to a "keystone habit" as a fundamental habit that, once established, can trigger the development of multiple positive behaviors and create widespread changes in a person's life. Keystone habits have a ripple effect, leading to the formation of additional good habits and positive changes that extend beyond the initial habit itself. For example, regular exercise is often cited as a keystone habit because it can lead to better eating habits, improved discipline in other areas, increased energy levels, and overall better mental health. What is your "keystone habit"?

DATE: _____

MEMORIES MADE, TOUGH TIMES, & LESSONS LEARNED:

Stressed   Angry   Tired   Sad   Happy   Excited

_____
_____
_____
_____
_____
_____
_____
_____

What are you grateful for today? _____

*"The future is always uncertain. Weather changes. Economic cycles are unpredictable. Disasters, accidents, and illness can change life quickly. These actions are largely beyond our control. But there are some things we can control, including how we spend our time each day." - Russell M. Nelson*

DATE: _____

MEMORIES MADE, TOUGH TIMES, & LESSONS LEARNED:

Stressed   Angry   Tired   Sad   Happy   Excited

_____
_____
_____
_____
_____
_____
_____

Prompt of the day:
Deepening Empathy: Write about an experience that deepened your empathy for others.

_____
_____
_____
_____
_____

What are you grateful for today? _____

Exercise sensitivity when discussing financial matters. Avoid prying into companions', members', or investigators' specific financial details like parents' incomes, home sizes, or vehicles. Similarly, don't brag about your own possessions or gifts received. While conversations about money aren't inherently inappropriate, digging into others' personal finances or making assumptions based on material wealth is unwise. Remember, a person's worth extends far beyond their monetary circumstances. As missionaries, your focus should remain on ministering to souls and helping others draw nearer to Christ - judging financial standings undermines that sacred purpose.

DATE: _____

MEMORIES MADE, TOUGH TIMES, & LESSONS LEARNED:

Stressed　Angry　Tired　Sad　Happy　Excited

_____
_____
_____
_____
_____
_____
_____
_____
_____

What are you grateful for today? _____

*"When you ... see our Father you will see a being with whom you have long been acquainted, and he will receive you into his arms, and you will be ready to fall into his embrace and kiss him." - Brigham Young*

DATE: _____

MEMORIES MADE, TOUGH TIMES, & LESSONS LEARNED:

Stressed　Angry　Tired　Sad　Happy　Excited

_____
_____
_____
_____
_____
_____
_____
_____

Prompt of the day:
Insights from Personal Study: Share insights or revelations you've gained from personal study and how they've influenced your mission.

_____
_____
_____
_____
_____

What are you grateful for today? _____

Avoid discouragement by remembering that it can weaken your faith, lower your expectations, decrease your effectiveness, and hinder your ability to follow the Spirit. When faced with trials or lack of apparent success, consciously choose to maintain a positive attitude and turn to the Lord for strength. Pray for the blessings and miracles you need, always submitting to God's will. Trust that as you work to strengthen your faith, your desire and capacity to serve effectively will increase, and you will recognize the Lord's hand guiding your daily efforts.

DATE: _____

MEMORIES MADE, TOUGH TIMES, & LESSONS LEARNED:

Stressed   Angry   Tired   Sad   Happy   Excited

_____
_____
_____
_____
_____
_____
_____

What are you grateful for today? _____

*"When we ponder His voluntary atonement, any sense of sacrifice on our part becomes completely overshadowed by a profound sense of gratitude for the privilege of serving Him." - Russell M. Nelson*

DATE: _____

MEMORIES MADE, TOUGH TIMES, & LESSONS LEARNED:

Stressed   Angry   Tired   Sad   Happy   Excited

_____
_____
_____
_____
_____
_____
_____

Prompt of the day:

Cultural Learning: Reflect on a cultural lesson you learned that surprised you or changed your perspective.

_____
_____
_____
_____

What are you grateful for today? _____

Do be consistent and reliable in your commitments and schedules with local members. Consistency builds trust and reliability. If plans change, be sure to let your leaders know, so that there are no miscommunications. Don't make promises you can't keep or overcommit yourself. It's better to be honest about your limitations and availability than to disappoint others by not following through.

DATE: _____

MEMORIES MADE, TOUGH TIMES, & LESSONS LEARNED:

Stressed   Angry   Tired   Sad   Happy   Excited

_____
_____
_____
_____
_____
_____
_____
_____

What are you grateful for today? _____

"Sometimes during our own challenges, we might feel like Christ is too late and our hope and faith might even feel challenged. My witness and testimony is that as we move forward with faith in Jesus Christ, the fourth day will always come." - W. Mark Bassett

DATE: _____

MEMORIES MADE, TOUGH TIMES, & LESSONS LEARNED:

Stressed   Angry   Tired   Sad   Happy   Excited

_____
_____
_____
_____
_____
_____
_____
_____

Prompt of the day:
Gifts of the Spirit: Write about what you have learned about the gifts of the Spirit, including any gifts you have recognized the Lord has blessed you with.

_____
_____
_____
_____
_____

What are you grateful for today? _____

Less stress? Learn the ABCs. Sue Johnson's ABCDE model involves five steps: Adversity, Beliefs, Consequences, Disputation, and Energization. It starts with identifying a challenging event (Adversity), examining the beliefs that arise from it (Beliefs), understanding the emotional and behavioral Consequences of those beliefs, actively challenging and Disputing irrational or unhelpful beliefs, and finally, feeling Energized or transformed by adopting more rational, supportive beliefs, leading to healthier emotional outcomes and behaviors.

DATE: _____

MEMORIES MADE, TOUGH TIMES, & LESSONS LEARNED:

Stressed    Angry    Tired    Sad    Happy    Excited

_____
_____
_____
_____
_____
_____
_____
_____

What are you grateful for today? _____

*"The greatest need in the world today is faith in God and courage to do his will."* - David O. McKay

DATE: _____

MEMORIES MADE, TOUGH TIMES, & LESSONS LEARNED:

Stressed    Angry    Tired    Sad    Happy    Excited

_____
_____
_____
_____
_____
_____
_____
_____

Prompt of the day:
The Significance of Names: Write about the significance of learning and remembering names in building relationships during your mission.

_____
_____
_____
_____
_____

What are you grateful for today? _____

When your own efforts to comfort or encourage others seem inadequate, turn to Jesus Christ and rely on His infinite capacity to heal and strengthen. There will be times when you feel helpless in the face of someone's pain or when your attempts to help seem to fall short. In these moments, remember that the Savior's power is limitless and that He can work miracles in the lives of those you serve. Pray for His guidance and intervention, and trust that He will supplement your efforts with His boundless love and grace. In the words of President Russell M. Nelson, "seek and expect miracles."

DATE: _____

MEMORIES MADE, TOUGH TIMES, & LESSONS LEARNED:   Stressed   Angry   Tired   Sad   Happy   Excited

_____
_____
_____
_____
_____
_____
_____
_____

What are you grateful for today? _____

"Giving help to others—making a conscientious effort to care about others as much as or more than we care about ourselves—is our joy. Especially, I might add, when it is not convenient and when it takes us out of our comfort zone. Living that second great commandment is the key to becoming a true disciple of Jesus Christ." - Russell M. Nelson

DATE: _____

MEMORIES MADE, TOUGH TIMES, & LESSONS LEARNED:   Stressed   Angry   Tired   Sad   Happy   Excited

_____
_____
_____
_____
_____
_____
_____
_____

Prompt of the day:
Cultivating Hope: Reflect on how you cultivate hope in yourself and those you teach, especially during challenging times.

_____
_____
_____
_____

What are you grateful for today? _____

Find strength in the Atonement of Jesus Christ during times of struggle, rejection, and discouragement. Christ understands your sorrows and afflictions, and His Atonement will carry you through the challenges of missionary work. When you face rejection, remember that you are standing with the Savior, who was also despised and rejected by many. Rely on His grace and power to help you overcome obstacles and continue in your sacred calling. The Atonement of Jesus Christ is not only for those you teach but also for you as a missionary, providing comfort, strength, and the assurance of Christ's love and understanding. In times of struggle, search inward, turn outward, look upward, and press forward.

DATE: _____

MEMORIES MADE, TOUGH TIMES, & LESSONS LEARNED:  Stressed  Angry  Tired  Sad  Happy  Excited

_____
_____
_____
_____
_____
_____
_____
_____

What are you grateful for today? _____

"If you have the Holy Ghost with you—and every one ought to have—I can say unto you that there is no greater gift, there is no greater blessing, there is no greater testimony given to any man on earth. You may have the administration of angels; you may see many miracles; you may see many wonders in the earth; but I claim that the gift of the Holy Ghost is the greatest gift that can be bestowed upon man" - Wilford Woodruff

DATE: _____

MEMORIES MADE, TOUGH TIMES, & LESSONS LEARNED:  Stressed  Angry  Tired  Sad  Happy  Excited

_____
_____
_____
_____
_____
_____
_____
_____

Prompt of the day:

Connecting with Local Communities: Share your experiences and feelings about connecting with local communities and how it has enriched your mission.

_____
_____
_____
_____

What are you grateful for today? _____

Acknowledge your discouragement and take responsibility for your role in it. Seek to learn from your experiences, both successes and failures, and use them as opportunities for growth. Remember that discouragement is a natural part of life and can be productive when you learn to work through it with faith and perseverance. As a missionary, you will face many challenges that may lead to feelings of discouragement, but by acknowledging these feelings and taking ownership of your response to them, you can develop greater resilience and a more positive outlook. Embrace the opportunity to learn and grow from every experience, and trust that the Lord will help you turn your discouragement into progress.

DATE: _____

MEMORIES MADE, TOUGH TIMES, & LESSONS LEARNED:

Stressed   Angry   Tired   Sad   Happy   Excited

_____
_____
_____
_____
_____
_____
_____
_____
_____

What are you grateful for today? _____

*"Our temple garment reminds us that the Savior and the blessings of His Atonement cover us throughout our lives. As we put on the garment of the holy priesthood each day, that beautiful symbol becomes a part of us." - J. Anette Dennis*

DATE: _____

MEMORIES MADE, TOUGH TIMES, & LESSONS LEARNED:

Stressed   Angry   Tired   Sad   Happy   Excited

_____
_____
_____
_____
_____
_____
_____
_____

Prompt of the day:
Memorable Spiritual Discussions: Share a memorable spiritual discussion you had and why it stands out to you.

_____
_____
_____
_____

What are you grateful for today? _____

Approach your weekly companionship inventory with a spirit of humility, love, and a sincere desire to grow and improve together. Remember that the purpose of this inspired practice is not to criticize or belittle one another, but rather to identify areas where you can work together to become more united, obedient, and effective missionaries. Be willing to listen to your companion's insights and observations with an open heart and mind, and be courageous in sharing your own thoughts and feelings in a kind and constructive manner. Focus your discussions on setting goals and making plans to help each other develop Christlike attributes and become the best possible representatives of the Savior. These discussions will prepare you well for marriage and the differences you will experience in the future.

DATE: _____

MEMORIES MADE, TOUGH TIMES, & LESSONS LEARNED:

Stressed    Angry    Tired    Sad    Happy    Excited

_____
_____
_____
_____
_____
_____
_____
_____

What are you grateful for today? _____

*"What does the Atonement [of Jesus Christ] have to do with missionary work? Any time we experience the blessings of [the Savior's] Atonement in our lives, we cannot help but have a concern for the welfare of [others]. ... A great indicator of one's personal conversion is the desire to share the gospel with others." - Howard W. Hunter.*

DATE: _____

MEMORIES MADE, TOUGH TIMES, & LESSONS LEARNED:

Stressed    Angry    Tired    Sad    Happy    Excited

_____
_____
_____
_____
_____
_____
_____

Prompt of the day:
Spiritual Discipline: Reflect on the discipline required for missionary work and how you've developed it.

_____
_____
_____
_____

What are you grateful for today? _____

Cultivate a spirit of gratitude as a missionary: Make gratitude a central part of your missionary experience. Take time each day to reflect on the blessings, miracles, and tender mercies you encounter. Express your gratitude to God through prayer, and share your appreciation with those around you. As you cultivate a spirit of gratitude, you'll find greater joy and contentment in your missionary service. Your thankful heart will be a light to others and a testament to the goodness of God.

DATE: _____

MEMORIES MADE, TOUGH TIMES, & LESSONS LEARNED:

Stressed  Angry  Tired  Sad  Happy  Excited

_____
_____
_____
_____
_____
_____
_____
_____

What are you grateful for today? _____

*"The highest achievement of spirituality comes as we conquer the flesh...As givers gain control of their desires and properly see other needs in light of their own wants, then the powers of the gospel are released in their lives." - Spencer W. Kimball*

DATE: _____

MEMORIES MADE, TOUGH TIMES, & LESSONS LEARNED:

Stressed  Angry  Tired  Sad  Happy  Excited

_____
_____
_____
_____
_____
_____
_____
_____

Prompt of the day:

Learning to Live in the Moment: Write about how your mission has taught you to live more in the moment and appreciate the present.

_____
_____
_____
_____
_____

What are you grateful for today? _____

Do follow the mission guidelines when it comes to visiting other houses of worship in your area. Show respect for these sacred spaces and the beliefs of others. Be mindful of your actions and words to avoid misinterpretation or offense. Don't disrespect local places of worship. Your respectful and considerate behavior can foster goodwill and understanding between different faith communities.

DATE: _____

MEMORIES MADE, TOUGH TIMES, & LESSONS LEARNED:

Stressed   Angry   Tired   Sad   Happy   Excited

_____
_____
_____
_____
_____
_____
_____
_____

What are you grateful for today? _____

"*When the Savior atoned for all mankind, He opened a way that those who follow Him can have access to His healing, strengthening, and redeeming power. These spiritual privileges are available to all who seek to hear Him and follow Him.*" - Russell M. Nelson

DATE: _____

MEMORIES MADE, TOUGH TIMES, & LESSONS LEARNED:

Stressed   Angry   Tired   Sad   Happy   Excited

_____
_____
_____
_____
_____
_____
_____
_____

Prompt of the day:
Gratitude for Challenges: Write about a challenge for which you're now grateful because of the growth it prompted.

_____
_____
_____
_____

What are you grateful for today? _____

Find joy in the plan of salvation as a missionary: Deepen your understanding and appreciation of God's eternal plan of happiness. Study the doctrines of the premortal life, the purpose of mortality, and the glorious potential of eternal life. Find joy in the knowledge that this plan provides meaning, direction, and hope for all of God's children. Share your testimony of the plan of salvation with others, inviting them to find the same joy and purpose in their lives. As you center your missionary work on the plan of salvation, you'll help others understand their divine identity and eternal destiny.

DATE: _____

MEMORIES MADE, TOUGH TIMES, & LESSONS LEARNED:

Stressed   Angry   Tired   Sad   Happy   Excited

_____
_____
_____
_____
_____
_____
_____
_____

What are you grateful for today?

"Overcoming the world is not an event that happens in a day or two. It happens over a lifetime as we repeatedly embrace the doctrine of Christ. We cultivate faith in Jesus Christ by repenting daily and keeping covenants that endow us with power. We stay on the covenant path and are blessed with spiritual strength, personal revelation, increasing faith, and the ministering of angels. Living the doctrine of Christ can produce the most powerful virtuous cycle, creating spiritual momentum in our lives." - Russell M. Nelson

DATE: _____

MEMORIES MADE, TOUGH TIMES, & LESSONS LEARNED:

Stressed   Angry   Tired   Sad   Happy   Excited

_____
_____
_____
_____
_____
_____
_____

Prompt of the day:

The Impact of Missionary Work on Future Plans: Reflect on how your experiences as a missionary might impact your future plans and aspirations.

_____
_____
_____
_____
_____
_____

What are you grateful for today? _____

You will experience many challenges and obstacles throughout your mission. Be patient through these tough times. Look upward. Think Celestial. Whether it is overwhelming schedules, daunting tasks, horrible weather, awful sickness, or less-than-ideal living situations. Remember that many of these challenges resolve over time. Focus your energy on what you can control and be patient with the processes that need more time to unfold. After every storm, the sun eventually shines again. By navigating the ups and downs with grace and resilience, you can maintain a positive outlook and effectively serve others throughout your mission.

DATE: _____

MEMORIES MADE, TOUGH TIMES, & LESSONS LEARNED:

Stressed   Angry   Tired   Sad   Happy   Excited

_____
_____
_____
_____
_____
_____
_____
_____

What are you grateful for today? _____

"Our Christlike example of kindness, righteousness, happiness, and sincere love for all people can create not only a guiding beacon light for them, but also an understanding that there is a safe harbor in the ordinances of salvation and exaltation of the restored gospel of Jesus Christ." - Quentin L. Cook

DATE: _____

MEMORIES MADE, TOUGH TIMES, & LESSONS LEARNED:

Stressed   Angry   Tired   Sad   Happy   Excited

_____
_____
_____
_____
_____
_____
_____
_____

Prompt of the day:
Missionary Work's Personal Benefits: Reflect on the unexpected personal benefits you've received from your missionary work.

_____
_____
_____
_____
_____

What are you grateful for today? _____

Myth: Once a mission is completed, the missionary's impact ends. Reality: The influence of your missionary service often continues long after the mission ends, affecting both the communities served and the missionaries themselves. You will see your time in the field as a foundation for a lifetime of service and discipleship. The relationships built, testimonies shared, and seeds of faith planted can continue to grow and bless lives long after you return home. You should strive to maintain the spiritual habits and Christlike attributes developed during your mission.

DATE: _____

MEMORIES MADE, TOUGH TIMES, & LESSONS LEARNED:  Stressed  Angry  Tired  Sad  Happy  Excited

_____
_____
_____
_____
_____
_____
_____
_____

What are you grateful for today? _____

*"...surely the thing God enjoys most about being God is the thrill of being merciful, especially to those who don't expect it and often feel they don't deserve it." - Jeffrey R. Holland*

DATE: _____

MEMORIES MADE, TOUGH TIMES, & LESSONS LEARNED:  Stressed  Angry  Tired  Sad  Happy  Excited

_____
_____
_____
_____
_____
_____
_____
_____

Prompt of the day:
Finding Strength in Weakness: Share an experience where you found strength in a weakness or vulnerability during your mission.

_____
_____
_____
_____

What are you grateful for today? _____

Focus on what you can control as a missionary: Direct your energy and attention to the aspects of your mission that you can influence. While you can't control every situation or outcome, you can control your attitude, effort, and obedience. Concentrate on your personal spiritual growth, your relationships with others, and your diligence in the work. Let go of the things beyond your control and trust in the Lord's plan. As you focus on what you can change, you'll find greater peace and purpose in your missionary service.

DATE: _____

MEMORIES MADE, TOUGH TIMES, & LESSONS LEARNED:    Stressed   Angry   Tired   Sad   Happy   Excited

_____
_____
_____
_____
_____
_____
_____
_____

What are you grateful for today? _____

"Our goal is to achieve eternal life. That is the greatest goal in the world. We are not opposed to goals. We do not want stake and full-time mission presidents to establish quotas for the missionaries. Rather, we expect them to inspire missionaries to set their own goals, and make them high enough to challenge their very best efforts, and work to achieve them. ... We look to you to teach these principles and follow up." - Spencer W. Kimball

DATE: _____

MEMORIES MADE, TOUGH TIMES, & LESSONS LEARNED:    Stressed   Angry   Tired   Sad   Happy   Excited

_____
_____
_____
_____
_____
_____
_____
_____

Prompt of the day:
Overcoming Personal Weaknesses: Share how your mission has helped you confront and overcome personal weaknesses.

_____
_____
_____
_____

What are you grateful for today? _____

You can read all the anxiety advice in the world, but none of it matters unless YOU. TAKE. ACTION. To feel better you have to ruthlessly focus your efforts on those things that reduce your anxiety, and increase positive emotions, and stop doing the things that keep you down, tense, and awake at night. One of the absolute best ways to start feeling better is exercise. And sleep. And eating right. Get those puppies in order and it will create an upward spiral. But if you want to feel better, you've got to change up some habits and take action my friend.

DATE: _____

MEMORIES MADE, TOUGH TIMES, & LESSONS LEARNED:

Stressed   Angry   Tired   Sad   Happy   Excited

_____
_____
_____
_____
_____
_____
_____
_____
_____

What are you grateful for today? _____

*"As disciples of Jesus Christ, we are to be examples of how to interact with others — especially when we have differences of opinion. One of the easiest ways to identify a true follower of Jesus Christ is how compassionately that person treats other people." - Russell M. Nelson*

DATE: _____

MEMORIES MADE, TOUGH TIMES, & LESSONS LEARNED:

Stressed   Angry   Tired   Sad   Happy   Excited

_____
_____
_____
_____
_____
_____
_____
_____

Prompt of the day:

The Role of Tradition in Faith: Reflect on the role of tradition in faith and how it has been evident in your missionary work.

_____
_____
_____
_____
_____

What are you grateful for today? _____

Sing to those you teach! I'll never forget a missionary companion who decided we should sing songs to those we were knocking doors. I didn't realize what was happening. On one particular door, the woman said she wasn't interested and as she was closing the door, my companion said, "Wait! Can we at least sing you a song?" I was stunned. He looked at me and said, we're going to sing "I am a child of God." And so we did. Unrehearsed. Right there on the porch. The spirit rushed in. She had tears in her eyes, and she thanked us and said she needed that. We sang at several doorsteps that week. There is a special spirit with music. Give it a try!

DATE: _____

MEMORIES MADE, TOUGH TIMES, & LESSONS LEARNED:

Stressed  Angry  Tired  Sad  Happy  Excited

_____
_____
_____
_____
_____
_____
_____
_____

What are you grateful for today? _____

*"Covenant-keeping men and women seek for ways to keep themselves unspotted from the world so there will be nothing blocking their access to the Savior's power." – Russell M. Nelson*

DATE: _____

MEMORIES MADE, TOUGH TIMES, & LESSONS LEARNED:

Stressed  Angry  Tired  Sad  Happy  Excited

_____
_____
_____
_____
_____
_____
_____

Prompt of the day:

Building Faith in Difficult Times: Reflect on a time when your faith was particularly challenged, and how you worked to strengthen it.

_____
_____
_____
_____
_____

What are you grateful for today? _____

Act with faith and hope, not fear. Trust in God's promises and continue to knock, knowing that your efforts will be rewarded. Rejection is not the end; Christ is with you, ready to comfort and strengthen you. Fear of rejection can paralyze you, hindering your engagement in the work. Act with faith, knowing your efforts are not in vain. Keep reaching out, trusting the Lord to guide you. When facing rejection, remember Christ understands your pain. Turn to Him in prayer for healing and courage to move forward in faith.

DATE: _____

MEMORIES MADE, TOUGH TIMES, & LESSONS LEARNED:   Stressed   Angry   Tired   Sad   Happy   Excited

_____
_____
_____
_____
_____
_____
_____
_____

What are you grateful for today? _____

*"Regardless of where we call home, members of the Church feel passionately about the fatherhood of God and the brotherhood of man. Thus, our greatest joy comes as we help our brothers and sisters, no matter where we live in this wonderful world." - Russell M. Nelson*

DATE: _____

MEMORIES MADE, TOUGH TIMES, & LESSONS LEARNED:   Stressed   Angry   Tired   Sad   Happy   Excited

_____
_____
_____
_____
_____
_____
_____

Prompt of the day:
Coping with the Unknown: Write about coping strategies you've developed for dealing with the unknown and uncertain aspects of missionary work.

_____
_____
_____
_____
_____

What are you grateful for today? _____

When going door-to-door proselytizing, greet each person who answers with an authentic, friendly big ol' smile. Offer a warm "hello" and make eye contact. Being kind and respectful from the start is so important. First impressions truly matter, so make sure yours feels welcoming and positive. A sincere smile paired with eye contact and a pleasant greeting immediately puts people at ease. Develop this habit of creating an inviting presence, as it's a valuable skill for life. Represent Christ's love through your warm and courteous approach when meeting new people at their doorstep.

DATE: _____

MEMORIES MADE, TOUGH TIMES, & LESSONS LEARNED:  Stressed  Angry  Tired  Sad  Happy  Excited

_____
_____
_____
_____
_____
_____
_____
_____

What are you grateful for today? _____

"Together, members and missionaries invite all to learn of God, of Jesus Christ, and of His gospel. Each inquiring individual should seek earnestly and pray fervently for the assurance that these things are true. The truth will be manifest by the power of the Holy Ghost." - Russell M. Nelson

DATE: _____

MEMORIES MADE, TOUGH TIMES, & LESSONS LEARNED:  Stressed  Angry  Tired  Sad  Happy  Excited

_____
_____
_____
_____
_____
_____
_____
_____

Prompt of the day:
Community Integration: Write about your efforts and experiences in integrating into the community you serve.

_____
_____
_____
_____

What are you grateful for today? _____

Myth: Missionaries always feel spiritually uplifted and happy.
Reality: While you often experience spiritual highs, you will also face challenges, homesickness, and regular emotional ups and downs like anyone else. It's normal for you to have days when you feel discouraged or exhausted. The key is to turn to God in prayer, find joy in serving others, and remember that personal growth often comes through overcoming trials. You should be kind to yourself and recognize that your worth is not determined by your temporary emotions.

DATE: _____

MEMORIES MADE, TOUGH TIMES, & LESSONS LEARNED:

Stressed  Angry  Tired  Sad  Happy  Excited

_____
_____
_____
_____
_____
_____
_____
_____

What are you grateful for today? _____

"You will have all kinds of trials to pass through. And it is quite as necessary for you to be tried as it was for Abraham and other men of God, and God will feel after you, and He will take hold of you and wrench your very heart strings, and if you cannot stand it you will not be fit for an inheritance in the Celestial Kingdom of God." - Joseph Smith

DATE: _____

MEMORIES MADE, TOUGH TIMES, & LESSONS LEARNED:

Stressed  Angry  Tired  Sad  Happy  Excited

_____
_____
_____
_____
_____
_____
_____
_____

Prompt of the day:
The Power of a Positive Attitude: Reflect on the power of maintaining a positive attitude, even when faced with challenges.

_____
_____
_____
_____

What are you grateful for today? _____

Use visualization techniques. Missionaries can manage stress by using visualization techniques, which involve creating a mental image of a positive outcome or serene environment. By vividly imagining a tranquil scene or envisioning yourself succeeding in a stressful scenario, you can lower anxiety levels, elevate your mood, and better equip yourself to face challenging situations with confidence and calmness. Incorporating this practice into your daily routine can lead to improved mental resilience and well-being throughout your mission.

DATE: _____

MEMORIES MADE, TOUGH TIMES, & LESSONS LEARNED:

Stressed   Angry   Tired   Sad   Happy   Excited

_____
_____
_____
_____
_____
_____
_____

What are you grateful for today? _____

*"When we kneel to pray, is it to replay the greatest hits of our own righteousness, or is it to confess our faults, plead for God's mercy, and shed tears of gratitude for the amazing plan of redemption? Salvation cannot be bought with the currency of obedience; it is purchased by the blood of the Son of God." - Dieter F. Uchtdorf*

DATE: _____

MEMORIES MADE, TOUGH TIMES, & LESSONS LEARNED:

Stressed   Angry   Tired   Sad   Happy   Excited

_____
_____
_____
_____
_____
_____
_____

Prompt of the day:
Spiritual Growth Milestones: Reflect on significant milestones in your spiritual growth during your mission.

_____
_____
_____
_____
_____

What are you grateful for today? _____

Avoid whispering in front of others as it creates discomfort, changes group dynamics, and can make people feel excluded and uncomfortable. Whispering may be acceptable in certain settings like at church, but in group situations as missionaries, choose better times for private conversations. When others are whispering, it's natural to assume they are talking about you. Consider how you would feel in those situations and strive to create an inclusive, welcoming environment. If a discussion isn't meant for the whole group, wait until later to have it privately. Prioritize making everyone feel valued by being mindful of how your actions could inadvertently alienate others.

DATE: _____

MEMORIES MADE, TOUGH TIMES, & LESSONS LEARNED:

Stressed   Angry   Tired   Sad   Happy   Excited

_____
_____
_____
_____
_____
_____
_____
_____

What are you grateful for today? _____

*"Our Father in Heaven is not an umpire who is trying to count us out. He is not a competitor who is trying to outsmart us. He is not a prosecutor who is trying to convict us. He is a Loving Father who wants our happiness and eternal progress and everlasting opportunity and glorious accomplishment, and who will help us all He can if we will but give Him, in our lives, the opportunity to do so with obedience and humility and faith and patience"* - Richard L. Evans

DATE: _____

MEMORIES MADE, TOUGH TIMES, & LESSONS LEARNED:

Stressed   Angry   Tired   Sad   Happy   Excited

_____
_____
_____
_____
_____
_____
_____
_____

Prompt of the day:

Witnessing Growth in Faith: Share an experience where you witnessed significant growth in someone's faith and how it affected you.

_____
_____
_____
_____
_____

What are you grateful for today? _____

These 3 words may be helpful as a missionary: Trust, Try, and Cry. Do we trust that God has all the answers, that He loves us, and that He will answer all our questions—in His way, on His timetable? Do we "think celestial?" Try: The Lord loves effort. The temple recommend questions include the word "strive." The primary children sing: "I'm trying to be like Jesus." We can follow their example. Cry: In the scriptures, the words pray and cry are often used interchangeably. But those that include the word "cry" suggest more than a request--there is a pleading urgency for mercy and help, right now. Even more desperate are prayers that begin with the letter "O." (look those up). We TRUST Jesus. We TRY to do all that is within our power to be obedient and stay on or come back to the covenant path. And we CRY and plead for help, forgiveness, grace, and strength.

DATE: _____

MEMORIES MADE, TOUGH TIMES, & LESSONS LEARNED:

Stressed   Angry   Tired   Sad   Happy   Excited

_____
_____
_____
_____
_____
_____
_____
_____

What are you grateful for today? _____

*"Solid, lasting missionary work is done on our knees."* - James O. Fraser

DATE: _____

MEMORIES MADE, TOUGH TIMES, & LESSONS LEARNED:

Stressed   Angry   Tired   Sad   Happy   Excited

_____
_____
_____
_____
_____
_____
_____
_____

Prompt of the day:
Memorable Conversations: Share a memorable conversation that had a profound impact on you or someone else.

_____
_____
_____
_____
_____

What are you grateful for today? _____

Be slow to judge and quick to love as a missionary: Approach others with compassion and understanding. Resist the temptation to judge or criticize those you meet. Instead, strive to see them as God sees them—as His beloved children with divine potential. Look for the good in others and focus on their strengths. As you extend love and acceptance, you'll create an environment where the Spirit can flourish. Your Christlike love will touch hearts and invite others to come unto Him.

DATE: _____

MEMORIES MADE, TOUGH TIMES, & LESSONS LEARNED:

Stressed  Angry  Tired  Sad  Happy  Excited

_____
_____
_____
_____
_____
_____
_____
_____

What are you grateful for today? _____

*"Even when you stumble, even when you turn away from Him, God loves you. If you are feeling lost, abandoned, or forgotten—fear not. The Good Shepherd will find you. He will lift you upon His shoulders. And He will carry you home." - Dieter F. Uchtdorf*

DATE: _____

MEMORIES MADE, TOUGH TIMES, & LESSONS LEARNED:

Stressed  Angry  Tired  Sad  Happy  Excited

_____
_____
_____
_____
_____
_____
_____

Prompt of the day:
The Role of Prayer in Community Building: Write about how prayer has played a role in building community and connections during your mission.

_____
_____
_____
_____
_____

What are you grateful for today? _____

Don't spread gossip and unhelpful information with other missionaries, members, or anyone else. Spreading rumors or talking behind others' back isn't being Christlike. Even if you mean well, it hurts everyone and creates unnecessary drama. If it's even potentially hurtful, don't say it and don't share it. Unless it is related to disobedience or other worthiness matters, you might think you're helping by sharing it with other missionaries, but it usually just backfires and makes things worse. Missionaries make mistakes, and sharing it makes it worse. Don't be part of it. Instead, be supportive and kind in your words and texts. Encourage others to do the same.

DATE: _____

MEMORIES MADE, TOUGH TIMES, & LESSONS LEARNED:

Stressed    Angry    Tired    Sad    Happy    Excited

_____
_____
_____
_____
_____
_____
_____
_____

What are you grateful for today? _____

*"There is not one of us but what God's love has been expended upon. There is not one of us that He has not cared for and caressed...We may be insignificant and contemptible in our own eyes, and in the eyes of others, but the truth remains that we are the children of God, and that He has actually given His angels—invisible beings of power and might—charge concerning us, and they watch over us and have us in their keeping." - George Q. Cannon*

DATE: _____

MEMORIES MADE, TOUGH TIMES, & LESSONS LEARNED:

Stressed    Angry    Tired    Sad    Happy    Excited

_____
_____
_____
_____
_____
_____
_____
_____

Prompt of the day:

Teaching Adaptability: Reflect on a time when you had to adapt your teaching approach on the spot. What prompted the change, and how did it go?

_____
_____
_____
_____
_____

What are you grateful for today? _____

Embrace the eternal significance of your missionary service: Remember that your mission is not just a temporary assignment, but an opportunity to participate in the Lord's eternal work of salvation. Recognize that your efforts, no matter how small they may seem, have the power to change lives and shape destinies. Find joy in the knowledge that your missionary service is laying the foundation for generations of faith and righteousness. As you embrace the eternal significance of your work, you'll approach each day with renewed dedication, gratitude, and joy.

DATE: _____

MEMORIES MADE, TOUGH TIMES, & LESSONS LEARNED:

Stressed   Angry   Tired   Sad   Happy   Excited

_____
_____
_____
_____
_____
_____
_____
_____
_____

What are you grateful for today? _____

"We need to pray from our hearts. Polite recitations of past and upcoming activities, punctuated with some requests for blessings, cannot constitute the kind of communing with God that brings enduring power. Are you willing to pray to know how to pray for more power? The Lord will teach you." - Russell M. Nelson

DATE: _____

MEMORIES MADE, TOUGH TIMES, & LESSONS LEARNED:

Stressed   Angry   Tired   Sad   Happy   Excited

_____
_____
_____
_____
_____
_____
_____
_____

Prompt of the day:
Reflections on Selflessness: Reflect on moments of self lessness you've experienced or witnessed during your mission and how they've impacted your perspective on service.

_____
_____
_____
_____
_____

What are you grateful for today? _____

When you experience dark and difficult days shift your focus to serving others (shine your companion's shoes!) and relying on Christ. When you feel overwhelmed or discouraged, turn your attention to the needs of those around you. Look for opportunities to perform acts of kindness, share your testimony, and invite others to come unto Christ. As you lose yourself in the service of others, you'll find that your own burdens become lighter. Remember that the Savior understands your struggles and has promised to help you carry your load. Rely on His grace and seek to develop a deeper relationship with Him through prayer, scripture study, and obedience to His commandments.

DATE: _____

MEMORIES MADE, TOUGH TIMES, & LESSONS LEARNED:

Stressed    Angry    Tired    Sad    Happy    Excited

_____
_____
_____
_____
_____
_____
_____

What are you grateful for today? _____

*"My dear brothers and sisters, with all the pleadings of my heart, I urge you to get on the covenant path and stay there. Experience the joy of repenting daily. Learn about God and how He works. Seek and expect miracles. Strive to end conflict in your life." - Russell M. Nelson*

DATE: _____

MEMORIES MADE, TOUGH TIMES, & LESSONS LEARNED:

Stressed    Angry    Tired    Sad    Happy    Excited

_____
_____
_____
_____
_____
_____

Prompt of the day:
Facing and Overcoming Fears: Write about facing a specific fear during your mission and the outcome.

_____
_____
_____
_____

What are you grateful for today? _____

As a missionary, create an "awe album" by collecting photos that inspire you and remind you of the grandeur of God's creations and the power of His work. Take time to scroll through your mission photos, selecting images that evoke feelings of wonder, gratitude, and reverence. As you curate your album, pause to relive, and savor each moment captured. Regularly view your "awe album," especially during times of stress or discouragement, to reconnect with the beauty and purpose of your missionary service. This visual reminder of inspiring moments will uplift your spirit and help you maintain an eternal perspective.

DATE: _____

MEMORIES MADE, TOUGH TIMES, & LESSONS LEARNED:

Stressed   Angry   Tired   Sad   Happy   Excited

_____
_____
_____
_____
_____
_____
_____
_____

What are you grateful for today? _____

*"People do not join the Church because of what they know. They join because of what they feel, what they see and want spiritually. Our spirit of testimony and happiness in that regard will come through to others if we let it." - Jeffrey R. Holland*

DATE: _____

MEMORIES MADE, TOUGH TIMES, & LESSONS LEARNED:

Stressed   Angry   Tired   Sad   Happy   Excited

_____
_____
_____
_____
_____
_____
_____
_____

Prompt of the day:

The Beauty of Diverse Perspectives: Write about how encountering diverse perspectives during your mission has enriched your understanding and empathy.

_____
_____
_____
_____
_____

What are you grateful for today? _____

Watch for the "one." Leaving out just one missionary is unkind. This is particularly true on preparation today when missionaries often get together. Be the one who makes room and includes others. If you have an issue with someone, talk to them instead of avoiding them. Imagine being in their shoes; someday, you might be left out too. Remember, there's space for one more. You can't always invite everyone, but leaving out one person is hurtful. Don't exclude someone from group messages or plans. You wouldn't want to be remembered as the person who made others feel small or unwanted. It's much better to be remembered for your kindness than your greatness.

DATE: _____

MEMORIES MADE, TOUGH TIMES, & LESSONS LEARNED:

Stressed   Angry   Tired   Sad   Happy   Excited

_____
_____
_____
_____
_____
_____
_____
_____

What are you grateful for today? _____

"If you have doubts about God the Father and His Beloved Son or the validity of the Restoration or the veracity of Joseph Smith's divine calling as a prophet, choose to believe and stay faithful. Take your questions to the Lord and to other faithful sources. Study with the desire to believe...Allow the Lord to lead you on your journey of spiritual discovery." - Russell M. Nelson

DATE: _____

MEMORIES MADE, TOUGH TIMES, & LESSONS LEARNED:

Stressed   Angry   Tired   Sad   Happy   Excited

_____
_____
_____
_____
_____
_____
_____

Prompt of the day:
Missionary Life's Simple Pleasures: Reflect on the simple pleasures of missionary life that bring you joy or comfort.

_____
_____
_____
_____

What are you grateful for today? _____

Let Him know you will act on the promptings that come. Over time, He will send more promptings because He knows and trusts you will act. He knows your heart. He knows sincere prayers and real intent. Pray for help. And then be still. And feel. And act.

DATE: _____

MEMORIES MADE, TOUGH TIMES, & LESSONS LEARNED:

Stressed   Angry   Tired   Sad   Happy   Excited

_____
_____
_____
_____
_____
_____
_____
_____

What are you grateful for today? _____

*"When we love somebody, we show it by doing something nice. So learn to serve: find a need and fulfill a need. Surprise people with a good deed they hadn't planned on. We have that opportunity at home, at school, and at church." - Russell M. Nelson*

DATE: _____

MEMORIES MADE, TOUGH TIMES, & LESSONS LEARNED:

Stressed   Angry   Tired   Sad   Happy   Excited

_____
_____
_____
_____
_____
_____
_____
_____

Prompt of the day:

Overcoming Prejudices: Reflect on a time when you or someone you encountered overcame prejudices, leading to growth and understanding.

_____
_____
_____
_____

What are you grateful for today? _____

The happiest missionaries are those who focus on their gifts and strengths and manage their weaknesses. Recognize your values, talents, and gifts, and find ways to utilize them creatively in your missionary service. Concentrating on your strengths and asking God how you can use them in His work will lead to more effectiveness as a missionary. Instead of dwelling on perceived weaknesses or limitations, identify the unique qualities and abilities you possess and explore how you can leverage them in your service. This could involve using your talents for teaching or even creative approaches to sharing the gospel message. By playing to your strengths, you'll not only contribute more effectively but also experience a greater sense of fulfillment and personal growth.

DATE: _____

MEMORIES MADE, TOUGH TIMES, & LESSONS LEARNED:

Stressed  Angry  Tired  Sad  Happy  Excited

_____
_____
_____
_____
_____
_____
_____
_____

What are you grateful for today? _____

*"There is no doubt, if a person lives according to the revelations given to God's people, he may have the Spirit of the Lord to signify to him his will, and to guide and to direct him in the discharge of his duties, in his temporal as well as his spiritual exercises. I am satisfied, however, that in this respect, we live far beneath our privileges." - Brigham Young*

DATE: _____

MEMORIES MADE, TOUGH TIMES, & LESSONS LEARNED:

Stressed  Angry  Tired  Sad  Happy  Excited

_____
_____
_____
_____
_____
_____
_____

Prompt of the day:
Role of Humor: Share how humor has played a role in your mission, either as a coping mechanism or in building relationships.

_____
_____
_____
_____

What are you grateful for today? _____

View rejection as an opportunity for growth. Reflect on your experiences and consider how you can adapt your approach or develop new skills to be more effective in your missionary work. While rejection can be painful, it can also be a valuable teacher. Ponder your experiences and identify areas where you can grow and improve. Work on your communication skills, your ability to connect with others, or your knowledge of the gospel. Try new methods or strategies in your missionary efforts. Above, plead for the Spirit to be with you. By viewing rejection as a chance to learn and develop, you can maintain a growth mindset and continue to progress in your abilities as a missionary.

DATE: _____

MEMORIES MADE, TOUGH TIMES, & LESSONS LEARNED:

Stressed  Angry  Tired  Sad  Happy  Excited

_____
_____
_____
_____
_____
_____
_____
_____

What are you grateful for today? _____

"*Your growing faith in Him will move mountains—not the mountains of rock that beautify the earth but the mountains of misery in your lives. Your flourishing faith will help you turn challenges into unparalleled growth and opportunity.*" - Russell M. Nelson

DATE: _____

MEMORIES MADE, TOUGH TIMES, & LESSONS LEARNED:

Stressed  Angry  Tired  Sad  Happy  Excited

_____
_____
_____
_____
_____
_____
_____
_____

Prompt of the day:

The Impact of Missionary Work on Personal Relationships: Share how your missionary work has affected your personal relationships, both with those back home and those you've met on your mission.

_____
_____
_____
_____

What are you grateful for today? _____

Accept that rejection is an inevitable part of missionary work and remember that it is not a reflection of your abilities or worth as a missionary. Even Jesus Christ, the perfect example and teacher, faced rejection during His mortal ministry. When people choose not to accept the gospel message, recognize that they are exercising their God-given agency, and trust that the seeds you have planted may still bear fruit in the future. Keep your focus on those who are prepared to receive the gospel, and find joy in the knowledge that you are doing your best to share the truth with all who will listen. It's sometimes difficult to realize many just don't want to hear it—right now. Their time may come.

DATE: _____

MEMORIES MADE, TOUGH TIMES, & LESSONS LEARNED:  Stressed  Angry  Tired  Sad  Happy  Excited

_____
_____
_____
_____
_____
_____
_____
_____

What are you grateful for today? _____

*"You can change human nature. No man who has felt in him the Spirit of Christ even for half a minute can deny this truth....You do change human nature, your own human nature, if you surrender it to Christ. Human nature can be changed here and now. Human nature has been changed in the past. Human nature must be changed on an enormous scale in the future, unless the world is to be drowned in its own blood. And only Christ can change it." - David O. McKay*

DATE: _____

MEMORIES MADE, TOUGH TIMES, & LESSONS LEARNED:  Stressed  Angry  Tired  Sad  Happy  Excited

_____
_____
_____
_____
_____
_____
_____
_____

Prompt of the day:
Reflecting on Pre-Mission Expectations: Reflect on your expectations before your mission and how they align with your actual experiences.

_____
_____
_____
_____

What are you grateful for today? _____

Focus on inviting people to take upon themselves the name of Christ through baptism, not just on "getting baptisms." Connect the ordinance to its Christ-centered meaning and purpose. Your goal is not a specific number, but helping people enter the path of discipleship. Teach them that baptism is a sacred covenant to follow Jesus Christ and receive a remission of sins through His Atonement. Emphasize that they are taking His name upon them. This doctrine-centered approach will bring more converts into the fold who are truly converted unto the Lord.

DATE: _____

MEMORIES MADE, TOUGH TIMES, & LESSONS LEARNED:    Stressed   Angry   Tired   Sad   Happy   Excited

_____
_____
_____
_____
_____
_____
_____
_____

What are you grateful for today? _____

*"With frightening speed, a testimony that is not nourished daily by the good word of God can crumble. Thus, the antidote to Satan's scheme is clear: we need daily experiences worshipping the Lord and studying His gospel. I plead with you to let God prevail in your life. Give Him a fair share of your time. As you do, notice what happens to your positive spiritual momentum."*
*- Russell M. Nelson*

DATE: _____

MEMORIES MADE, TOUGH TIMES, & LESSONS LEARNED:    Stressed   Angry   Tired   Sad   Happy   Excited

_____
_____
_____
_____
_____
_____
_____
_____

Prompt of the day:

Spiritual Resilience in the Face of Hardship: Write about an instance that tested your spiritual resilience and what you learned from it.

_____
_____
_____
_____
_____

What are you grateful for today? _____

Is your scripture study a ritual or relationship? Sometimes when someone is struggling spiritually, we reduce our recommendations to only one phrase: "Read your scriptures and pray." Certainly, scripture study and prayer are fundamental practices for spiritual well-being and growth. But sometimes we forget that it is not scripture study and prayer that heal us. God does. He is the Great Physician whose wisdom and power will provide us with customized guidance and mending. We use scripture study and prayer to help us discover Him and His will. By emphasizing the practices themselves rather than the purpose of those practices, we ritualize the behavior. We run the substantial risk that we will start to associate the practices with righteousness, holiness and spiritual power. The practices can become our god. Yet the heavenly directive is to come unto Him. Learn to love the scriptures because they help you as a missionary to know, love, and learn from the Lord Jesus Christ. Jesus changes everything.

DATE: _____

**MEMORIES MADE, TOUGH TIMES, & LESSONS LEARNED:**

Stressed   Angry   Tired   Sad   Happy   Excited

_____
_____
_____
_____
_____
_____
_____
_____
_____

What are you grateful for today? _____

*"Nothing opens the heavens quite like the combination of increased purity, exact obedience, earnest seeking, daily feasting on the words of Christ in the Book of Mormon, and regular time committed to temple and family history work." - Russell M. Nelson*

DATE: _____

**MEMORIES MADE, TOUGH TIMES, & LESSONS LEARNED:**

Stressed   Angry   Tired   Sad   Happy   Excited

_____
_____
_____
_____
_____
_____
_____
_____

Prompt of the day:
Inspirational Missionary Stories: Write about an inspirational story or anecdote from another missionary that has motivated you.

_____
_____
_____
_____

What are you grateful for today? _____

Allow yourself mental vacations. Missionary work can be emotionally and mentally taxing. When you feel overwhelmed, take a brief mental vacation. Find a quiet spot, close your eyes, and picture a peaceful scene like the temple grounds. Breathe deeply and enjoy the calm for a few minutes. After your mental break, choose a small task to help your day run more smoothly. These short respites can help you recharge and approach challenges with renewed energy and focus.

DATE: _____

MEMORIES MADE, TOUGH TIMES, & LESSONS LEARNED:

Stressed   Angry   Tired   Sad   Happy   Excited

_____
_____
_____
_____
_____
_____
_____
_____

What are you grateful for today? _____

*"Though a man should say but a few words, and his sentences and words be ever so ungrammatical, if he speaks by the power of the Holy Ghost, he will do good." - Brigham Young*

DATE: _____

MEMORIES MADE, TOUGH TIMES, & LESSONS LEARNED:

Stressed   Angry   Tired   Sad   Happy   Excited

_____
_____
_____
_____
_____
_____
_____
_____

Prompt of the day:
The Role of Music in Worship and Fellowship: Reflect on the role of music in your mission, whether in worship, fellowship, or personal reflection.

_____
_____
_____
_____

What are you grateful for today? _____

Let go of what you can't control. Concentrate your efforts on aspects within your control, like your behavior, choices, and attitude. Worrying about external factors you can't influence only leads to frustration and emotional drain. As a missionary, you'll encounter various situations and challenges that are beyond your control, such as the reactions of others, unexpected events, or cultural differences. Instead of expending valuable energy and emotional resources on these uncontrollable factors, focus your attention and energy on the things you can actively shape and improve. This includes your own actions, mindset, and responses to adversity. By letting go of what you can't control and embracing what you can, you'll maintain a greater sense of empowerment, inner peace, and emotional resilience.

DATE: _____

MEMORIES MADE, TOUGH TIMES, & LESSONS LEARNED:

Stressed    Angry    Tired    Sad    Happy    Excited

_____
_____
_____
_____
_____
_____
_____
_____

What are you grateful for today? _____

*"As we diligently focus on the Savior and then follow His pattern of focusing on joy, we need to avoid those things that can interrupt our joy...Anything that opposes Christ or His doctrine will interrupt our joy...If we look to the world and follow its formulas for happiness, we will never know joy." - Russell M. Nelson*

DATE: _____

MEMORIES MADE, TOUGH TIMES, & LESSONS LEARNED:

Stressed    Angry    Tired    Sad    Happy    Excited

_____
_____
_____
_____
_____
_____
_____
_____

Prompt of the day:

Embracing Uncertainty: Reflect on a time when you had to embrace uncertainty in your mission. How did you find peace or clarity in that situation?

_____
_____
_____
_____
_____

What are you grateful for today? _____

Do actively listen to the members' stories, challenges, and feedback. Show genuine interest, ask follow-up questions, and seek to understand their perspectives. Being good listeners can help you build trust and tailor your service to their needs. Don't shine the spotlight on yourself when talking with members, remember this mission is not about YOU!

DATE: _____

MEMORIES MADE, TOUGH TIMES, & LESSONS LEARNED:

Stressed  Angry  Tired  Sad  Happy  Excited

_____
_____
_____
_____
_____
_____
_____
_____
_____

What are you grateful for today? _____

*"Preach the first principles of the Gospel—preach them over again: you will find that day after day new ideas and additional light concerning them will be revealed to you. You can enlarge upon them so as to comprehend them clearly. You will then be able to make them more plainly understood by those [you] teach."* - Hyrum Smith

DATE: _____

MEMORIES MADE, TOUGH TIMES, & LESSONS LEARNED:

Stressed  Angry  Tired  Sad  Happy  Excited

_____
_____
_____
_____
_____
_____
_____
_____

Prompt of the day:
Experiencing the Power of the Sacrament: Share an experience where the sacrament had a profound impact on you during your mission.

_____
_____
_____
_____
_____

What are you grateful for today? _____

Find joy in the Book of Mormon as a missionary: Develop a deep love for the Book of Mormon during your mission. Make daily study of this sacred scripture a priority, pondering its teachings and applying them to your life. Share your testimony of the Book of Mormon with those you teach, inviting them to discover its truth for themselves. As you immerse yourself in the Book of Mormon, you'll find wisdom, comfort, and spiritual power. Your growing love for this book of scripture will bring you joy and strengthen your faith in Jesus Christ.

DATE: _____

MEMORIES MADE, TOUGH TIMES, & LESSONS LEARNED:

Stressed    Angry    Tired    Sad    Happy    Excited

_____
_____
_____
_____
_____
_____
_____
_____

What are you grateful for today? _____

*"Keeping divine commandments brings blessings, every time! Breaking divine commandments brings a loss of blessings, every time!" - Russell M. Nelson*

DATE: _____

MEMORIES MADE, TOUGH TIMES, & LESSONS LEARNED:

Stressed    Angry    Tired    Sad    Happy    Excited

_____
_____
_____
_____
_____
_____
_____
_____

Prompt of the day:

Personal Traditions: Have you developed any personal traditions or routines during your mission? Describe them and their significance.

_____
_____
_____
_____
_____

What are you grateful for today? _____

Strive for perfection while understanding it's a lifelong process. Maintain your integrity, live by the Spirit, and keep the commandments to stand blameless before God. Give Him your faith and loyalty each day. Remember that perfection is the goal, but it takes time to achieve. Be patient with yourself and others as you all progress towards this goal. You are doing AWESOME!

DATE: _____

MEMORIES MADE, TOUGH TIMES, & LESSONS LEARNED:

Stressed   Angry   Tired   Sad   Happy   Excited

_____
_____
_____
_____
_____
_____
_____
_____
_____

What are you grateful for today? _____

*"Daily immersion in the word of God is crucial for spiritual survival, especially in these days of increasing upheaval. As we feast on the words of Christ daily, the words of Christ will tell us how to respond to difficulties we never thought we would face." - Russell M. Nelson*

DATE: _____

MEMORIES MADE, TOUGH TIMES, & LESSONS LEARNED:

Stressed   Angry   Tired   Sad   Happy   Excited

_____
_____
_____
_____
_____
_____
_____
_____
_____

Prompt of the day:
Lessons Learned from Local Traditions: Write about lessons learned from local traditions and how they've broadened your view of worship and community.

_____
_____
_____
_____
_____

What are you grateful for today? _____

Communicate openly withcompanions and establish ground rules. Whew…this is one is HUGE! Talk about things early and often. Don't let frustrations bottle up. Consider setting aside a regular time each week (Sunday nights?) to sit down and chat about how things are going, from dirty dishes to annoying habits. Happy companions intentionally create organization, cleaning charts, and rules that everyone makes and lives by. Trust me, be open with each other and don't talk behind each other's backs!

DATE: _____

MEMORIES MADE, TOUGH TIMES, & LESSONS LEARNED:

Stressed  Angry  Tired  Sad  Happy  Excited

_____
_____
_____
_____
_____
_____
_____
_____

What are you grateful for today? _____

*"Salvation depends on the only TWO things that human beings can do well; and for the blessed opportunity of exercising those peculiar talents they are envied by the angels... Those two things are 1) to REPENT, and 2) to FORGIVE." - Hugh Nibley*

DATE: _____

MEMORIES MADE, TOUGH TIMES, & LESSONS LEARNED:

Stressed  Angry  Tired  Sad  Happy  Excited

_____
_____
_____
_____
_____
_____
_____
_____

Prompt of the day:
Impact of Service Projects: Share about a service project that particularly moved you or changed your perspective on service.

_____
_____
_____
_____

What are you grateful for today? _____

There are roots and there are fruits of missionary work. The "fruits" include the joy of witnessing people's lives change, make covenants, receive ordinances, and play a small part in bringing God's children back to Him. It's the Spirit that brings tears to your eyes as you realize how small you are and how wonderful God is. So, what are the "roots?" The roots of missionary work include prayer, fasting, studying, testifying, obedience, sacrifice, listening, loving, learning, acting, doing and covenant-keeping. There is a reason it is called missionary "work." Water the "roots" with hard work and by-and-by you will taste of the sweet fruits of your labor. And thank God for the privilege.

DATE: _____

MEMORIES MADE, TOUGH TIMES, & LESSONS LEARNED:

Stressed   Angry   Tired   Sad   Happy   Excited

_____
_____
_____
_____
_____
_____
_____
_____

What are you grateful for today? _____

"If we look to the world and follow its formulas for happiness, we will never know joy. The unrighteous may experience any number of emotions and sensations, but they will never experience joy! Joy is a gift for the faithful. It is the gift that comes from intentionally trying to live a righteous life, as taught by Jesus Christ." - Russell M. Nelson

DATE: _____

MEMORIES MADE, TOUGH TIMES, & LESSONS LEARNED:

Stressed   Angry   Tired   Sad   Happy   Excited

_____
_____
_____
_____
_____
_____
_____
_____

Prompt of the day:
The Impact of Missionary Work on Worldview: Write about how your missionary work has expanded your worldview and understanding of global interconnectedness.

_____
_____
_____
_____

What are you grateful for today? _____

Use good manners in public and when eating out. You are a representative of the Church always. And people are watching you—always! Smile and make eye contact with your server. Clearly say your order, and if you're unsure, ask questions politely. Order quickly or ask for more time, but don't keep the server or cashier waiting. Know how you like your food cooked. When served, say "thank you." Keep noise down to not disturb others. Put away your phones. Don't make a big mess and don't forget to leave a tip. Always treat those serving you with kindness and respect.

DATE: _____

MEMORIES MADE, TOUGH TIMES, & LESSONS LEARNED:

Stressed   Angry   Tired   Sad   Happy   Excited

_____
_____
_____
_____
_____
_____
_____
_____

What are you grateful for today? _____

*"All missionaries, younger and older, serve with the sole hope of making life better for other people." - Russell M. Nelson*

DATE: _____

MEMORIES MADE, TOUGH TIMES, & LESSONS LEARNED:

Stressed   Angry   Tired   Sad   Happy   Excited

_____
_____
_____
_____
_____
_____
_____
_____

Prompt of the day:

Dealing with Homesickness: Write about how you deal with homesickness, especially during important family dates or holidays.

_____
_____
_____
_____

What are you grateful for today? _____

Love and serve your companion. Strive to be your companion's friend, regardless of how well your personalities mesh. Encourage and support them without being critical, remembering that you are both giving the Lord your time to spread the gospel of Jesus Christ. Build a strong relationship founded on mutual respect, trust, and a shared commitment to the work. Look for ways to uplift and inspire your companion, and be quick to forgive and move past any differences. A loving, unified companionship will be a powerful tool in bringing others unto Christ.

DATE: _____

MEMORIES MADE, TOUGH TIMES, & LESSONS LEARNED:

Stressed  Angry  Tired  Sad  Happy  Excited

_____
_____
_____
_____
_____
_____
_____
_____
_____

What are you grateful for today? _____

*"I haven't met anyone who found the gospel later in life who didn't wish it could have been earlier." - Elder D. Todd Christofferson*

DATE: _____

MEMORIES MADE, TOUGH TIMES, & LESSONS LEARNED:

Stressed  Angry  Tired  Sad  Happy  Excited

_____
_____
_____
_____
_____
_____
_____
_____

Prompt of the day:
The Joy of Priesthood Blessings: Write about at time where you gave someone a priesthood blessing. What was that experience like?

_____
_____
_____
_____

What are you grateful for today? _____

As a missionary, strengthening your faith is essential for your personal well-being and your ability to effectively serve others. Engage in regular spiritual practices such as prayer, scripture study, and attending Church meetings. These activities have been shown to improve mental and physical health, foster better relationships, and increase overall happiness. Invite your companions and those you teach to join you in these faith-building practices, as sharing your spiritual journey can deepen your own conviction and create a supportive environment for growth. By making your faith a priority, you'll be better equipped to face challenges, find joy, and fulfill your divine purpose as a missionary.

DATE: _____

MEMORIES MADE, TOUGH TIMES, & LESSONS LEARNED:

Stressed   Angry   Tired   Sad   Happy   Excited

_____
_____
_____
_____
_____
_____
_____
_____

What are you grateful for today? _____

"Charity is the antidote to contention. Charity is the spiritual gift that helps us to cast off the natural man, who is selfish, defensive, prideful, and jealous. Charity is the principal characteristic of a true follower of Jesus Christ. Charity defines a peacemaker. When we humble ourselves before God and pray with all the energy of our hearts, God will grant us charity." - Russell M. Nelson

DATE: _____

MEMORIES MADE, TOUGH TIMES, & LESSONS LEARNED:

Stressed   Angry   Tired   Sad   Happy   Excited

_____
_____
_____
_____
_____
_____
_____

Prompt of the day:
Teaching Success Stories: Share a success story from your teaching efforts. What made this experience successful, and what did you learn?

_____
_____
_____
_____
_____

What are you grateful for today? _____

Jeff Olson, the creator of Live Happy, points out that it's the little adjustments made consistently over time that lead to real change. Just as a single greasy meal won't ruin your health, one healthy smoothie won't make you fit overnight. Similarly, a single workout session won't build your muscles instantly, nor will one good moment instantly strengthen a relationship or boost long-term happiness. True progress in overall well-being rarely happens in an instant; it requires steady and persistent effort. We created the acronym S.C.A.R.E.D. Small Changes Are Really Effective…Dude (or Daily).

DATE: _____

MEMORIES MADE, TOUGH TIMES, & LESSONS LEARNED:

| Stressed | Angry | Tired | Sad | Happy | Excited |
|----------|-------|-------|-----|-------|---------|

_____
_____
_____
_____
_____
_____
_____
_____

What are you grateful for today? _____

"Saints can be happy under every circumstance. We can feel joy even while having a bad day, a bad week, or even a bad year! My dear brothers and sisters, the joy we feel has little to do with the circumstances of our lives and everything to do with the focus of our lives." - Russell M. Nelson

DATE: _____

MEMORIES MADE, TOUGH TIMES, & LESSONS LEARNED:

| Stressed | Angry | Tired | Sad | Happy | Excited |
|----------|-------|-------|-----|-------|---------|

_____
_____
_____
_____
_____
_____
_____
_____

Prompt of the day:
Adapting to Different Worship Styles: Write about your experiences adapting to different worship styles and what you've learned from them.

_____
_____
_____
_____

What are you grateful for today? _____

As a missionary, make it a habit to express gratitude and appreciation for those who support and assist you in your efforts to share the gospel. Regularly thank your companions for their dedication, teamwork, and friendship. Show appreciation to members who offer their time, talents, and resources to help further the missionary work in their area. Acknowledge the kindness, hospitality, and assistance of those who welcome you into their homes or provide referrals. A sincere "thank you" can go a long way in strengthening relationships, fostering a spirit of unity, and demonstrating Christlike love. Remember that expressing gratitude is a powerful way to invite the Spirit and show others that you value and appreciate their contributions to the Lord's work.

DATE: _____

MEMORIES MADE, TOUGH TIMES, & LESSONS LEARNED:

Stressed   Angry   Tired   Sad   Happy   Excited

_____
_____
_____
_____
_____
_____
_____
_____
_____

What are you grateful for today? _____

*"If you have sincere questions about the gospel or the Church, as you choose to let God prevail, you will be led to find and understand the absolute, eternal truths that will guide your life and help you stay firmly on the covenant path." - Russell M. Nelson*

DATE: _____

MEMORIES MADE, TOUGH TIMES, & LESSONS LEARNED:

Stressed   Angry   Tired   Sad   Happy   Excited

_____
_____
_____
_____
_____
_____
_____
_____

Prompt of the day:

The Power of Listening: Reflect on a time when active listening played a crucial role in your missionary work.

_____
_____
_____
_____
_____

What are you grateful for today? _____

Remember that your primary role as a missionary is to help bring others, including your companion, closer to Christ. When your companion is struggling with obedience or other challenges, resist the temptation to judge or shame them. Instead, focus on creating an environment of love, understanding, and encouragement. Pray for your companion, and look for opportunities to share your testimony and to remind them of their divine worth and potential. Trust that as you extend Christlike love and compassion, your companion will be more likely to open their heart to the Savior's healing influence and to make positive changes in their life. When prompted, talk to your mission president for guidance.

DATE: _____

MEMORIES MADE, TOUGH TIMES, & LESSONS LEARNED:  Stressed   Angry   Tired   Sad   Happy   Excited

_____
_____
_____
_____
_____
_____
_____
_____

What are you grateful for today? _____

"As we strive to live the higher laws of Jesus Christ, our hearts and our very natures begin to change. The Savior lifts us above the pull of this fallen world by blessing us with greater charity, humility, generosity, kindness, self-discipline, peace, and rest." - Russell M. Nelson

DATE: _____

MEMORIES MADE, TOUGH TIMES, & LESSONS LEARNED:  Stressed   Angry   Tired   Sad   Happy   Excited

_____
_____
_____
_____
_____
_____
_____
_____

Prompt of the day:
Finding Commonality in Diversity: Reflect on moments when you found common ground with others despite cultural, linguistic, or other differences.

_____
_____
_____
_____

What are you grateful for today? _____

Remember to celebrate the individual milestones and achievements of local members and those you teach, both spiritual and secular. Recognize birthdays, special occasions, and the keeping of commitments, no matter how small or large. Show genuine happiness and support for their accomplishments. Your attentiveness to their individual journeys can strengthen your relationships and inspire continued growth.

DATE: _____

MEMORIES MADE, TOUGH TIMES, & LESSONS LEARNED:

Stressed   Angry   Tired   Sad   Happy   Excited

_____
_____
_____
_____
_____
_____
_____
_____

What are you grateful for today? _____

*"We are commanded by God to take this gospel to all the world. That is the cause that must unite us today. Only the gospel will save the world from the calamity of its own self-destruction. Only the gospel will unite men of all races and nationalities in peace. Only the gospel will bring joy, happiness, and salvation to the human family." - Ezra Taft Benson*

DATE: _____

MEMORIES MADE, TOUGH TIMES, & LESSONS LEARNED:

Stressed   Angry   Tired   Sad   Happy   Excited

_____
_____
_____
_____
_____
_____
_____
_____

Prompt of the day:
Building Lasting Relationships: Write about a relationship you've built during your mission that you believe will last beyond your missionary service.

_____
_____
_____
_____

What are you grateful for today? _____

As a missionary, cultivate self-compassion by treating yourself with the same kindness and understanding you would offer a good friend, particularly in challenging moments. Recognize that facing stress is a natural aspect of the mission journey, and it's normal to have ups and downs. Remind yourself that perfection is unattainable and unnecessary for growth and learning. Embracing your imperfections and viewing setbacks as opportunities to develop resilience can significantly reduce stress and foster a healthier, more forgiving self-attitude.

DATE: _____

MEMORIES MADE, TOUGH TIMES, & LESSONS LEARNED:

Stressed    Angry    Tired    Sad    Happy    Excited

_____
_____
_____
_____
_____
_____
_____
_____

What are you grateful for today? _____

*"The best antidote I know for worry is work. The best cure for weariness is the challenge of helping someone who is even more tired. One of the great ironies of life is this: He or she who serves almost always benefits more than he or she who is served." - Gordon B. Hinckley*

DATE: _____

MEMORIES MADE, TOUGH TIMES, & LESSONS LEARNED:

Stressed    Angry    Tired    Sad    Happy    Excited

_____
_____
_____
_____
_____
_____
_____
_____

Prompt of the day:

The Power of Simple Gestures: Share how simple gestures, whether given or received, have made a significant impact during your mission.

_____
_____
_____
_____

What are you grateful for today? _____

Observe then serve. When you've been invited over to someone's place for a meal, be quick to help out. Ask what they need help with, or just jump up and pitch in! This manner is super important! A great way to build a relationship and make a good first impression is to help out. It could be as simple as helping to set the table or fill glasses with water. And always clean up after yourself. Don't be the one relaxing while others are working. A little help goes a long way.

DATE: _____

MEMORIES MADE, TOUGH TIMES, & LESSONS LEARNED:

Stressed   Angry   Tired   Sad   Happy   Excited

_____
_____
_____
_____
_____
_____
_____
_____

What are you grateful for today? _____

*"If the Saints could realize things as they are when they are called to pass through trials, and to suffer what they call sacrifices, they would acknowledge them to be the greatest blessings that could be bestowed upon them...We are the happiest people when we have what are called trials; for then the Spirit of God is more abundantly bestowed upon the faithful." - Brigham Young*

DATE: _____

MEMORIES MADE, TOUGH TIMES, & LESSONS LEARNED:

Stressed   Angry   Tired   Sad   Happy   Excited

_____
_____
_____
_____
_____
_____
_____
_____

Prompt of the day:

Learning from Mistakes: Share a mistake you made on your mission and what you learned from it.

_____
_____
_____
_____
_____

What are you grateful for today? _____

The ripple effects of enhanced physical activity extend far beyond just fitness improvements. Research indicates that engaging in regular exercise can lead to a cascade of positive lifestyle changes, including healthier eating habits, increased productivity, more patience, lower stress levels, and even improved financial management. These interconnected benefits underscore the profound impact that physical well-being can have on various aspects of our lives, promoting a holistic approach to health and personal development.

DATE: _____

MEMORIES MADE, TOUGH TIMES, & LESSONS LEARNED:   Stressed   Angry   Tired   Sad   Happy   Excited

_____
_____
_____
_____
_____
_____
_____
_____
_____

What are you grateful for today? _____

"One of the things the Spirit has repeatedly impressed upon my mind...is how willing the Lord is to reveal His mind and will. The privilege of receiving revelation is one of the greatest gifts of God to His children. Through the manifestations of the Holy Ghost, the Lord will assist us in all our righteous pursuits." - Russell M. Nelson

DATE: _____

MEMORIES MADE, TOUGH TIMES, & LESSONS LEARNED:   Stressed   Angry   Tired   Sad   Happy   Excited

_____
_____
_____
_____
_____
_____
_____
_____
_____

Prompt of the day:
Embracing Moments of Quiet Reflection: Write about the importance and impact of moments of quiet reflection amidst the busyness of missionary work.

_____
_____
_____
_____

What are you grateful for today? _____

Pay attention to the significance of non-verbal cues in communication. Be attentive to body language, facial expressions, and other non-verbal signals that can convey important messages. Use these cues to enhance your understanding of others' feelings and needs, and to build rapport and trust. By being sensitive to these unspoken messages, you can communicate more effectively and compassionately.

DATE: _____

MEMORIES MADE, TOUGH TIMES, & LESSONS LEARNED:  Stressed  Angry  Tired  Sad  Happy  Excited

_____
_____
_____
_____
_____
_____
_____
_____
_____

What are you grateful for today? _____

*"I plead with you to be the men and young men the Lord needs you to be. Make your focus on daily repentance so integral to your life that you can exercise the priesthood with greater power than ever before. This is the only way you will keep yourself and your family spiritually safe in the challenging days ahead." - Russell M. Nelson*

DATE: _____

MEMORIES MADE, TOUGH TIMES, & LESSONS LEARNED:  Stressed  Angry  Tired  Sad  Happy  Excited

_____
_____
_____
_____
_____
_____
_____
_____

Prompt of the day:
Local Cuisine: Describe your experiences with the local cuisine. Have you found a new favorite food?

_____
_____
_____
_____

What are you grateful for today? _____

Pay attention to emotional signals. Just as a car's dashboard alerts you to various conditions, your emotions act as signals telling you when something needs attention. Stress, worry, sadness, disgust, and fear are crucial indicators that, when acknowledged, can help you better understand your needs and navigate life more effectively. As a missionary, when you feel stressed, pause and ask yourself what these emotional signals are telling you. By doing so, you can gain valuable insights and address the root causes of your stress.

DATE: _____

MEMORIES MADE, TOUGH TIMES, & LESSONS LEARNED:

Stressed   Angry   Tired   Sad   Happy   Excited

_____
_____
_____
_____
_____
_____
_____
_____

What are you grateful for today? _____

*"We need to reach out and extend our friendship to others regardless of whether they are interested in the gospel or not. We must not be too selective in identifying those we feel are worthy or appreciative of our attention. The spirit of true Christian fellowship must include everyone."* M. Russell Ballard

DATE: _____

MEMORIES MADE, TOUGH TIMES, & LESSONS LEARNED:

Stressed   Angry   Tired   Sad   Happy   Excited

_____
_____
_____
_____
_____
_____
_____
_____

Prompt of the day:
The Role of Patience in Building Faith: Reflect on how patience has been crucial in building your faith and the faith of others during your mission.

_____
_____
_____
_____

What are you grateful for today? _____

Understand that rejection is not a reflection of your worth in God's eyes. When faced with rejection, turn to the Lord and seek His love and validation, remembering that you are of infinite worth to Him. As a missionary, you may experience rejection on a daily basis, whether through doors slammed in your face or people who are not interested in your message. It's easy to internalize this rejection and feel discouraged, but it's crucial to remember that your value and identity are not determined by others' opinions. Instead, find your sense of worth in the knowledge that you are a beloved child of God, and that He sees your efforts and sacrifices. Pray for the strength to withstand rejection and for the ability to see yourself as God sees you.

DATE: _____

MEMORIES MADE, TOUGH TIMES, & LESSONS LEARNED:

Stressed   Angry   Tired   Sad   Happy   Excited

_____
_____
_____
_____
_____
_____
_____
_____

What are you grateful for today? _____

"Man is a spiritual being, a soul, and at some period of his life everyone is possessed with an irresistible desire to know his relationship to the Infinite. . . . There is something within him which urges him to rise above himself, to control his environment, to master the body and all things physical and live in a higher and more beautiful world." - David O. McKay

DATE: _____

MEMORIES MADE, TOUGH TIMES, & LESSONS LEARNED:

Stressed   Angry   Tired   Sad   Happy   Excited

_____
_____
_____
_____
_____
_____
_____
_____

Prompt of the day:
Spiritual Conversations with Strangers: Share an impactful spiritual conversation you had with a stranger.

_____
_____
_____
_____
_____

What are you grateful for today? _____

Prioritize your physical health and well-being by maintaining a balanced diet, exercising regularly, and getting sufficient sleep, as these factors play a crucial role in supporting your mental and emotional resilience. Recognize that the demands of missionary work can be taxing on both body and spirit, and that taking care of your physical health is essential for your overall well-being and effectiveness as a missionary. Make conscious choices to eat nutritious meals, engage in the daily exercise outlined in your missionary schedule, and adhere to a consistent sleep routine. As you do so, you will find that you have greater energy, focus, and spiritual strength to face the challenges of each day.

DATE: _____

MEMORIES MADE, TOUGH TIMES, & LESSONS LEARNED:

Stressed   Angry   Tired   Sad   Happy   Excited

_____
_____
_____
_____
_____
_____
_____
_____
_____

What are you grateful for today? _____

"You can never get enough of what you don't need, because what you don't need won't satisfy you." - Dallin H. Oaks

DATE: _____

MEMORIES MADE, TOUGH TIMES, & LESSONS LEARNED:

Stressed   Angry   Tired   Sad   Happy   Excited

_____
_____
_____
_____
_____
_____
_____
_____

Prompt of the day:
Witnessing the Impact of Service on the Community: Share observations of how service projects or acts of kindness have impacted the community you're serving.

_____
_____
_____
_____
_____

What are you grateful for today? _____

As a missionary, offer to help when you are a guest in someone's home. When invited to dinner or to share a message, show appreciation for their hospitality by asking how you can assist. Even if they initially decline, find a way to contribute, such as setting the table or washing dishes. Your thoughtfulness and willingness to serve will be remembered and can touch hearts. Hosting missionaries can be demanding, so your offer to help demonstrates your gratitude and recognition of their efforts. By serving others, you exemplify Christlike love and may open doors to further gospel conversations.

DATE: _____

MEMORIES MADE, TOUGH TIMES, & LESSONS LEARNED:

Stressed    Angry    Tired    Sad    Happy    Excited

_____
_____
_____
_____
_____
_____
_____
_____
_____

What are you grateful for today? _____

"You can show your reverence for the book as you quote from it and demonstrate your Nephi-like ability to 'liken' the scriptures. We can, unapologetically, showcase the Book of Mormon much better than we now do. It is, after all, 'a marvelous work and a wonder.'" - Neal A. Maxwell

DATE: _____

MEMORIES MADE, TOUGH TIMES, & LESSONS LEARNED:

Stressed    Angry    Tired    Sad    Happy    Excited

_____
_____
_____
_____
_____
_____
_____
_____

Prompt of the day:

Adapting to Local Customs: Write about your experience adapting to a local custom that was initially foreign to you.

_____
_____
_____
_____
_____

What are you grateful for today? _____

Focus on the BIG 3: Research suggests that whether a stressor results in a crisis depends on three factors: resources, relationships, and prior experiences with that stressor. As a missionary, focus on building the resources you have to lean on and nurturing relationships with others. Especially Jesus. He can take your humble heart and change it in wonderful ways. If you have managed challenges in the past, you'll be better equipped to handle stresses because you know what to do and understand that you can survive. Prioritize these BIG 3 throughout your mission and life for improved stress management.

DATE: _____

MEMORIES MADE, TOUGH TIMES, & LESSONS LEARNED:

Stressed   Angry   Tired   Sad   Happy   Excited

_____
_____
_____
_____
_____
_____
_____
_____
_____

What are you grateful for today? _____

"During the sacrament, which I call the heart of the Sabbath, I have found that after I pray for forgiveness of sins, it is instructive for me to ask Heavenly Father, 'Father, is there more?' When we are yielded and still, our minds can be directed to something more we may need to change—something that is limiting our capacity to receive spiritual guidance or even healing and help." - Neill F. Marriott

DATE: _____

MEMORIES MADE, TOUGH TIMES, & LESSONS LEARNED:

Stressed   Angry   Tired   Sad   Happy   Excited

_____
_____
_____
_____
_____
_____
_____
_____

Prompt of the day:
The Challenge and Reward of Forgiveness: Write about a personal challenge related to forgiveness you've faced on your mission and the rewards of overcoming it.

_____
_____
_____
_____
_____

What are you grateful for today? _____

In the scriptures, we are commanded to do only two things "always." First, we are commanded to "pray always." (3 Nephi 18:15; D&C 31:12). The second is found in the sacrament prayer. We covenant to "always remember Him." (D&C 20:77;79). Both have to do with the Godhead—praying and remembering. Make time to study the definition of "prayer" in the Bible Dictionary. You will learn that it is a form of work. Learn to talk with God. And may we never offer a prayer where we only mention our Savior's name as we close it. Express your deep heartfelt gratitude for Jesus Christ. Occasionally offer a prayer of only gratitude. Don't ask for anything.

DATE: _____

MEMORIES MADE, TOUGH TIMES, & LESSONS LEARNED:

Stressed   Angry   Tired   Sad   Happy   Excited

_____
_____
_____
_____
_____
_____
_____
_____

What are you grateful for today? _____

"*We will attain our exaltation in the Celestial Kingdom only on the condition that we share with our Father's other children the blessings of the Gospel of Jesus Christ and observe the commandments that will enrich our lives here and hereafter.*" - *George Albert Smith*

DATE: _____

MEMORIES MADE, TOUGH TIMES, & LESSONS LEARNED:

Stressed   Angry   Tired   Sad   Happy   Excited

_____
_____
_____
_____
_____
_____
_____
_____

Prompt of the day:
Reflections on Solitude: Reflect on moments of solitude and what they've taught you about yourself and your mission.

_____
_____
_____
_____

What are you grateful for today? _____

It's good to be grateful. President Henry B. Eyring once said that we should never fail to thank those who have taught us well. Whenever anyone does anything kind, be sure to express gratitude. A handwritten note is awesome, but if that's not doable, just send a sincere text pronto. Receive a gift from someone or a package in the mail from your parents? Make sure to let them know the next time you talk with them. Sooner is better, but some research suggests thanking someone long after it occurred still makes an impact— the person may feel happy that you still remembered the kindness long after it occurred. Gratitude is the key!

DATE: _____

MEMORIES MADE, TOUGH TIMES, & LESSONS LEARNED:   Stressed   Angry   Tired   Sad   Happy   Excited

_____
_____
_____
_____
_____
_____
_____
_____

What are you grateful for today? _____

*"...to effectively serve others we must see them through...Heavenly Father's eyes. Only then can we begin to comprehend the true worth of a soul. Only then can we sense the love that Heavenly Father has for all of His children. Only then can we sense the Savior's caring concern for them. We cannot completely fulfill our covenant obligation to mourn with those who mourn and comfort those who stand in need of comfort unless we see them through God's eyes." - Dale G. Renlund*

DATE: _____

MEMORIES MADE, TOUGH TIMES, & LESSONS LEARNED:   Stressed   Angry   Tired   Sad   Happy   Excited

_____
_____
_____
_____
_____
_____
_____
_____

Prompt of the day:

The Dynamics of Missionary Teamwork: Reflect on the dynamics of working as part of a missionary team, including the challenges and triumphs.

_____
_____
_____
_____

What are you grateful for today? _____

When discussing the Atonement of Jesus Christ, emphasize that Jesus Christ Himself is the source of healing and forgiveness, not some abstract concept. Connect the doctrine of the Atonement directly to the Savior. Teach investigators that it is through Jesus Christ's sacrifice that we can be forgiven, find peace, and overcome challenges. Avoid shorthand phrases like "the Atonement" that omit His name. Instead, talk about "the atoning sacrifice of Jesus Christ." This reinforces His role as our Redeemer and invites people to build a personal relationship with Him.

DATE: _____

MEMORIES MADE, TOUGH TIMES, & LESSONS LEARNED:

Stressed   Angry   Tired   Sad   Happy   Excited

_____
_____
_____
_____
_____
_____
_____

What are you grateful for today? _____

*"Contention drives away the Spirit—every time. Contention reinforces the false notion that confrontation is the way to resolve differences; but it never is. Contention is a choice. Peacemaking is a choice. You have your agency to choose contention or reconciliation. I urge you to choose to be a peacemaker, now and always." - Russell M. Nelson*

DATE: _____

MEMORIES MADE, TOUGH TIMES, & LESSONS LEARNED:

Stressed   Angry   Tired   Sad   Happy   Excited

_____
_____
_____
_____
_____
_____
_____

Prompt of the day:
Elder or Sister's Influence: Write about an Elder or Sister whose influence has been particularly meaningful to you.

_____
_____
_____
_____

What are you grateful for today? _____

Get outside yourself. As a missionary, it's easy to get caught up in your own challenges. Take a step back and focus on serving others. Bake cookies for investigators, volunteer in the community, or help a fellow missionary. While you shouldn't overextend yourself, taking time to serve others can bring peace and satisfaction. It helps you see the bigger picture and find greater meaning in your mission. By focusing on others, you'll gain a fresh perspective on your own struggles. Remember President Hinckley's father's advice to him as a young missionary: "Forget yourself and go to work."

DATE: _____

MEMORIES MADE, TOUGH TIMES, & LESSONS LEARNED:

Stressed   Angry   Tired   Sad   Happy   Excited

_____
_____
_____
_____
_____
_____
_____
_____

What are you grateful for today? _____

"When our Savior Jesus Christ looks upon us, He sees and understands the pain and burden of our sins. He sees our addictions and challenges. He sees our struggles and afflictions of any kind—and He is filled with compassion toward us." - Peter F. Meurs

DATE: _____

MEMORIES MADE, TOUGH TIMES, & LESSONS LEARNED:

Stressed   Angry   Tired   Sad   Happy   Excited

_____
_____
_____
_____
_____
_____
_____
_____

Prompt of the day:
Personal Growth Through Daily Challenges: Share how facing and overcoming daily challenges during your mission has contributed to your personal growth.

_____
_____
_____
_____
_____

What are you grateful for today? _____

Reread your patriarchal blessing. Remember who you are but more importantly remember who God is and your relationship with Him. He will answer the prayers of His people, especially His missionaries. Look back on the tender mercies and mini miracles. Jesus is in the very details of your life and the lives of those you teach. Your character will change but only as you go all-in and obey the first and second great commandments: Love God with all your heart, might, mind, and strength. And love your neighbor, companion, other missionaries, members, investigators, and others. Let your guard down, give Him everything because He has given you everything already. And reread your patriarchal blessing regularly for that reminder. You are not a mere mortal. You are a divine being with Heavenly Parents.

DATE: _____

MEMORIES MADE, TOUGH TIMES, & LESSONS LEARNED:

Stressed   Angry   Tired   Sad   Happy   Excited

_____
_____
_____
_____
_____
_____
_____
_____

What are you grateful for today? _____

*"The key to successful missionary work is a close relationship between the missionaries and the members. Creating an environment in working with members that will bring more into the Church." - Richard G. Scott*

DATE: _____

MEMORIES MADE, TOUGH TIMES, & LESSONS LEARNED:

Stressed   Angry   Tired   Sad   Happy   Excited

_____
_____
_____
_____
_____
_____
_____
_____

Prompt of the day:

Challenges in Teamwork: Reflect on a challenge you faced in teamwork, either with your companion or in a group, and how you resolved it.

_____
_____
_____
_____
_____

What are you grateful for today? _____

Do encourage and facilitate local members' involvement in teaching and leadership roles within missionary activities. Invite members to lessons frequently, as this is one of the best ways to do missionary work. Try to avoid "burning out" the members. When you do have lessons with members, plan ahead of time what you will be teaching so that the member feels comfortable in the lesson. Don't overburden local members with constant requests for assistance or participation. Be mindful of their commitments and personal circumstances. Pray to know when and how to involve them appropriately.

DATE: _____

MEMORIES MADE, TOUGH TIMES, & LESSONS LEARNED:    Stressed   Angry   Tired   Sad   Happy   Excited

_____
_____
_____
_____
_____
_____
_____
_____

## What are you grateful for today?

*"The first thing you will do when an investigator tells you he or she had not read and prayed about the Book of Mormon is be devastated! ... Much of the time we are just too casual about all of this. This is eternal life. This is the salvation of the children of God. Eternity hangs in the balance. ... It is the most important path this investigator will ever walk. But if he or she doesn't know that, at least you do! ... So take control of this situation. Teach with power and authority, and then be devastated if the first steps toward commandment-keeping and covenant-keeping have not been successfully begun." - Jeffrey R. Holland*

DATE: _____

MEMORIES MADE, TOUGH TIMES, & LESSONS LEARNED:    Stressed   Angry   Tired   Sad   Happy   Excited

_____
_____
_____
_____
_____
_____
_____
_____

## Prompt of the day:

The Influence of Missionary Work on Prayer Life: Write about how your missionary work has influenced and deepened your prayer life.

_____
_____
_____
_____

What are you grateful for today? _____

It's natural to feel tired, both physically and emotionally, during your mission. Listen to your body and give yourself permission to rest when needed. Prioritize your health by eating well, exercising regularly, and getting enough sleep. Seek out opportunities for rejuvenation, such as spending time in nature or engaging in activities that bring you joy. Remember that it's okay to take breaks and care for yourself, as your well-being is essential to your effectiveness as a missionary.

DATE: _____

MEMORIES MADE, TOUGH TIMES, & LESSONS LEARNED:

Stressed  Angry  Tired  Sad  Happy  Excited

_____
_____
_____
_____
_____
_____
_____
_____

What are you grateful for today? _____

"*The voices and pressures of the world are engaging and numerous. But too many voices are deceptive, seductive, and can pull us off the covenant path. To avoid the inevitable heartbreak that follows, I plead with you today to counter the lure of the world by making time for the Lord in your life—each and every day.*" - Russell M. Nelson

DATE: _____

MEMORIES MADE, TOUGH TIMES, & LESSONS LEARNED:

Stressed  Angry  Tired  Sad  Happy  Excited

_____
_____
_____
_____
_____
_____
_____
_____

Prompt of the day:
The Role of Faith in Everyday Life: How has your mission deepened your understanding of the role of faith in everyday life?

_____
_____
_____
_____

What are you grateful for today? _____

Do promote and encourage family involvement in church activities and missionary work, strengthening family bonds. The family is one of the most important units in God's plan. Create a huge emphasis on this when you are teaching, or when you are with members. It is vital! Don't neglect the importance of family in your teachings and interactions. Recognize and respect the unique challenges and dynamics of each family, and strive to support and strengthen them in their spiritual journey.

DATE: _____

MEMORIES MADE, TOUGH TIMES, & LESSONS LEARNED:

Stressed  Angry  Tired  Sad  Happy  Excited

_____
_____
_____
_____
_____
_____
_____
_____

What are you grateful for today? _____

*"Warn them that they will encounter people who pick which commandments they will keep and ignore others that they choose to break. I call this the cafeteria approach to obedience. This practice of picking and choosing will not work. It will lead to misery." - Russell M. Nelson*

DATE: _____

MEMORIES MADE, TOUGH TIMES, & LESSONS LEARNED:

Stressed  Angry  Tired  Sad  Happy  Excited

_____
_____
_____
_____
_____
_____
_____
_____

Prompt of the day:
Developing Empathy Through Service: Reflect on how serving others during your mission has helped develop your empathy and understanding.

_____
_____
_____
_____

What are you grateful for today? _____

Earn others' trust. This is critical for the work to move forward. Whether it's a companion, mission president, church leader, member or those you teach. The foundation of all relationships is trust. If someone shares something in confidence. Be respectful and keep it 100% confidential. Keep secrets and what others say confidential unless there is a serious safety risk or there are matters of disobedience. Pay attention to the Spirit and the nudges it offers. Trust not only forms the foundation of relationships in the mission field but the foundation of romantic and all other relationships. Trust is slowly earned and easily burned. Breaking trust strains relationships—especially those you are living with or serve closely with. Strive to embody the loyalty and trustworthiness you seek in others.

DATE: _____

MEMORIES MADE, TOUGH TIMES, & LESSONS LEARNED:   Stressed   Angry   Tired   Sad   Happy   Excited

_____
_____
_____
_____
_____
_____
_____
_____

What are you grateful for today? _____


*"Even if everyone is doing it, wrong is never right....Rationalization is one of the real obstacles to obedience." - Russell M. Nelson*


DATE: _____

MEMORIES MADE, TOUGH TIMES, & LESSONS LEARNED:   Stressed   Angry   Tired   Sad   Happy   Excited

_____
_____
_____
_____
_____
_____
_____
_____

Prompt of the day:
Observations of Local Faith Practices: Share your observations of local faith practices and what you've learned from them.

_____
_____
_____
_____

What are you grateful for today? _____

Be mindful of your nonverbal cues—voice tone, facial expressions, and body language—as they greatly impact how others perceive you. Be aware of your tone, as it may come across as harsh or snarky. Seek input from companions and others who care about you and be open to improvement. There's nothing wrong with being yourself; the key is ensuring your external presentation aligns with your true self. If people often misunderstand you, it could be due to your tone or body language. Exercising humility and embracing feedback helps make small adjustments, and becoming more Christlike.

DATE: _____

MEMORIES MADE, TOUGH TIMES, & LESSONS LEARNED:

Stressed   Angry   Tired   Sad   Happy   Excited

_____
_____
_____
_____
_____
_____
_____
_____

What are you grateful for today? _____

*"As you think celestial, your heart will gradually change. You will want to pray more often and more sincerely. Please don't let your prayers sound like a shopping list. The Lord's perspective transcends your mortal wisdom. His response to your prayers may surprise you and will help you to think celestial."* - Russell M. Nelson

DATE: _____

MEMORIES MADE, TOUGH TIMES, & LESSONS LEARNED:

Stressed   Angry   Tired   Sad   Happy   Excited

_____
_____
_____
_____
_____
_____
_____
_____

Prompt of the day:
The Role of Faith in Overcoming Language Barriers: Share experiences where faith played a key role in overcoming language barriers and facilitating communication.

_____
_____
_____
_____
_____

What are you grateful for today? _____

Find joy in the miracles of missionary work: Keep your eyes open for the daily miracles that occur during your missionary service. Recognize the hand of God in the lives of those you teach, in the answers to your prayers, and in the growth of your own testimony. Celebrate the small victories and the moments of divine intervention. As you acknowledge and appreciate these miracles, you'll find increased joy and gratitude in your missionary work. Remember that you are part of a marvelous work and a wonder, guided by the hand of the Lord.

DATE: _____

MEMORIES MADE, TOUGH TIMES, & LESSONS LEARNED:

Stressed   Angry   Tired   Sad   Happy   Excited

_____
_____
_____
_____
_____
_____
_____
_____

What are you grateful for today? _____

*"Never let your faith be difficult to detect." - J. Reuben Clark*

DATE: _____

MEMORIES MADE, TOUGH TIMES, & LESSONS LEARNED:

Stressed   Angry   Tired   Sad   Happy   Excited

_____
_____
_____
_____
_____
_____
_____
_____

Prompt of the day:
Maintaining Balance: Write about how you strive to maintain a balance between missionary work, personal time, and rest.

_____
_____
_____
_____

What are you grateful for today? _____

Find strength in your companion and others. Your companion and other missionaries can be a great source of strength during challenging times. When you feel discouraged, turn to them for support. Share your feelings, listen to their insights, and pray together. Build each other up and focus on the positive. Remember that you're not alone in this work; lean on the love and encouragement of those around you, and together you can face any challenge with faith.

DATE: _____

MEMORIES MADE, TOUGH TIMES, & LESSONS LEARNED:

Stressed  Angry  Tired  Sad  Happy  Excited

_____
_____
_____
_____
_____
_____
_____
_____

What are you grateful for today? _____

*"When the Spirit is present, people are not offended when you share your feelings about the gospel."* - M. Russell Ballard

DATE: _____

MEMORIES MADE, TOUGH TIMES, & LESSONS LEARNED:

Stressed  Angry  Tired  Sad  Happy  Excited

_____
_____
_____
_____
_____
_____
_____
_____

Prompt of the day:
Adapting to Mission Life's Routine: Write about the process of adapting to the routine of mission life and how it has shaped your daily practices.

_____
_____
_____
_____
_____

What are you grateful for today? _____

Sister Emily Belle Freeman once shared an experience about a missionary who really struggled his first 6 months or so. He decided to petition the Lord repeatedly until he received answers. He set a timer every 15 minutes, starting at 6:30am and prayed for help and answers to his questions to show the Lord his sincerity. On the 43rd prayer of the day, He felt the Spirit say, "You have been praying all day, but the focus has only been on yourself. Try praying for someone else and serve someone else." In his quest to know answers for himself he wasn't focusing on others like Jesus did. He was consumed only with himself. He decided to forget himself and serve and love others and expect nothing in return. This wasn't a bargain with the Lord, this wasn't "I'll try losing myself, Lord, and only focus on helping others IF you'll bless me with answers to my questions and concerns." He decided to go all in, no bargaining or begging, and in his compassionate quest to bless, he was blessed with promptings to help, lift, serve, teach and testify. His testimony as a missionary grew slowly over time.

DATE: _____

MEMORIES MADE, TOUGH TIMES, & LESSONS LEARNED:  Stressed  Angry  Tired  Sad  Happy  Excited

_____
_____
_____
_____
_____
_____
_____
_____

What are you grateful for today? _____

*"It is important for you to know who you are and who you may become. It is more important than what you do, even as vital as your work is and will be....Your life will be a blessed and balanced experience if you first honor your identity and priority." - Russell M. Nelson*

DATE: _____

MEMORIES MADE, TOUGH TIMES, & LESSONS LEARNED:  Stressed  Angry  Tired  Sad  Happy  Excited

_____
_____
_____
_____
_____
_____
_____
_____

Prompt of the day:

Strengthening Testimony: Reflect on a specific experience that significantly strengthened your testimony.

_____
_____
_____
_____

What are you grateful for today? _____

Show loyalty to the Lord by sustaining His chosen leaders. The Lord inspires and empowers those He calls to lead His children. Pray for your leaders and sustain them, knowing that the Lord is pleased with all who magnify their callings, regardless of their visibility. Have faith that the Lord will bless you as you support and follow His servants—even though they are imperfect. Occasionally, you may struggle with a leader. In Adjusting to Missionary Life it states, "realize that leaders are human. If we think leaders are supposed to be much better than other people, we will become disappointed and become critical." Look for the good in others and pray for charity and patience!

DATE: _____

MEMORIES MADE, TOUGH TIMES, & LESSONS LEARNED:

Stressed   Angry   Tired   Sad   Happy   Excited

_____
_____
_____
_____
_____
_____
_____
_____

What are you grateful for today? _____

"Let us never lose sight of what the Lord is doing for us now. He is making His temples more accessible. He is accelerating the pace at which we are building temples. He is increasing our ability to help gather Israel. He is also making it easier for each of us to become spiritually refined. I promise that increased time in the temple will bless your life in ways nothing else can." - Russell M. Nelson

DATE: _____

MEMORIES MADE, TOUGH TIMES, & LESSONS LEARNED:

Stressed   Angry   Tired   Sad   Happy   Excited

_____
_____
_____
_____
_____
_____
_____
_____

Prompt of the day:

The Significance of Missionary Work in Personal Testimony: Reflect on how your missionary work has deepened or reshaped your personal testimony.

_____
_____
_____
_____

What are you grateful for today? _____

Center your teaching on the Atonement of Jesus Christ, as it is the central doctrine of the gospel and the foundation of all other truths. Help investigators understand that through Christ's sacrifice, they can overcome sin, find hope, and return to their Heavenly Father. The Atonement is the "good news" that death and hell can be escaped, mistakes and sins can be overcome, and everyone has the opportunity to become clean and pure, returning to the presence of God. Emphasize this message of hope and salvation in all your teachings. The center of all your teaching is the focus on Jesus Christ.

DATE: _____

MEMORIES MADE, TOUGH TIMES, & LESSONS LEARNED:   Stressed   Angry   Tired   Sad   Happy   Excited

_____
_____
_____
_____
_____
_____
_____

What are you grateful for today? _____

*"All missionaries teach and testify of the Savior. The spiritual darkness in the world makes the light of Jesus Christ needed more than ever. Everyone deserves the chance to know about the restored gospel of Jesus Christ. Every person deserves to know where they can find the hope and peace that [pass] all understanding." - Russell M. Nelson*

DATE: _____

MEMORIES MADE, TOUGH TIMES, & LESSONS LEARNED:   Stressed   Angry   Tired   Sad   Happy   Excited

_____
_____
_____
_____
_____
_____
_____

Prompt of the day:
Cultural Exchange: Have you taught someone about your own culture? Describe that experience and its impact.

_____
_____
_____
_____

What are you grateful for today? _____

Be on time. This is a HUGE life lesson as well as missionary lesson! Use a schedule, reminders, and alarms. Learn to leave early for most everything in life. If you're running behind, stuck in traffic or know you'll be late, tell those waiting ASAP and thank them and apologize when you arrive. If you're late for church, slip in quietly. If being late turns into a habit, consider some tweaks in your routines like wake-up time or drive time. Remember, everyone's time is valuable, not just yours. Punctuality shows good time management, responsibility, and consideration for others. Strive to exemplify this virtue as a missionary representing the Lord.

DATE: _____

MEMORIES MADE, TOUGH TIMES, & LESSONS LEARNED:

Stressed    Angry    Tired    Sad    Happy    Excited

_____
_____
_____
_____
_____
_____
_____
_____

What are you grateful for today? _____

*"I promise that as you increase your capacity to receive revelation, the Lord will bless you with increased direction for your life and with boundless gifts of the Spirit." - Russell M. Nelson*

DATE: _____

MEMORIES MADE, TOUGH TIMES, & LESSONS LEARNED:

Stressed    Angry    Tired    Sad    Happy    Excited

_____
_____
_____
_____
_____
_____
_____
_____

Prompt of the day:
Looking back: Write about advice you would give to priests who are getting ready to serve missions. What would you tell them and why?

_____
_____
_____
_____
_____

What are you grateful for today? _____

Take your action plans to the Lord, whether it involves finding new ways to share the gospel, improving your teaching skills, or working on personal growth. Dedicate time and effort to making progress, just as you would to any other important task. Celebrate small victories along the way and remain committed to your goals, even when progress seems slow. As a missionary, your time is dedicated to the Lord's work, so make sure that your efforts to overcome discouragement are focused on becoming a more effective instrument in His hands. Set aside time each day to work on your plan, and be diligent in your efforts, trusting that the Lord will magnify your abilities as you strive to serve Him.

DATE: _____

MEMORIES MADE, TOUGH TIMES, & LESSONS LEARNED:  Stressed  Angry  Tired  Sad  Happy  Excited

_____
_____
_____
_____
_____
_____
_____
_____

What are you grateful for today? _____

"There are several reasons for bearing testimony. One is that when you declare the truth, it will bring an echo, a memory, even if it is an unconscious memory to the investigator, that they have heard this truth before—and of course they have. A missionary's testimony invokes a great legacy of testimony dating back to the councils in heaven before this world was. There, in an earlier place, these same people heard this same plan outlined and heard there the role that Jesus Christ would play in their salvation..." - Jeffrey R. Holland

DATE: _____

MEMORIES MADE, TOUGH TIMES, & LESSONS LEARNED:  Stressed  Angry  Tired  Sad  Happy  Excited

_____
_____
_____
_____
_____
_____
_____
_____

Prompt of the day:

Zone Conference Insights: Reflect on a recent zone conference or meeting. What did you learn, and how do you plan to implement this in your mission work?

_____
_____
_____
_____

What are you grateful for today? _____

Stay positive: Maintain a positive attitude, even when faced with difficulties. Your optimism will not only uplift those around you but also help you find joy in the journey. Positivity is a choice, and it can make a significant difference in how you experience your mission. Things won't always go the way you planned, and that is to be expected. Look for the good in every situation and focus on the blessings and opportunities that come your way. Your positive attitude will not only make your mission more enjoyable but also make you a more effective instrument in the Lord's hands.

DATE: _____

MEMORIES MADE, TOUGH TIMES, & LESSONS LEARNED:

Stressed　Angry　Tired　Sad　Happy　Excited

_____
_____
_____
_____
_____
_____
_____
_____
_____

What are you grateful for today? _____

*"A pivotal spiritual attribute is that of self-mastery—the strength to place reason over appetite. Self-mastery builds a strong conscience. And your conscience determines your moral responses in difficult, tempting, and trying situations." - Russell M. Nelson*

DATE: _____

MEMORIES MADE, TOUGH TIMES, & LESSONS LEARNED:

Stressed　Angry　Tired　Sad　Happy　Excited

_____
_____
_____
_____
_____
_____
_____
_____

Prompt of the day:
Learning from Failure: Write about a time when what seemed like a failure turned into a learning opportunity during your mission.

_____
_____
_____
_____
_____

What are you grateful for today? _____

Embrace boredom and downtime as a skill. Many of us automatically reach for our phones when we become bored, whether we are with others or alone. Instead of reaching for your phone when you're bored, try catching yourself and just be still for a few minutes. Take a few deep breaths and spend a few minutes with uninterrupted thinking. Some research even suggests free-time and boredom aids brain function, sparking solutions, boosting mental health, unveiling new hobbies, clarifying thoughts, and promoting mindfulness. A few minutes of downtime daily yields numerous positive benefits. Take lunch and dinner breaks as an opportunity to rest.

DATE: _____

MEMORIES MADE, TOUGH TIMES, & LESSONS LEARNED:  Stressed  Angry  Tired  Sad  Happy  Excited

_____
_____
_____
_____
_____
_____
_____
_____

What are you grateful for today? _____

*"Our Heavenly Father is more liberal in His views, and boundless in His mercies and blessings, than we are ready to believe or receive; and, at the same time, is more terrible to the workers of iniquity, more awful in the executions of His punishments, and more ready to detect every false way, than we are apt to suppose Him to be." - Joseph Smith*

DATE: _____

MEMORIES MADE, TOUGH TIMES, & LESSONS LEARNED:  Stressed  Angry  Tired  Sad  Happy  Excited

_____
_____
_____
_____
_____
_____
_____
_____

Prompt of the day:
Personal Reflections on Conversion: Reflect on your personal journey of conversion and how it has evolved during your mission.

_____
_____
_____
_____

What are you grateful for today? _____

Serve others by focusing on their needs, offering kind words, acts of charity, or friendship. Shifting your attention to those you minister to can help alleviate feelings of discomfort and strengthen your sense of purpose as a missionary. Look for opportunities to uplift and support your companion, investigators, and members of the community. By immersing yourself in the work of serving others, you will find joy and fulfillment in your missionary efforts and be better equipped to handle the challenges of adjusting to missionary life.

DATE: _____

MEMORIES MADE, TOUGH TIMES, & LESSONS LEARNED:   Stressed   Angry   Tired   Sad   Happy   Excited

_____
_____
_____
_____
_____
_____
_____
_____

What are you grateful for today? _____

"*Every woman and every man who makes covenants with God and keeps those covenants, and who participates worthily in priesthood ordinances, has direct access to the power of God. Those who are endowed in the house of the Lord receive a gift of God's priesthood power by virtue of their covenant, along with a gift of knowledge to know how to draw upon that power.*" - *Russell M. Nelson*

DATE: _____

MEMORIES MADE, TOUGH TIMES, & LESSONS LEARNED:   Stressed   Angry   Tired   Sad   Happy   Excited

_____
_____
_____
_____
_____
_____
_____
_____

Prompt of the day:
Reflect on a Leader: Write about an influential leader you have met and admire on your mission. Write about the impact the leader has had on you.

_____
_____
_____
_____

What are you grateful for today? _____

Recognize the profound impact of small, everyday acts of kindness. Whether it's a simple gesture of service to your companion, such as shining their shoes or preparing breakfast, or a thoughtful deed for a member or friend, these seemingly minor actions can build goodwill and strengthen relationships. Your consistent efforts to serve and care for others will leave a lasting impression.

DATE: _____

MEMORIES MADE, TOUGH TIMES, & LESSONS LEARNED: Stressed   Angry   Tired   Sad   Happy   Excited

_____
_____
_____
_____
_____
_____
_____
_____

What are you grateful for today? _____

*"The Lord will bless you with miracles if you believe in Him, 'doubting nothing.' Do the spiritual work to seek miracles. Prayerfully ask God to help you exercise that kind of faith...Few things will accelerate your spiritual momentum more than realizing the Lord is helping you to move a mountain in your life." - Russell M. Nelson*

DATE: _____

MEMORIES MADE, TOUGH TIMES, & LESSONS LEARNED: Stressed   Angry   Tired   Sad   Happy   Excited

_____
_____
_____
_____
_____
_____
_____
_____

Prompt of the day:
The Importance of Patience: How have you seen yourself grow since the beginning of your mission? Consider aspects such as spiritual maturity, resilience, and interpersonal skills.

_____
_____
_____
_____
_____

What are you grateful for today? _____

First impressions are vital as missionaries. Whether teaching investigators, meeting new members, or introducing yourself in any setting, start strong. Confidently make an excellent first impression by shaking hands firmly, smiling, making eye contact, and clearly stating your name and calling. A positive initial impression helps you be taken seriously from the start. Master the art of a self-assured self-introduction, even if it feels awkward at first. This simple skill, when practiced, significantly shapes how others perceive you as a representative of the Lord's Church. Nail that critical first moment by exuding confidence and warmth.

DATE: _____

MEMORIES MADE, TOUGH TIMES, & LESSONS LEARNED:

Stressed    Angry    Tired    Sad    Happy    Excited

_____
_____
_____
_____
_____
_____
_____
_____
_____

What are you grateful for today? _____

"When we choose Heavenly Father to be our God and when we can feel the Savior's Atonement working in our lives, we will be filled with joy... every time we forgive someone or ask for forgiveness, we can feel joy. Every day that you and I choose to live celestial laws, every day that we keep our covenants and help others to do the same, joy will be ours." - Russell M. Nelson

DATE: _____

MEMORIES MADE, TOUGH TIMES, & LESSONS LEARNED:

Stressed    Angry    Tired    Sad    Happy    Excited

_____
_____
_____
_____
_____
_____
_____
_____

Prompt of the day:

Building Interpersonal Relationships: Share insights on building strong interpersonal relationships during your mission and their impact on your work.

_____
_____
_____
_____
_____

What are you grateful for today? _____

Cultivate a love for the Savior as a missionary: Make your mission a time to deepen your personal relationship with Jesus Christ. Study His life and teachings, striving to understand His character and emulate His example. Feel His love for you and for those you serve. As you cultivate a genuine love for the Savior, you'll find greater joy and purpose in your missionary work. Your love for Christ will shine through in your words and actions, inviting others to come unto Him and experience His redeeming grace.

DATE: _____

MEMORIES MADE, TOUGH TIMES, & LESSONS LEARNED:

Stressed   Angry   Tired   Sad   Happy   Excited

_____
_____
_____
_____
_____
_____
_____
_____

What are you grateful for today? _____

"When you face adversity, you can be led to ask many questions. Some serve a useful purpose; others do not. To ask, Why does this have to happen to me? Why do I have to suffer this, now? What have I done to cause this? will lead you into blind alleys. It really does no good to ask questions that reflect opposition to the will of God. Rather ask, What am I to do? What am I to learn from this experience? What am I to change? Whom am I to help? How can I remember my many blessings in times of trial?" - Richard G. Scott

DATE: _____

MEMORIES MADE, TOUGH TIMES, & LESSONS LEARNED:

Stressed   Angry   Tired   Sad   Happy   Excited

_____
_____
_____
_____
_____
_____
_____

Prompt of the day:

Impact of Technology in Missionary Work: Reflect on how technology has impacted your missionary work, both positively and negatively.

_____
_____
_____
_____

What are you grateful for today? _____

Do practice patience and understanding. Patience fosters a more forgiving and cooperative atmosphere. Being patient with your companion is important too, address problems in the relationship, and try your best to be patient when issues arise. Don't let frustration or anger get the best of you when faced with challenges or misunderstandings. Take a step back, pray for guidance, and approach the situation with a calm and open heart. Just breathe!

DATE: _____

MEMORIES MADE, TOUGH TIMES, & LESSONS LEARNED:

Stressed  Angry  Tired  Sad  Happy  Excited

_____
_____
_____
_____
_____
_____
_____
_____
_____

What are you grateful for today? _____

*"Put yourself in a position to begin having experiences with Him. Humble yourself. Pray to have eyes to see God's hand in your life and in the world around you. Ask Him to tell you if He is really there—if He knows you. Ask Him how He feels about you. And then listen." - Russell M. Nelson*

DATE: _____

MEMORIES MADE, TOUGH TIMES, & LESSONS LEARNED:

Stressed  Angry  Tired  Sad  Happy  Excited

_____
_____
_____
_____
_____
_____
_____
_____
_____

Prompt of the day:

Fasting and Prayer: Write about how your attitude and approach to fasting and prayer have changed over time.

_____
_____
_____
_____
_____

What are you grateful for today? _____

Get the door for others. Whether it is your companion, someone at church or you see someone at a store with their arms full or someone pushing a stroller, observe what's going on and jump at the chance to help someone with the door. Keep your eyes up and attuned to the needs of others. See a person in a wheelchair or an elderly person getting ready to enter a building? Hop up and hold the door open. Notice when there is someone coming in behind you and open the door for them. These small acts of service contribute to creating a better, kinder world and make a great impression.

DATE: _____

MEMORIES MADE, TOUGH TIMES, & LESSONS LEARNED:

Stressed   Angry   Tired   Sad   Happy   Excited

_____
_____
_____
_____
_____
_____
_____
_____

What are you grateful for today? _____

*"We are followers of Jesus Christ. The most important truth the Holy Ghost will ever witness to you is that Jesus is the Christ, the Son of the living God. He lives! He is our Advocate with the Father, our Exemplar, and our Redeemer." - Russell M. Nelson*

DATE: _____

MEMORIES MADE, TOUGH TIMES, & LESSONS LEARNED:

Stressed   Angry   Tired   Sad   Happy   Excited

_____
_____
_____
_____
_____
_____
_____
_____

Prompt of the day:
Learning from the Elderly: Write about a meaningful interaction you had with an elderly person and what you learned from it.

_____
_____
_____
_____
_____

What are you grateful for today? _____

Do recognize the unifying power of group singing and prayer in strengthening community bonds and providing spiritual upliftment. Embrace opportunities to join in these collective activities, whether in church services, devotionals, or other gatherings. Encourage participation and lead by example in creating a spirit of unity and devotion. Don't dismiss the significance of these shared spiritual experiences in fostering a sense of belonging and purpose among members and friends. Your enthusiasm and reverence can inspire others to draw closer to God and to each other.

DATE: _____

MEMORIES MADE, TOUGH TIMES, & LESSONS LEARNED:

Stressed   Angry   Tired   Sad   Happy   Excited

_____
_____
_____
_____
_____
_____
_____
_____

What are you grateful for today? _____

*"Spending more time in the temple builds faith...The temple is a place of revelation. There you are shown how to progress toward a celestial life. There you are drawn closer to the Savior and given greater access to His power. There you are guided in solving the problems in your life, even your most perplexing problems." - Russell M. Nelson*

DATE: _____

MEMORIES MADE, TOUGH TIMES, & LESSONS LEARNED:

Stressed   Angry   Tired   Sad   Happy   Excited

_____
_____
_____
_____
_____
_____
_____
_____

Prompt of the day:

The Role of General Conference: Reflect on your observations and experiences with General Conference and how your attitude has changed over time.

_____
_____
_____
_____

What are you grateful for today? _____

As a missionary, demonstrate respect for others' property and resources. When visiting homes or using items provided by members or those you teach, treat them with care and gratitude. If you borrow something, such as a book or a tool, return it promptly and in the same or better condition than when you received it. Remember that as a missionary, you often rely on the generosity and support of others. Show your appreciation by being a good steward of the resources they share with you. By respecting others' property and using it responsibly, you demonstrate integrity, trustworthiness, and gratitude, which are essential qualities for building strong relationships and effectively sharing the gospel message.

DATE: _____

MEMORIES MADE, TOUGH TIMES, & LESSONS LEARNED:

Stressed　Angry　Tired　Sad　Happy　Excited

_____
_____
_____
_____
_____
_____
_____
_____

What are you grateful for today? _____

*"God loves us. He is watching us. He wants us to succeed. We will know someday that He has not left one thing undone for the eternal welfare of each of us. If we only knew it, heavenly hosts are pulling for us—friends in heaven we cannot now remember, who yearn for our victory." - Ezra Taft Benson*

DATE: _____

MEMORIES MADE, TOUGH TIMES, & LESSONS LEARNED:

Stressed　Angry　Tired　Sad　Happy　Excited

_____
_____
_____
_____
_____
_____
_____
_____

Prompt of the day:

Finding Common Ground: Share an experience where you found common ground with someone vastly different from you.

_____
_____
_____
_____
_____

What are you grateful for today? _____

Seek personalized guidance. Remember that scripture study and prayer are not just about the actions themselves, but about seeking personal guidance from God. Pray for the ability to understand His will for you and the people you serve. Trust that God, the Great Physician, knows you and your needs intimately, and will provide customized guidance and healing as you seek Him through scripture study and prayer. It's true. It's all true. Believe it. Learn it. Live it and you'll love it. The answers will come, but often they come when we forget about the worry and wondering and give our will to Him. He is Wonderful and He will do anything to bring you home and He loves that you are gathering His children. Watch for His heavenly hugs—they come frequently!

DATE: _____

MEMORIES MADE, TOUGH TIMES, & LESSONS LEARNED:

Stressed   Angry   Tired   Sad   Happy   Excited

_____
_____
_____
_____
_____
_____
_____
_____
_____

What are you grateful for today? _____

"All of God's faculties, all of his inclinations are poised and bent on blessing at the slightest provocation. Oh, how God loves to be merciful and bless his children! Perhaps that is his greatest joy. It is the inherent quality that drives him with tireless vigilance to save his children." - Tad R. Callister

DATE: _____

MEMORIES MADE, TOUGH TIMES, & LESSONS LEARNED:

Stressed   Angry   Tired   Sad   Happy   Excited

_____
_____
_____
_____
_____
_____
_____
_____

Prompt of the day:
Cultivating a Sense of Community: Share how you and your fellow missionaries have worked to cultivate a sense of community among yourselves and with those you serve.

_____
_____
_____
_____
_____

What are you grateful for today? _____

Notice the good and seek out the positive. Instead of joining the trend of constant complaints and criticisms, actively look for, find, and express the good. Be generous in giving sincere compliments and expressing gratitude to others. Look for the silver lining in less-than-ideal situations. This positive attitude pleasantly surprises others and a positive person draws people in instead of pushing people away. Avoid being a constant complainer and drainer, as most people can't stand negativity. You'll always find what you're looking for so search for the good.

DATE: _____

MEMORIES MADE, TOUGH TIMES, & LESSONS LEARNED:

Stressed   Angry   Tired   Sad   Happy   Excited

_____
_____
_____
_____
_____
_____
_____
_____

What are you grateful for today? _____

"A hallmark of the Lord's true and living Church will always be an organized, directed effort to minister to individual children of God and their families. Because it is His Church, we as His servants will minister to the one, just as He did. We will minister in His name, with His power and authority, and with His loving-kindness." - Russell M. Nelson

DATE: _____

MEMORIES MADE, TOUGH TIMES, & LESSONS LEARNED:

Stressed   Angry   Tired   Sad   Happy   Excited

_____
_____
_____
_____
_____
_____
_____

Prompt of the day:
Dealing with Doubts: How do you deal with doubts, whether your own or those of the people you teach?

_____
_____
_____
_____

What are you grateful for today? _____

It's important to understand that you may not develop a close friendship with every missionary companion you are assigned. Having some companions whom you don't naturally get along with as well is normal and okay. Don't force a bond that doesn't come naturally. However, you should still strive to be respectful, patient, and work together effectively despite personal differences. Focus on your shared purpose as missionaries and find ways to support each other in that work. With an attitude of understanding and Christ-like love, even difficult companionships can be navigated successfully. Have patience, put forth your best effort, and trust that you'll learn valuable lessons regardless of how well you click personally.

DATE: _____

MEMORIES MADE, TOUGH TIMES, & LESSONS LEARNED:

Stressed   Angry   Tired   Sad   Happy   Excited

_____
_____
_____
_____
_____
_____
_____
_____

What are you grateful for today? _____

*"True disciples of Jesus Christ are willing to stand out, speak up, and be different from the people of the world. They are undaunted, devoted, and courageous...There is nothing easy or automatic about becoming such powerful disciples. Our focus must be riveted on the Savior and His gospel." - Russell M. Nelson*

DATE: _____

MEMORIES MADE, TOUGH TIMES, & LESSONS LEARNED:

Stressed   Angry   Tired   Sad   Happy   Excited

_____
_____
_____
_____
_____
_____
_____
_____

Prompt of the day:

Personal Reflections on Missionary Work's Legacy: Write about your thoughts on the legacy you hope to leave through your missionary work.

_____
_____
_____
_____

What are you grateful for today? _____

You will get to know and love those you teach. You will feel a deep divine love for them. It will be a feeling so strong, perhaps unlike any kind of love you have felt before. You want more than anything for them to accept the message you are sharing about Jesus Christ. And just when you feel they are embracing the message, there will be some who tell you no more. They are finished. They don't want you to return. Those will be heart-wrenching moments that will tear you apart emotionally. It may be confusing and frustrating as you don't understand why they suddenly changed their mind. The Spirit will direct you in what to do or say—whether to leave them alone and pray for them, or to bear testimony, or even sing them a song. Rely on and follow the promptings of the Spirit in those tough times.

DATE: _____

MEMORIES MADE, TOUGH TIMES, & LESSONS LEARNED: Stressed Angry Tired Sad Happy Excited

_____
_____
_____
_____
_____
_____
_____
_____

What are you grateful for today? _____

"Of all the training I have received in my Church assignments, none has been more important to me than the training I received as a nineteen-year-old elder serving a full-time mission." - M. Russell Ballard

DATE: _____

MEMORIES MADE, TOUGH TIMES, & LESSONS LEARNED: Stressed Angry Tired Sad Happy Excited

_____
_____
_____
_____
_____
_____
_____

Prompt of the day:
The Joy of Teaching: Reflect on a moment when teaching brought you immense joy or satisfaction.

_____
_____
_____
_____

What are you grateful for today? _____

Develop patience: Missionary work requires a lot of patience, whether it's waiting for investigators to progress or dealing with challenging companions. Cultivate patience in all aspects of your mission, and you'll find that you're better able to handle the ups and downs that come your way. Patience is not just about waiting; it's also about maintaining a positive attitude and trusting in the Lord's timing. Use your moments of waiting as opportunities to learn and grow, both spiritually and personally. The lessons you learn in patience will serve you well in life—marriage, parenting, and work.

DATE: _____

MEMORIES MADE, TOUGH TIMES, & LESSONS LEARNED:  Stressed  Angry  Tired  Sad  Happy  Excited

_____
_____
_____
_____
_____
_____
_____
_____
_____

What are you grateful for today? _____

"I have often said that one of the greatest secrets of missionary work is work! If a missionary works, he will get the Spirit; if he gets the Spirit, he will teach by the Spirit; and if he teaches by the Spirit, he will touch the hearts of the people and he will be happy. Work, work, work—there is no satisfactory substitute, especially in missionary work." - Ezra Taft Benson

DATE: _____

MEMORIES MADE, TOUGH TIMES, & LESSONS LEARNED:  Stressed  Angry  Tired  Sad  Happy  Excited

_____
_____
_____
_____
_____
_____
_____
_____

Prompt of the day:
The Impact of Daily Scripture Study: Reflect on the impact that daily scripture study has had on your mission, both personally and in your teachings.

_____
_____
_____
_____
_____

What are you grateful for today? _____

Strengthen your relationship with Heavenly Father by seeking His Spirit through personal prayer, scripture study, uplifting music, and reading your patriarchal blessing. Developing a deep connection with God will provide comfort, guidance, and strength during difficult times. Make time each day to commune with your Heavenly Father and to seek His direction. As you do so, you will feel His love and support, and you will be better equipped to face the challenges and opportunities of missionary life with faith and courage.

DATE: _____

MEMORIES MADE, TOUGH TIMES, & LESSONS LEARNED:

Stressed    Angry    Tired    Sad    Happy    Excited

_____
_____
_____
_____
_____
_____
_____

What are you grateful for today? _____

"When the focus of our lives is on God's plan of salvation ... and Jesus Christ and His gospel, we can feel joy regardless of what is happening — or not happening — in our lives." - Russell M. Nelson

DATE: _____

MEMORIES MADE, TOUGH TIMES, & LESSONS LEARNED:

Stressed    Angry    Tired    Sad    Happy    Excited

_____
_____
_____
_____
_____
_____
_____

Prompt of the day:
Coping with Rejection: Share how you cope with rejection in your missionary work and remain positive.

_____
_____
_____
_____

What are you grateful for today? _____

Do offer your support and assistance during difficult times, showing that your care extends beyond church-related activities. Offer this support to your companion, the members, the friends you are teaching, and even those that you have only met once. Christlike care is important! But remember, don't overextend yourself or neglect your own well-being while supporting others. Remember to take care of your own physical, emotional, and spiritual needs so that you can effectively serve others.

DATE: _____

MEMORIES MADE, TOUGH TIMES, & LESSONS LEARNED:

Stressed   Angry   Tired   Sad   Happy   Excited

_____
_____
_____
_____
_____
_____
_____
_____

What are you grateful for today? _____

"With the increase of missionary work throughout the world, there must be a comparable increase in the effort to make every convert feel at home in his or her ward or branch. . . . I invite every member to reach out in friendship and love for those who come into the Church as converts." - Gordon B. Hinckley

DATE: _____

MEMORIES MADE, TOUGH TIMES, & LESSONS LEARNED:

Stressed   Angry   Tired   Sad   Happy   Excited

_____
_____
_____
_____
_____
_____
_____
_____

Prompt of the day:
Navigating Transitions Within the Mission: Share your experiences and insights on navigating transitions, such as changing areas or companions, within your mission.

_____
_____
_____
_____

What are you grateful for today? _____

Four important words to be aware of in this great work. Inspection. Connection. Direction. Distraction. It starts with Inspection. Getting our hearts right as missionaries is fundamental. Are you clean? Humble? Obedient? Full of compassion? Willing to submit everything on the alter? Then Connection. The Atonement of Jesus Christ is all about connection, becoming one with God. Lack of attention leads to loss of connection. Give the Lord your all-in attention. And seek unity with your companion and others. People are more willing to listen to your message when they feel genuinely Connected with you. Build a relationship of trust. When you are Connected, then you'll be Directed. Seek His Direction and guidance of the Spirit. And beware of Distraction. The adversary aims for distraction with "flashy misery." Don't be distracted by less important things. The joy you feel and the growth you experience as a missionary depends on your relationship with Jesus Christ. Period.

DATE: _____

MEMORIES MADE, TOUGH TIMES, & LESSONS LEARNED:  Stressed  Angry  Tired  Sad  Happy  Excited

_____
_____
_____
_____
_____
_____
_____
_____

What are you grateful for today? _____

"What we need now is the greatest generation of missionaries in the history of the Church. We need worthy, qualified, spiritually energized missionaries who, like Helaman's 2,000 stripling warriors, are 'exceedingly valiant for courage, and also for strength and activity' and who are 'true at all times in whatsoever thing they [are] entrusted' (Alma 53:20)." - M. Russell Ballard

DATE: _____

MEMORIES MADE, TOUGH TIMES, & LESSONS LEARNED:  Stressed  Angry  Tired  Sad  Happy  Excited

_____
_____
_____
_____
_____
_____
_____

Prompt of the day:

Overcoming Fear of Public Speaking: Write about your experiences overcoming the fear of public speaking through teaching and sharing your testimony.

_____
_____
_____
_____
_____

What are you grateful for today? _____

Resilience is our ability to recover from difficulties, strengthened by proactive habits such as regular exercise, practicing mindfulness, maintaining a healthy diet, and ensuring adequate sleep. These positive routines boost our overall wellbeing, making us better equipped to handle life's stresses and challenges. Additionally, reactive strategies, such as deep breathing during stressful moments, or changing your posture, which will change how you feel, helps manage negative emotions on the spot. Together, these practices fortify our mental and emotional resilience, enabling us to navigate adversity more effectively.

DATE: _____

MEMORIES MADE, TOUGH TIMES, & LESSONS LEARNED:

Stressed    Angry    Tired    Sad    Happy    Excited

_____
_____
_____
_____
_____
_____
_____
_____

What are you grateful for today? _____

"Are you willing to let God prevail in your life? Are you willing to let God be the most important influence in your life? Will you allow His words, His commandments, and His covenants to influence what you do each day? Will you allow His voice to take priority over any other? Are you willing to let whatever He needs you to do take precedence over every other ambition? Are you willing to have your will swallowed up in His?" - Russell M. Nelson

DATE: _____

MEMORIES MADE, TOUGH TIMES, & LESSONS LEARNED:

Stressed    Angry    Tired    Sad    Happy    Excited

_____
_____
_____
_____
_____
_____
_____

Prompt of the day:

Embracing Moments of Spontaneity: Reflect on a time when a spontaneous moment led to an unexpected positive outcome or deepened a relationship during your mission.

_____
_____
_____
_____

What are you grateful for today? _____

Make baptismal services Christ-centered, spiritual experiences that focus on the significance of the ordinance and the Atonement of Jesus Christ. Many investigators who attend a baptismal service will go on to their own baptisms if the service is a strong teaching moment centered on faith in Christ and repentance. Ensure that the prayers, hymns, and talks at the baptismal service emphasize the cleansing power of Christ, the remission of sins, and the importance of this sacred ordinance in the plan of salvation. A spiritually uplifting baptismal service can have a profound impact on both the convert and those in attendance. Pray to be guided on how you can help make these sacred experiences powerful experiences.

DATE: _____

MEMORIES MADE, TOUGH TIMES, & LESSONS LEARNED:  Stressed  Angry  Tired  Sad  Happy  Excited

_____
_____
_____
_____
_____
_____
_____
_____

What are you grateful for today? _____

"I plead with you now—to take charge of your own testimony of Jesus Christ and His gospel. Work for it. Nurture it so that it will grow. Feed it truth. Don't pollute it with false philosophies of unbelieving men and women. As you make the continual strengthening of your testimony of Jesus Christ your highest priority, watch for miracles to happen in your life."
- Russell M. Nelson

DATE: _____

MEMORIES MADE, TOUGH TIMES, & LESSONS LEARNED:  Stressed  Angry  Tired  Sad  Happy  Excited

_____
_____
_____
_____
_____
_____
_____
_____

Prompt of the day:
The Impact of Local Festivities: Share how participating in or observing local festivities has enriched your understanding of the community and its culture.

_____
_____
_____
_____
_____

What are you grateful for today? _____

Plan ahead for stressful situations. Missionaries can benefit from planning ahead to handle stress better. Before entering a potentially stressful situation, think about what might go wrong and prepare for it. This method, called "prospective hindsight" or "pre-mortem," can help you stay calm and make smarter choices when stress hits. By having a plan ready in advance, you'll be better equipped to deal with stressful situations effectively. Remember that stress can make it hard to think clearly and make good decisions, so preparing beforehand is crucial. Embrace this strategy to enhance your stress resilience and maintain focus on your mission.

DATE: _____

MEMORIES MADE, TOUGH TIMES, & LESSONS LEARNED:

Stressed   Angry   Tired   Sad   Happy   Excited

_____
_____
_____
_____
_____
_____
_____
_____

What are you grateful for today? _____

*"All of those called to the ministry...are given the gifts needed to perform the work whereunto they are called. These gifts are always the ones needed for the particular work at hand." - Bruce R. McConkie*

DATE: _____

MEMORIES MADE, TOUGH TIMES, & LESSONS LEARNED:

Stressed   Angry   Tired   Sad   Happy   Excited

_____
_____
_____
_____
_____
_____
_____
_____

Prompt of the day:
Witnessing Small Miracles: Write about a "small miracle" you witnessed that reaffirmed your faith or brought joy to your mission.

_____
_____
_____
_____

What are you grateful for today? _____

Deal with rejection in a Christlike way. Rejection is a common part of missionary work, but it doesn't define your success. When people turn away from your message, remember they're not rejecting you personally. Focus on the present and those who are ready to hear the gospel. Pray for those who reject you and trust in the Lord's plan. Continue to love and serve as Christ did. By managing rejection with faith and compassion, you'll maintain a positive attitude throughout your mission.

DATE: _____

MEMORIES MADE, TOUGH TIMES, & LESSONS LEARNED:

Stressed   Angry   Tired   Sad   Happy   Excited

_____
_____
_____
_____
_____
_____
_____
_____

What are you grateful for today? _____

*"Every generation since time began has had some things to overcome and some problems to work out. Furthermore, every individual person has a particular set of challenges that sometimes seem to be earmarked for us personally. We understood that in our pre-mortal existence." - Howard W. Hunter*

DATE: _____

MEMORIES MADE, TOUGH TIMES, & LESSONS LEARNED:

Stressed   Angry   Tired   Sad   Happy   Excited

_____
_____
_____
_____
_____
_____
_____

Prompt of the day:

Learning from Interfaith Dialogues: Reflect on what you've learned from interfaith dialogues and how these conversations have shaped your approach to missionary work.

_____
_____
_____
_____

What are you grateful for today? _____

Center everything you do on Jesus Christ. When your service is connected to the Savior, it has greater power and impact. Strive to keep Christ at the heart of your missionary efforts. Remember that your ultimate goal is to bring others unto Him. He changes hearts. He offers hope, healing, and happiness. By focusing on the Savior in your teaching, invitations, and personal interactions, you will find greater purpose and effectiveness in your work. Your love for those you serve will be magnified as you help them develop a relationship with Jesus Christ. They will see Him in your eyes and feel His Spirit through you.

DATE: _____

MEMORIES MADE, TOUGH TIMES, & LESSONS LEARNED:

Stressed    Angry    Tired    Sad    Happy    Excited

_____
_____
_____
_____
_____
_____
_____
_____
_____

What are you grateful for today? _____

"When we have faith in the Lord Jesus Christ, we must have trust in him. We must trust him enough that we are content to accept his will, knowing that he knows what is best for us." - Dallin H. Oaks

DATE: _____

MEMORIES MADE, TOUGH TIMES, & LESSONS LEARNED:

Stressed    Angry    Tired    Sad    Happy    Excited

_____
_____
_____
_____
_____
_____
_____
_____

Prompt of the day:

The Role of Heritage in Faith: Share how your personal or cultural heritage has played a role in your approach to missionary work.

_____
_____
_____
_____

What are you grateful for today? _____

Find joy in the restoration of the gospel as a missionary: Deepen your understanding and appreciation of the restored gospel of Jesus Christ. Study the events and revelations of the Restoration, from the First Vision to the present day. Recognize the joy and blessings that come from living in a time when the fullness of the gospel is available. Share your testimony of the Restoration with others, inviting them to experience the same joy and peace that comes from this knowledge. As you find joy in the Restoration, your missionary service will be infused with greater purpose and enthusiasm.

DATE: _____

MEMORIES MADE, TOUGH TIMES, & LESSONS LEARNED:

Stressed  Angry  Tired  Sad  Happy  Excited

_____
_____
_____
_____
_____
_____
_____
_____

What are you grateful for today? _____

*"Every person who has made covenants with God has promised to care about others and serve those in need. We can demonstrate faith in God and always be ready to respond to those who ask about 'the hope that is in [us].' Each of us has a role to play in the gathering of Israel." - Russell M. Nelson*

DATE: _____

MEMORIES MADE, TOUGH TIMES, & LESSONS LEARNED:

Stressed  Angry  Tired  Sad  Happy  Excited

_____
_____
_____
_____
_____
_____
_____

Prompt of the day:
Spiritual Practices Beyond Mission: How do you plan to continue certain spiritual practices you've developed on your mission once you return home?

_____
_____
_____
_____

What are you grateful for today? _____

Remember that your Heavenly Father wants you to experience joy and happiness during your missionary service, even amidst the challenges and trials you may face. When you find yourself struggling with discouragement, homesickness, or self-doubt, turn to Him in sincere prayer and ask for His help in managing your expectations, attitudes, and emotions. Trust that He is aware of your needs and desires, and that He will provide you with the strength, comfort, and guidance you need to press forward with faith and optimism. Seek to recognize His hand in your daily experiences, and cultivate a grateful heart for the blessings and miracles, both large and small, that He brings into your life.

DATE: _____

MEMORIES MADE, TOUGH TIMES, & LESSONS LEARNED:

Stressed  Angry  Tired  Sad  Happy  Excited

_____
_____
_____
_____
_____
_____
_____
_____

What are you grateful for today? _____

*"Attempts to create a list of specific steps of repentance may be helpful to some, but it may also lead to a mechanical, check-off-the-boxes approach with no real feeling or change. True repentance is not superficial." - D. Todd Christofferson*

DATE: _____

MEMORIES MADE, TOUGH TIMES, & LESSONS LEARNED:

Stressed  Angry  Tired  Sad  Happy  Excited

_____
_____
_____
_____
_____
_____
_____
_____

Prompt of the day:
Learning Through Language Blunders: Share a humorous or insightful language blunder and what it taught you about communication and humility.

_____
_____
_____
_____
_____

What are you grateful for today? _____

Martin Seligman's concept of "Learned Optimism" suggests that being positive isn't just something you're born with; you can actually learn to be more optimistic. We can train our brain to see challenges as temporary setbacks, not permanent defeats. It's like building mental muscles through techniques like identifying unhelpful thought patterns, reframing events, and celebrating small wins. This helps you handle tough times better and makes you feel happier overall. It's all about training your brain to focus on the good side of things instead of the bad.

DATE: _____

MEMORIES MADE, TOUGH TIMES, & LESSONS LEARNED:

Stressed  Angry  Tired  Sad  Happy  Excited

_____
_____
_____
_____
_____
_____
_____
_____

What are you grateful for today? _____

*"I renew my plea for you to do whatever it takes to increase your spiritual capacity to receive personal revelation. Doing so will help you know how to move ahead with your life, what to do during times of crisis, and how to discern and avoid the temptations and the deceptions of the adversary." - Russell M. Nelson*

DATE: _____

MEMORIES MADE, TOUGH TIMES, & LESSONS LEARNED:

Stressed  Angry  Tired  Sad  Happy  Excited

_____
_____
_____
_____
_____
_____
_____
_____

Prompt of the day:

The Role of Personal Reflection: Share the role that personal reflection plays in your daily missionary routine and its impact on your spiritual growth.

_____
_____
_____
_____

What are you grateful for today? _____

Cultivate the qualities the Lord has outlined for His servants: faith, hope, charity, love, virtue, knowledge, temperance, patience, brotherly kindness, godliness, humility, and diligence. Keep your eye single to the glory of God, and let these attributes guide your missionary work. As you develop these Christlike qualities, you will be better prepared to serve the Lord and bless the lives of those you teach. Pray for opportunities to exercise these attributes, and seek feedback from your companion and mission leaders on areas where you can improve. Remember that becoming a successful missionary is a process of personal growth and refinement, and the Lord will help you every step of the way.

DATE: _____

MEMORIES MADE, TOUGH TIMES, & LESSONS LEARNED:

Stressed    Angry    Tired    Sad    Happy    Excited

_____
_____
_____
_____
_____
_____
_____
_____
_____

What are you grateful for today? _____

*"I plead with you to increase your spiritual capacity to receive revelation. Choose to do the spiritual work required to enjoy the gift of the Holy Ghost and hear the voice of the Spirit more frequently and more clearly." - Russell M. Nelson*

DATE: _____

MEMORIES MADE, TOUGH TIMES, & LESSONS LEARNED:

Stressed    Angry    Tired    Sad    Happy    Excited

_____
_____
_____
_____
_____
_____
_____
_____

Prompt of the day:
Preach My Gospel: Reflect on all that you have learned and summarize one or two of the most important lessons learned from studying from it daily.

_____
_____
_____
_____

What are you grateful for today? _____

As a missionary, don't chase happiness as the ultimate goal. While you may experience joy in your service, pursuing happiness for its own sake can be counterproductive. Just as chasing a butterfly can cause it to flutter away, focusing too intently on being happy can lead to disappointment. Instead, immerse yourself in serving others, expressing gratitude, and showing kindness. Lose yourself in the work of inviting others to come unto Christ, and you'll find that feelings of peace, joy, and contentment often follow naturally. Remember, true happiness comes as a byproduct of living the gospel and focusing on others, not as an end goal.

DATE: _____

MEMORIES MADE, TOUGH TIMES, & LESSONS LEARNED:

Stressed   Angry   Tired   Sad   Happy   Excited

_____
_____
_____
_____
_____
_____
_____
_____

What are you grateful for today? _____

*"Faith comes by hearing the word of God through the testimony of the servants of God. That testimony is always attended by the Spirit of Prophecy and Revelation." - Joseph Smith*

DATE: _____

MEMORIES MADE, TOUGH TIMES, & LESSONS LEARNED:

Stressed   Angry   Tired   Sad   Happy   Excited

_____
_____
_____
_____
_____
_____
_____

Prompt of the day:
The Role of Storytelling in Connecting with Others: Share how storytelling, whether your own stories or those of the gospel, has played a role in connecting with others.

_____
_____
_____
_____
_____

What are you grateful for today? _____

Remember your divine calling and the trust God has placed in you. You were called to this mission for a reason, and the Lord knows your potential. Search inward and ask God for help to magnify your calling and to use the strengths and gifts He has blessed you with. Look at the progress you have made with His help, rather than comparing yourself to others or dwelling on your shortcomings. Pray for guidance and strength, and know that your efforts, no matter how small they may seem, are valuable in the eyes of God. Trust in His plan and timing and have faith that He will help you overcome your challenges, doubts, and discouragement.

DATE: _____

MEMORIES MADE, TOUGH TIMES, & LESSONS LEARNED: 

Stressed  Angry  Tired  Sad  Happy  Excited

_____
_____
_____
_____
_____
_____
_____
_____

What are you grateful for today? _____

*"The future is bright for God's covenant-keeping people. The Lord will increasingly call upon His servants who worthily hold the priesthood to bless, comfort, and strengthen mankind and to help prepare the world and its people for His Second Coming. It behooves each of us to measure up to the sacred ordination we have received. We can do this!" - Russell M. Nelson*

DATE: _____

MEMORIES MADE, TOUGH TIMES, & LESSONS LEARNED: 

Stressed  Angry  Tired  Sad  Happy  Excited

_____
_____
_____
_____
_____
_____
_____
_____

Prompt of the day:

Overcoming Personal Insecurities: Write about overcoming personal insecurities through your missionary work and how it has led to growth.

_____
_____
_____
_____

What are you grateful for today? _____

Say it with confidence. Practice confident communication as a missionary with basic courtesies. Make eye contact when speaking to others, and speak loudly and clearly enough to be understood. This is especially important when making comments or being called on in meetings - don't mumble or look down. Speak up and make eye contact. Use these same practices in noisy environments too. If someone asks you to repeat yourself, don't get annoyed. Just restate what you said in a louder, clearer voice. Developing poise in how you communicate will help your messages be effectively delivered. Master these skills now, and you'll carry them into future responsibilities and interactions long after your mission.

DATE: _____

MEMORIES MADE, TOUGH TIMES, & LESSONS LEARNED:

Stressed   Angry   Tired   Sad   Happy   Excited

_____
_____
_____
_____
_____
_____
_____
_____
_____

What are you grateful for today? _____

"We think we must climb to a certain height of goodness before we can reach God. But He says not 'at the end of the way you may find Me;' He says, 'I am the Way; I am the road under your feet, the road that begins just as low down as you happen to be.' If we are in a hole, then the Way begins in the hole. The moment we set our face in the same direction as His, we are walking with God." - Helen Woodhouse

DATE: _____

MEMORIES MADE, TOUGH TIMES, & LESSONS LEARNED:

Stressed   Angry   Tired   Sad   Happy   Excited

_____
_____
_____
_____
_____
_____
_____
_____

Prompt of the day:

The Power of Patience in Teaching: Write about a time when patience in teaching led to breakthroughs or deepened understanding for someone you were teaching.

_____
_____
_____
_____
_____

What are you grateful for today? _____

Happy people learn to focus their time and attention on what is really important and what they can control. While there will be many times you wish you could control your companions, members or those you teach, you will be happier when you focus on what you can control. And there are very few things in life that are really super duper important. Stay calm and keep the big picture in mind. What is important? What can you control? Shift from worrying about little things and trying to control people to focusing your energy on doing the Lord's work and listening to and acting on the promptings of the Spirit.

DATE: _____

MEMORIES MADE, TOUGH TIMES, & LESSONS LEARNED:

Stressed    Angry    Tired    Sad    Happy    Excited

_____
_____
_____
_____
_____
_____
_____
_____

What are you grateful for today? _____

"Whether you are diligently moving along the covenant path, have slipped or stepped from the covenant path, or can't even see the path from where you are now, I plead with you to repent. Experience the strengthening power of daily repentance—of doing and being a little better each day." - Russell M. Nelson

DATE: _____

MEMORIES MADE, TOUGH TIMES, & LESSONS LEARNED:

Stressed    Angry    Tired    Sad    Happy    Excited

_____
_____
_____
_____
_____
_____
_____
_____

Prompt of the day:
The Power of Anecdotes in Teaching: Share how using personal anecdotes or stories has enhanced your teaching and connected with others.

_____
_____
_____
_____
_____

What are you grateful for today? _____

Recognize that Jesus Christ, through His Atonement, has experienced the pain and consequences of all mankind's sins, sorrows, and troubles. He is the ultimate example of empathy and understanding. When you encounter someone who is struggling with a particular challenge, remember that the Savior has felt their pain and knows exactly what they are going through. He has the power to heal, comfort, and strengthen them, and He can guide you in your efforts to minister to their needs. Trust in His infinite love and compassion, and strive to be an instrument in His hands.

DATE: _____

MEMORIES MADE, TOUGH TIMES, & LESSONS LEARNED:

Stressed    Angry    Tired    Sad    Happy    Excited

_____
_____
_____
_____
_____
_____
_____
_____

What are you grateful for today? _____

*"If the setting is right you might ask what their fears are, what they yearn for, or what they feel is missing in their lives. I promise you that something in what they say will always highlight a truth of the gospel about which you can bear testimony and about which you can then offer more."* - Jeffrey R. Holland

DATE: _____

MEMORIES MADE, TOUGH TIMES, & LESSONS LEARNED:

Stressed    Angry    Tired    Sad    Happy    Excited

_____
_____
_____
_____
_____
_____
_____

Prompt of the day:
The Significance of Handwritten Letters: Share the significance of sending or receiving handwritten letters during your mission and the personal touch they add.

_____
_____
_____
_____

What are you grateful for today? _____

This tip is for next year!
Give yourself the gift of time to adjust to life after your mission. There's no rush to revert to who you were before; instead, focus on becoming an improved version of yourself. Allow yourself the space to grow, learn, and evolve, embracing the changes that come your way. Remember that progress takes time, and each step forward is a step toward becoming the best version of yourself. So be patient with yourself as you navigate this new chapter, and trust that the journey ahead holds endless opportunities for growth and fulfillment. Remember, this time in the mission field isn't the best two years of your life, but they are the best years and months FOR your life!

DATE: _____

MEMORIES MADE, TOUGH TIMES, & LESSONS LEARNED:

Stressed   Angry   Tired   Sad   Happy   Excited

_____
_____
_____
_____
_____
_____
_____
_____
_____

What are you grateful for today? _____

*"And now, I ask, how righteousness and truth are going to sweep the earth as with a flood? I will answer. Men and angels are to be co-workers in bringing to pass this great work, and Zion is to be prepared..."* - Joseph Smith

DATE: _____

MEMORIES MADE, TOUGH TIMES, & LESSONS LEARNED:

Stressed   Angry   Tired   Sad   Happy   Excited

_____
_____
_____
_____
_____
_____
_____
_____

Prompt of the day:
Adapting to Missionary Work's Intensity: Reflect on how you've adapted to the intensity of missionary work and the coping mechanisms you've developed.

_____
_____
_____
_____

What are you grateful for today? _____

Make time to review and study "The Living Christ." Ponder it's words and you may even want to challenge yourself to memorize it. Think about it: The birth, life, teachings, atoning sacrifice, death, resurrection, and eternal role of Jesus Christ are central to human history. As the creator, Jehovah, Messiah, and Redeemer, He brought a message of peace, healed the sick, set a perfect example, and gave His life to atone for the sins of all mankind. Modern prophets testify He lives, His Church is restored, and He will return in glory to reign and judge each of us. It is a beautiful message you can share with others.

DATE: _____

MEMORIES MADE, TOUGH TIMES, & LESSONS LEARNED:  Stressed  Angry  Tired  Sad  Happy  Excited

_____
_____
_____
_____
_____
_____
_____
_____
_____

What are you grateful for today? _____

*"There has never been a time in the history of the world when knowledge of our Savior is more personally vital and relevant to every human soul. Imagine how quickly the devastating conflicts throughout the world—and those in our individual lives—would be resolved if we all chose to follow Jesus Christ and heed His teachings." - Russell M. Nelson*

DATE: _____

MEMORIES MADE, TOUGH TIMES, & LESSONS LEARNED:  Stressed  Angry  Tired  Sad  Happy  Excited

_____
_____
_____
_____
_____
_____
_____
_____

Prompt of the day:

The Joy of Returning to Familiar Areas: Write about the joy and reflections that come with returning to familiar areas during your mission and witnessing changes or growth.

_____
_____
_____
_____

What are you grateful for today? _____

Search for meaning in your missionary service: Reflect on the deeper significance of your missionary work. Consider how your efforts contribute to the eternal salvation of others and to the building of God's kingdom on earth. Look for ways to use your unique strengths and talents to bless the lives of those you serve. As you find meaning and purpose in your mission, you'll experience a profound sense of fulfillment and joy. Embrace the opportunity to be an instrument in God's hands and to make a lasting difference in the world.

DATE: _____

MEMORIES MADE, TOUGH TIMES, & LESSONS LEARNED:

Stressed   Angry   Tired   Sad   Happy   Excited

_____
_____
_____
_____
_____
_____
_____
_____

What are you grateful for today? _____

"As we look at the periods past and our own era in the Church, it is our responsibility to participate in the ever-reaching destiny of the Church. It would seem to me that as we follow the direction of our present prophet, this will be a time of declaring the word of the Lord to the people of the earth with more boldness and more courage than we have ever known before. We have the doctrinal base; we have the organization." - L. Tom Perry

DATE: _____

MEMORIES MADE, TOUGH TIMES, & LESSONS LEARNED:

Stressed   Angry   Tired   Sad   Happy   Excited

_____
_____
_____
_____
_____
_____
_____
_____

Prompt of the day:
The Role of Tradition in Missionary Work: Write about how you've observed or integrated traditional practices into your missionary efforts.

_____
_____
_____
_____
_____

What are you grateful for today? _____

Express gratitude for past experiences and people: Reflect on the individuals and experiences that have shaped your life and brought you to your mission. Write letters or emails expressing your gratitude to family members, friends, teachers, or leaders who have influenced you for good. Share specific memories and the impact they've had on your life. As you express gratitude, you'll feel a greater sense of connection and purpose. Recognizing the blessings in your life can bring you happiness and motivation as you serve.

DATE: _____

MEMORIES MADE, TOUGH TIMES, & LESSONS LEARNED:  Stressed  Angry  Tired  Sad  Happy  Excited

_____
_____
_____
_____
_____
_____
_____
_____

What are you grateful for today? _____

"My dear brothers and sisters, the joy we feel has little to do with the circumstances of our lives and everything to do with the focus of our lives." - Russell M. Nelson

DATE: _____

MEMORIES MADE, TOUGH TIMES, & LESSONS LEARNED:  Stressed  Angry  Tired  Sad  Happy  Excited

_____
_____
_____
_____
_____
_____
_____

Prompt of the day:
Reflection on Leadership: If you've had leadership responsibilities, reflect on what these duties have taught you about leadership, service, and humility.

_____
_____
_____
_____
_____

What are you grateful for today? _____

Trust that Heavenly Father and Jesus Christ care about you and those you serve. They want to strengthen you in your weaknesses and make you an instrument in Their hands to bless others. When you feel inadequate or discouraged, remember that God has called you to this sacred work and that He will qualify you for the tasks He has given you. Seek His guidance and direction daily and have faith that He will help you become the missionary and minister He knows you can be. As you trust in His love and rely on His enabling power, you will find joy and fulfillment in your service.

DATE: _____

MEMORIES MADE, TOUGH TIMES, & LESSONS LEARNED:

Stressed  Angry  Tired  Sad  Happy  Excited

_____
_____
_____
_____
_____
_____
_____
_____

What are you grateful for today? _____

*"Your devotion to duty and your selfless service are just as important in your callings as ours are in our callings. Through a lifetime of service in this Church, I have learned that it really doesn't matter where one serves. What the Lord cares about is how one serves." - Russell M. Nelson*

DATE: _____

MEMORIES MADE, TOUGH TIMES, & LESSONS LEARNED:

Stressed  Angry  Tired  Sad  Happy  Excited

_____
_____
_____
_____
_____
_____
_____

Prompt of the day:
Lessons Learned: Summarize some of the greatest lessons learned on your mission.

_____
_____
_____
_____

What are you grateful for today? _____

Find comfort in knowing that even the greatest individuals, including Jesus Christ, have experienced rejection. Don't let rejection discourage you from continuing to serve and share the gospel with others. When you feel disheartened by rejection, remember that you are in good company. Many of the most righteous and faithful individuals throughout history, including prophets and apostles, have faced rejection and persecution. Even the Savior Himself was "despised and rejected of men" (Isaiah 53:3). Take heart in the knowledge that your experiences are not unique and that you can find strength in the examples of those who have gone before you. Keep pressing forward in faith, knowing that your efforts are not in vain and that the Lord is pleased with your dedication.

DATE: _____

MEMORIES MADE, TOUGH TIMES, & LESSONS LEARNED:

Stressed   Angry   Tired   Sad   Happy   Excited

_____
_____
_____
_____
_____
_____
_____
_____
_____

What are you grateful for today? _____

*"The Lord needs selfless men who put the welfare of others ahead of their own. He needs men who intentionally work to hear the voice of the Spirit with clarity. He needs men of the covenant who keep their covenants with integrity. The Lord needs men eager to repent—men with a zeal to serve and be part of the Lord's battalion of worthy priesthood bearers." - Russell M. Nelson*

DATE: _____

MEMORIES MADE, TOUGH TIMES, & LESSONS LEARNED:

Stressed   Angry   Tired   Sad   Happy   Excited

_____
_____
_____
_____
_____
_____
_____
_____

Prompt of the day:
Adapting Gospel Messages for Children: Share your experiences and strategies for adapting gospel messages to be engaging and understandable for children.

_____
_____
_____
_____

What are you grateful for today? _____

Elder Jeffrey R. Holland talked once about being on the Lord's team. He said, "The future of this world has long been declared; the final outcome between good and evil is already known. There is absolutely no question as to who wins because the victory has already been posted on the scoreboard. The only really strange thing in all of this is that we are still down here on the field trying to decide which team's jersey we want to wear!" But how do you get on the Lord's team? I want one of those jerseys! I want to be on His team and go where He goes and play where He plays! It requires an invitation to be on the Lord's team. BUT please don't be discouraged. Here's all that is required to receive an invite. Listen for the invitation in the Book of Mormon. Look up Alma 5:33 and ponder what that means in your life.

DATE: _____

MEMORIES MADE, TOUGH TIMES, & LESSONS LEARNED:  Stressed  Angry  Tired  Sad  Happy  Excited

_____
_____
_____
_____
_____
_____
_____
_____
_____

What are you grateful for today? _____

*"Your life will be a blessed and balanced experience if you first honor your identity and priority. It is important for you to know who you are and who you may become. It is more important than what you do, even as vital as your work is and will be. - Russell M. Nelson*

DATE: _____

MEMORIES MADE, TOUGH TIMES, & LESSONS LEARNED:  Stressed  Angry  Tired  Sad  Happy  Excited

_____
_____
_____
_____
_____
_____
_____
_____
_____

Prompt of the day:
Adjusting to Return Home: Anticipate the adjustment of returning home after your mission. What do you expect to be the most challenging and rewarding aspects?

_____
_____
_____
_____

What are you grateful for today? _____

Find joy in the doctrine of Christ as a missionary: Deepen your understanding and appreciation of the doctrine of Christ during your mission. Study and ponder the principles of faith, repentance, baptism, the gift of the Holy Ghost, and enduring to the end. Recognize the beauty and power of these teachings in your own life and in the lives of those you teach. As you find joy in living and sharing the doctrine of Christ, you'll experience a greater sense of purpose and fulfillment in your missionary work.

DATE: _____

MEMORIES MADE, TOUGH TIMES, & LESSONS LEARNED:  Stressed  Angry  Tired  Sad  Happy  Excited

_____
_____
_____
_____
_____
_____
_____
_____

What are you grateful for today? _____

*"Anytime we do anything that helps anyone—on either side of the veil—to make and keep their covenants with God, we are helping to gather Israel."* - Russell M. Nelson

DATE: _____

MEMORIES MADE, TOUGH TIMES, & LESSONS LEARNED:  Stressed  Angry  Tired  Sad  Happy  Excited

_____
_____
_____
_____
_____
_____
_____

Prompt of the day:
The Role of Silence and Listening: Share the importance of silence and active listening in your missionary work and how it has facilitated deeper understanding and connections.

_____
_____
_____
_____
_____
_____

What are you grateful for today? _____

This tip is for this time next year! (don't peek! ;)

As your mission journey enters its final stretch, it's natural to feel a bit trunky — that longing for home or the comforts you miss. But remember, there's still important work to be done and precious moments to savor. Embrace each remaining day with gratitude and enthusiasm. Focus on the needs of those you're teaching, and serve the members with love and dedication. By staying engaged and purposeful, you'll find fulfillment and a sense of accomplishment. Keep your schedule filled with meaningful opportunities to bring others closer to Christ, and live each day to the fullest. You've come this far, and you've got what it takes to finish strong. Keep shining bright!

DATE: _____

MEMORIES MADE, TOUGH TIMES, & LESSONS LEARNED:

Stressed   Angry   Tired   Sad   Happy   Excited

_____
_____
_____
_____
_____
_____
_____
_____

What are you grateful for today? _____

"...my call to you...is to start today to increase your faith. Through your faith, Jesus Christ will increase your ability to move the mountains in your life, even though your personal challenges may loom as large as Mount Everest. Your mountains may be loneliness, doubt, illness, or other personal problems. Your mountains will vary, and yet the answer to each of your challenges is to increase your faith." - Russell M. Nelson

DATE: _____

MEMORIES MADE, TOUGH TIMES, & LESSONS LEARNED:

Stressed   Angry   Tired   Sad   Happy   Excited

_____
_____
_____
_____
_____
_____
_____
_____

Prompt of the day:

Maintaining Relationships with Converts: Reflect on how you maintain and nurture relationships with converts, ensuring their continued growth and support.

_____
_____
_____
_____

What are you grateful for today? _____

This message is for this time next year! (don't read it until then ;)

Ok, do not get too excited… but dating time is right around the corner. But wait! Don't start looking now. Stay focused on your mission until you are released. But, it is good to remember that you have an important goal in mind. You have a covenant in mind. This covenant is to get sealed in the temple for all time and eternity. Take your upcoming decisions, concerning dating, seriously as they will have an eternal impact on your life. Choose wisely those that you date, keep your standards high and have fun!

DATE: _____

MEMORIES MADE, TOUGH TIMES, & LESSONS LEARNED:

Stressed   Angry   Tired   Sad   Happy   Excited

_____
_____
_____
_____
_____
_____
_____
_____
_____

What are you grateful for today? _____

"Our ultimate quest in life is to prepare to meet our Maker. We do this by striving daily to become more like our Savior, Jesus Christ.2 And we do that as we repent daily and receive His cleansing, healing, and strengthening power. Then we can feel enduring peace and joy, even during turbulent times." - Russell M. Nelson

DATE: _____

MEMORIES MADE, TOUGH TIMES, & LESSONS LEARNED:

Stressed   Angry   Tired   Sad   Happy   Excited

_____
_____
_____
_____
_____
_____
_____
_____

Prompt of the day:
The Challenge of Digital Detox: Reflect on the challenges and benefits of a digital detox or limited digital access during your mission, and how it has affected your personal growth.

_____
_____
_____
_____
_____

What are you grateful for today? _____

This tip is for this time next year as well!

Let's ensure both you and your companion avoid feeling trunky! It can be tough when your companion is counting down the days till home, obsessing over movies or songs. Remember to be present and engage with each other spiritually. Share your excitement for the remaining days of your mission together, involving the Lord in every step. Let's make these days count!

DATE: _____

MEMORIES MADE, TOUGH TIMES, & LESSONS LEARNED:

Stressed    Angry    Tired    Sad    Happy    Excited

_____
_____
_____
_____
_____
_____
_____
_____

What are you grateful for today? _____

*"If we are going to fill the world with goodness and truth, then we must be worthy to receive inspiration so we can bless the lives of our Heavenly Father's children." - M. Russell Ballard*

DATE: _____

MEMORIES MADE, TOUGH TIMES, & LESSONS LEARNED:

Stressed    Angry    Tired    Sad    Happy    Excited

_____
_____
_____
_____
_____
_____
_____
_____

Prompt of the day:
The Impact of Missionary Work on Future Career Paths: Reflect on how your missionary experiences might influence your future career paths and aspirations.

_____
_____
_____
_____

What are you grateful for today? _____

(Also a message for this time next year!)

Navigating media and social media wisely is crucial as you transition from your mission to everyday life. Apply the principles you've learned to discern truth from falsehood and prioritize uplifting content. Set boundaries for screen time and commit to using technology for positive purposes, such as sharing the gospel and connecting with loved ones. Cultivate habits of mindfulness and moderation, ensuring that your online activities align with your values and goals. By exercising caution and intentionality, you can harness the power of media to inspire and uplift others while maintaining the habits of righteousness you developed on your mission. Stay vigilant, stay connected, and stay true to your mission!

DATE: _____

MEMORIES MADE, TOUGH TIMES, & LESSONS LEARNED:

Stressed   Angry   Tired   Sad   Happy   Excited

_____
_____
_____
_____
_____
_____
_____
_____
_____

What are you grateful for today? _____

"He [Christ] has infinite attention to spare for each one of us. He does not have to deal with us in the mass. You are as much alone with Him as if you were the only being He had ever created. When Christ dies, He died for you individually just as much as if you had been the only man in the world." - Tad R. Callister

DATE: _____

MEMORIES MADE, TOUGH TIMES, & LESSONS LEARNED:

Stressed   Angry   Tired   Sad   Happy   Excited

_____
_____
_____
_____
_____
_____
_____
_____
_____

Prompt of the day:

The Role of Personal Testimonies in Conversion: Write about the power of personal testimony in your own conversion.

_____
_____
_____
_____
_____

What are you grateful for today? _____

This tip is for this time next year too!

Returning home from your mission marks the beginning of a new chapter filled with possibilities! To maintain the good habits you've cultivated, it's essential to create a solid plan. Start by reflecting on the routines that served you well on your mission. Then, identify how you can adapt them to your life at home. Set specific, achievable goals for daily scripture study, prayer, service, and personal development. Surround yourself with supportive friends and family who share your values and can help keep you motivated. Remember, consistency is key, so stay committed to your plan and adjust as needed.

DATE: _____

MEMORIES MADE, TOUGH TIMES, & LESSONS LEARNED:

Stressed    Angry    Tired    Sad    Happy    Excited

_____
_____
_____
_____
_____
_____
_____
_____
_____

What are you grateful for today? _____

"The mountains in our lives do not always move how or when we would like. But our faith will always propel us forward. Faith always increases our access to godly power." - Russell M. Nelson

DATE: _____

MEMORIES MADE, TOUGH TIMES, & LESSONS LEARNED:

Stressed    Angry    Tired    Sad    Happy    Excited

_____
_____
_____
_____
_____
_____
_____
_____

Prompt of the day:
Building Interpersonal Skills: Write about how your missionary work has helped develop your interpersonal skills, such as empathy, communication, and conflict resolution.

_____
_____
_____
_____

What are you grateful for today? _____

(Also message for next year!)

Recognize that others may not grasp the depth of your journey as they haven't walked alongside you every step of the way. Rather than seeking to explain, prioritize remembering. Heed the Savior's guidance to recall the lessons learned and experiences gained, using them to propel your growth. Embrace the new opportunities for personal development that await you post-mission, understanding that these years should be just as fulfilling, in different ways, as your time in the field.

DATE: _____

MEMORIES MADE, TOUGH TIMES, & LESSONS LEARNED:

Stressed   Angry   Tired   Sad   Happy   Excited

_____
_____
_____
_____
_____
_____
_____
_____

What are you grateful for today? _____

*"Talk about the temple with your family and friends. Because Jesus Christ is at the center of everything we do in the temple, as you think more about the temple you will be thinking more about Him. Study and pray to learn more about the power and knowledge with which you have been endowed." - Russell M. Nelson*

DATE: _____

MEMORIES MADE, TOUGH TIMES, & LESSONS LEARNED:

Stressed   Angry   Tired   Sad   Happy   Excited

_____
_____
_____
_____
_____
_____
_____
_____

Prompt of the day:

As your mission comes to a close, write about some of your most powerful experiences.

_____
_____
_____
_____

What are you grateful for today? _____

# GOALS AS YOU TRANSITION HOME

(WHAT ARE YOU COMMITTING TO DO MORE OR LESS OF
WHEN YOU RETURN HOME? WHAT DOES THE NEXT
MONTH OR YEAR LOOK LIKE? WHAT DO YOU HOPE TO DO?)

_____
_____
_____
_____
_____
_____
_____
_____
_____
_____
_____
_____
_____
_____
_____
_____
_____
_____

# YOUR TESTIMONY - LAST DAY

(REVISIT YOUR TESTIMONY FROM DAY 1)

_____
_____
_____
_____
_____
_____
_____
_____
_____
_____
_____
_____
_____
_____
_____
_____
_____
_____

# NOTES

# NOTES

# NOTES

# NOTES

# NOTES

# NOTES

# NOTES

# NOTES

# NOTES

# NOTES

# NOTES

# NOTES

# NOTES

# NOTES

# NOTES

# NOTES

**ENJOY THE JOURNAL!**
**FROM THE SCHRAMM-FAM**
**DAVE, JAMIE, CHANDLER, MALLORY, AUBREY AND HAYDEN!**